Alpines

Alpines

Lionel Bacon

DAVID & CHARLES : NEWTON ABBOT

ISBN 0 7153 5947 9

Set in 11 on 12pt Bembo
and printed in Great Britain
by Latimer Trend & Company Ltd Plymouth
For David & Charles (Holdings) Limited
South Devon House Newton Abbot Devon

Contents

List of Illustrations

Plates

In Text

Introduction

There are many books on alpines, but this specialised subject is a vast one and there are still a great many unanswered questions about alpine plants and their cultivation. The longer one gardens, and the wider the range of plants cultivated, the more does one encounter puzzles and inconsistencies which cannot be disentangled by reference to the literature. Sometimes the books are silent: more often there is information for the seeking, but it is contradictory or perhaps does not accord with one's own experience. No book will answer all questions and solve all difficulties, but if it faithfully records what the author has himself observed it may shed some fresh light or perhaps set up a new train of thought and inquiry in the reader's mind.

If this book is to justify itself it must truly reflect my own experiences, which began in August 1923 when as a schoolboy I saw my first spring gentian on the Rochers de Naye above Lake Geneva. I can see it still. A few years later my father treated me to a load of Westmorland limestone and I built my first rock garden at our home in north London. It was a shrewd move on his part; it kept me occupied through a university long vacation and cleaned up an untidy bank. I do not know how good or bad the rock work was, but the important thing was that I read everything I could on the subject before constructing or planting the garden. Here is a point upon which I would lay emphasis: however much the writer of a book of this sort may seek to lean upon his own experience, he is inevitably indebted to and influenced by all that he has read and all that he has been told. There is one thing that I do remember about that first rock garden—and I still shudder to think of it! It was an imitation mountain range. The Jungfrau, the Mönch and the Eiger were all there: I have forgotten which

Swiss lake the tiny pool represented, but a couple of vertical leaning slabs constituted the Aarschlucht. Of course it all became nonsense as soon as the first plant was put in; but I still have to struggle with a tendency to try to build mountains in miniature.

It was not until 1948 that my wife and I first had our own garden, and started to cultivate alpines on almost naked chalk on a Chiltern hillside. Three years later we moved to Hampshire, and it is here that most of our experience has been gained. Our garden is upon chalky marl, well drained but lacking in humus. The Hampshire climate is mild, encouraging winter growth. We are very susceptible to frosts, which in June or September can be devastating. Occasionally, but seldom, we reach zero Fahrenheit in mid-winter, and we have little snow protection. This is not a book about our garden, but since it is upon experience in this garden that the book is based these brief data may help the reader to judge its applicability to his own conditions. Like most gardeners we have not contented ourselves with growing those plants which are best suited to our own conditions, but have made numerous attempts to cater for lime-hating and for frost-tender plants as well as the other special provision—screes and moraine, bog, copse, etc—considered in this book. In 1967 my wife acquired an alpine house. This extension of our experience has proved particularly interesting: certainly she has been able to grow successfully many plants which were more or less failures in the open garden, and the reasons why this should be so are I believe at the heart of any consideration of the cultivation of alpine plants. Chapter Six is based largely upon her experience, and I am indebted to her not only for this but also for her constructive criticism of the whole text.

For many years we have spent our main holidays in the mountains, and have devoted much time to seeking, photographing and studying alpine plants in the wild. I have become firmly convinced that it is in the hills if anywhere that we shall find answers to the problems of cultivating alpines in our gardens. I do not mean that we can hope to reproduce precisely in the garden the conditions under which plants grow in the wild; but the more carefully we study and assess these, the more hope have we of modifying the conditions in our rock gardens in favour of the plants. It has seemed logical therefore to start this book with a consideration of alpine plants in the wild.

There is so much that we do not know about alpines; and so there is need for research. The plant physiologists in their laboratories are continuously at work, and from time to time results emerge which are of interest to the gardener; but inevitably their work leans towards the solution of problems of economic importance, and only now and again has it something to offer to the rock gardener. In earlier times, before the advent of research specialists, a great deal of valuable study was carried out by practical gardeners and botanists in the field. I believe that this is still possible and still needed, and that if we are able and prepared to devote the time to careful observation and recording, and to set up deliberate homely experiments, there is much which we may learn.

There is a dilemma that confronts the rock gardener. The demands of alpine plants and of the garden are conflicting. To achieve a colourful and effective rock garden one should concentrate upon a relatively few of the easier and more showy plants, and many of the rarer and more difficult species upon which we lavish the majority of our time and affection really make very little contribution to the effectiveness of the garden as a whole. The more plants one grows the greater does the dilemma become. The rock garden tends to be a plant collection, and many of the plants assessible as 'collector's pieces'. It is not just a question of which plants one chooses to grow, or the allocation of time as between the garden and the plants. It must affect one's whole attitude towards the way the garden is constructed and maintained. A little while ago I started realigning all the rockwork in my garden, using a compass. The improvement in appearance was considerable—so was the time expended. An experienced and successful gardener commented 'Why bother? Surely the important thing is to provide good homes for your plants in which they will grow successfully.' One can see his point: but for my part, despite the clamant demands of the 'plant collection', I still prefer to strive towards the satisfaction of a well constructed garden. So I have devoted a considerable amount of space in Chapter Three to the actual building of the rock garden, and in this I must acknowledge my indebtedness to a work which I read many years ago, *Natural Rock Gardening* by B. H. B. Symons-Jeune (1932). This develops the concept of rock garden construction on the 'rectangular' principle, and I do not myself believe that this method of construction can be bettered.

In writing any book one should have a clear idea as to the class of reader for whom it is intended. I have tried to make it useful for, and readable by, 'beginners' by keeping technical terms to a minimum and

by starting from first principles. Nevertheless, it is something more
than a first introduction to the subject. Nobody can become interested
in alpines without soon wanting to extend the range of species grown,
and this necessitates making special provision for them. The simple
'rockery' rapidly evolves into the rock garden with its scree beds, etc.
When does one cease to be a 'beginner'? If the characteristics of a
beginner are a recognition of ignorance and a desire to learn more the
answer should surely be 'never'. I hope therefore that this book may
command the interest, though not necessarily the agreement, of readers
who are already well steeped in the subject. On the other hand I have
made no attempt to go deeply into its specialised aspects: it is not a
work of reference on abstruse points. The Bibliography contains
suggestions for further reading.

There are some deliberate omissions. The enthusiast for dwarf
conifers, for instance, will find nothing here to help him. The garden
pool is mentioned as an embellishment of the rock garden, but its construction, planting and maintenance have been regarded as outside the
scope of this book. The gardener upon acid soils whose interests are
centred upon the *Ericaceae* may feel that these have received less than
due consideration. Of ferns I have made no mention, though some are
well at home in the rock garden. Such limitations as these are necessary
in a small book on a large subject.

I have made occasional references to the Alpine Garden Society.
This society in England has its counterparts in some other countries of
the world, including Scotland, the United States and France. Among
the members of these societies there is a fine camaraderie: not only are
rare plants obtainable by private gift and exchange, and through the
societies' seed exchanges, but also there is a ready and unstinted release
of experience, knowledge and opinion. I acknowledge my indebtedness to many fine and generous gardeners who, with the readiness of
the enthusiast and the humility of the real expert, have allowed me to
benefit from their knowledge.

Acknowledgements

My grateful thanks are due to Mr and Mrs Gerard Parker, Lt-Col L. H.
Brammall, and Mr F. W. Bacon for permission to use photographs
taken in their gardens (Plates, p 89, p 72 *upper* and p 72 *lower*, respectively); and to Mrs Parker and Mr Lyn Weeks for reading the proofs.

One

Alpine Plants in the Wild

What is an 'alpine'?

Their name implies that alpine plants are those which grow in the 'alps', that is to say, the mountain pastures. Though these pastures cover a wide range of altitude, the definition is too narrow for the gardener: it excludes those mountain flowers which grow in other habitats than the pastures—those of the screes, the rock-faces and crevices, the mountain forests and woodlands, the stream-sides and bogs. 'Alpines' have also been defined as plants growing above some specified level of altitude, irrespective of their habitat: but this again is unsatisfactory because it takes no account of latitude, and the same plants which are found typically at high levels in, for instance, the European Alps may grow by the sea shore in the Arctic zone.

A wider definition would be 'those plants whose natural habitat is mountains and rocky places'. This opens the field to include a large number of plants, for instance many of those which are found on the rocky hills bordering the Mediterranean, which are not hardy in more northerly gardens. The rock gardener who acquires an alpine house (particularly if he is not one of those purists who spurn all heating in it) usually extends his sphere of interest to include some of these plants of doubtful hardiness, and they are accepted and frequently appear on the Alpine Garden Society's show benches. Nevertheless in a book of this sort some limitation must be imposed, and therefore, except when considering the alpine house, I shall treat mainly of plants which have been found to survive with minimal protection in the open, in most winters in temperate gardens subject to frost. And this implies another criterion; the plants to be considered must in addition look well and grow well in a rock garden, though the latter term will also be interpreted widely to include such extensions as woodland and water-side which are not only components of the mountain scene but also form a very satisfying part of the setting of a rock garden.

Some characteristics of alpine plants

The plants which fall within the above loose definition are exceedingly varied; nevertheless they tend to have some common characteristics. This is not a botanical treatise, and the following discussion of some of the growing conditions and characteristics of alpine plants in the wild is confined to those which are significant in relation to their cultivation. There is nothing like seeing a plant growing in its natural habitat (pro-vided that one observes it with a sufficiently critical eye) to enable one to grow it better.

FIG 1   The Spring Gentian, *Gentiana verna* (scale × ¾)

THE ALPINE MEADOW

Let us start with a typical alpine plant—a plant of the alpine meadows —such as the spring gentian (*Gentiana verna*—Fig 1). It is growing in rich soil. The humus content is maintained at a high level, in spite of heavy grazing and mowing, both by the annual dying down of the lush vegetation and by the excreta of the grazing flocks and herds. The mineral content is also high: every spring, and in many situations for a great part of the year, the meadows are dowsed with snow-water carrying down dissolved minerals from the heights. Yet rich though the soil of the pastures may be it is rarely sour or stagnant: characteristically the meadows are more or less steeply sloping and have a high content of broken rock, so that drainage is fast; the importance of drainage in growing alpines cannot be over-stressed—though it can be overdone.

The chemistry of the soil in alpine meadows varies according to the nature of the underlying rock and other factors, and tends to be more alkaline on calcareous formations; but mountain limestones are generally hard and probably release calcium far more slowly than the chalks of the lower hills, and the alkalinity tends to be neutralised by the organic acids of the humus, so that extremes of alkalinity such as one may meet in a chalk garden are probably rare in the mountains. Certainly there are differences in the wild flora of the alkaline and acid formations, but these are more apparent when one comes to consider the plants that grow on rock or in scree than among those of the alpine meadows.

Let us consider for a moment the annual cycle of a plant such as the spring gentian. For many months it is snow-covered, and this provides it with important winter protection against both cold and excessive humidity. The soil temperatures under snow do not fall greatly below freezing point, but these temperatures are low enough to ensure that there is little unfrozen moisture around the leaves and crowns of the plants. Alpine plants do not have to be very hardy, and frequently are not so. In these winter conditions they are at rest; some, such as the spring gentian, retain their foliage, while others die down to a resting rootstock. The duration of this winter snow cover varies widely according to such factors as aspect, latitude and altitude. On a south-facing slope in a southerly range such as the Apennines at low levels (say under 1,000m) the spring gentians are in fine flower in early April. The visitor to the Alps in August must take himself up to more than twice that height to find gentians opening their flowers as the last of the impermanent snow recedes: by this time those of the lower meadows will have set and perhaps shed their seed. The summer temperatures at the lower levels are high, particularly on southerly faces, and many alpine plants, including the spring gentian, would be subject to scorching were they not protected from direct heat by their habit of growing pressed low against the soil among the grasses. The plants of the higher alps must make their growth in a shorter season: this they are able to do, growing in closer and less abundant turf, exposed to hot sun with a high ultraviolet light content, yet protected from drought by their proximity to the melting snows above.

The mountain pastures, particularly at the lower levels, carry not only a varied but also an abundant vegetation. Competition appears to be intense—but the plants seem to do very well on it, and I wonder to what extent they are dependent upon one another for their successful growth. Certainly there is a view widely held among rock gardeners that the spring gentian does not like to be alone, and there is room for study and experimentation to try to determine whether the interdependence of alpine plants is purely physical (a need for root-anchorage and protection from excessive heat) or whether there are in addition chemical and biological factors, such as sharing of nutrients, neutralisation of unwanted chemicals, the provision of a suitable balance of fungal elements which provide an essential root-association for some plants, and in some instances (such as the louseworts and rattles which form an extensive part of the alpine meadow population) frank parasitism.

The majority of plants in the alpine meadows which are of interest to the rock gardener are perennial. They are largely dormant under the snow, but resume growth immediately the snow melts providing abundant moisture coupled with rising temperatures. Such plants in temperate gardens tend to make new growth in warm and moist spells during the winter. This young growth may then be vulnerable to hard frosts or cold drying winds, and one of the major problems of the cultivation of alpines in some gardens is the damage occasioned in this way by 'stop and start' winters. Many other of the alpine meadow plants are leaf-losing and therefore perhaps rather less vulnerable to such winter conditions. A large component of the alpine meadow vegetation is provided by bulbous or tuberous rooted plants, such as orchids, spring crocuses, lilies, narcissi, and colchicums, most of which are able to protect themselves against summer drought by making their leaf-growth in the spring and early summer and then losing their foliage; but some of these also are susceptible to damage by late spring frosts in the garden.

THE HIGHER ALPS

As one ascends to the higher levels of the Alps, the vegetation becomes less lush and the plants progressively more specialised. Increasingly they acquire the characteristics which the rock gardener

Page 17 The author's rock garden in Hampshire, built mainly of Purbeck limestone on a level site. To the left of the pool is an underwatered scree ('moraine')

Page 18 The stones are laid to give the impression of a single rock-mass beneath

values in alpine plants—small, neat, compact growth and abundant, brightly-coloured flowers of large size in relation to the whole plant. Insect life becomes progressively sparser as one ascends, and presumably competition for the attention of insects to secure fertilisation becomes greater. To the attraction of large flowers is sometimes added that of scent. Many of our loveliest plants for the rock garden come from the high level turf, but it is also true to say that plants from the higher levels exist in more specialised conditions, more different from those of our gardens, and tend therefore to be more difficult to cultivate. As one proceeds upwards from the highest turf into the screes and rock crevices the specialisation becomes yet greater, and so do the horticultural problems.

FIXED SCREES

At their upper edges the high Alps become more stony and grade into scree. The lower and less steep screes tend to be 'fixed'—that is to say there is relatively little movement in the rocks and stones that compose them. There is some humus from decaying vegetation, and at the lower levels, where they grade into the pastures, the stones are bound with turf. The plants of these fixed screes differ from those of the high pastures. They tend to have longer root-systems, providing anchorage as well as feeding. They clearly do not need, and probably cannot tolerate, the close competitive growth of the turf. They are in a medium which contains more air and less moisture, and indeed is never, even temporarily, water-logged.

MOVING SCREES

Characteristically screes are formed by the shedding of stone fractured from steep rock faces. As you approach the rock face, climbing higher, the scree becomes steeper, newer and less settled. The rocks are more liable to move under your feet. The plants are yet sparser, growing as individuals rather than as communities. There is very little visible soil. There are capacious air-spaces between the rocks. Moisture in the main exists only as a thin film on the faces of the stones. The plants are yet more specialised, with anchorage and feeding roots which may extend for several feet into the jumbled stone: they do not go down vertically, but tend to travel away up the slope, as a result of the downward movement of the crown of the plant, carried by the sliding scree.

B

MORAINES

Screes are infinitely variable. One specialised type carrying a particularly interesting flora is the glacier moraine—the great banks of boulders cast out over the centuries by the glaciers at their sides and feet as they advance down the mountain sides. The distinctive feature of these moraines as compared with other forms of scree is that they are heavily filled with silt, and constantly permeated with running snow water.

SUMMIT SCREES

Yet another specialised habitat which may be thought of as a form of fixed scree is to be found on rounded ridges and summits, particularly on schists and other very fragmented formations, where the stones are more or less bound together by a soil which is largely a mineral sludge, containing very little humus. Drainage is fast, but the growth mixture is reasonably compact, and shallow-rooted plants (including some annuals) can survive in these conditions. *Ranunculus parnassifolius* (Fig 2) favours the summit screes.

FIG 2   *Ranunculus parnassifolius* (scale × 1)

ROCK CREVICES

Above and between the screes are the rock faces. Some of the igneous rocks, such as granites, are unfissured and scarcely porous, and carry very little vegetation: others, such as limestones, dolomite, shales, etc, have larger or smaller cracks and fissures, horizontal or vertical or both, which provide a root-hold for plants. These crevice-plants show a type and degree of adaptation which can be thought of as an extreme form of the specialisation of the plants of the moving screes, although indeed the rock in which they grow is fixed and rigid. Some,

FIG 3   *Phyteuma comosum* at home in a dolomite crevice (scale × ⅓)

such as for instance *Campanula zoysii* in the Dolomites, occupy narrow fissures through which they force minute frail-looking roots and stems, the latter emerging at intervals so that the crevice becomes lined with the plant. Others, like *Phyteuma comosum* (Fig 3) and *Saxifraga longifolia*, emerge from a single crown which may build up to a considerable size. In either case the fissure may be so minute as to be almost invisible: one can only wonder first that any seedling should ever have succeeded in gaining a footing there and secondly at the tremendous slow force exerted by the plant in its growth. Such plants do not have, nor do they need, the long thick thong-like anchorage roots of the moving scree plants; nevertheless their tiny thin feeding roots penetrate far into the rock where so far as can be seen the only nutriment available to them is the minerals dissolved in a minutely thin film of moisture. Such moisture is found deeply within the rock, and it would seem that to support vegetation a rock face must be not only fissured but also to some degree porous. Like the scree plants, these crevice plants can therefore resist surface drought, yet they are never subject to stagnant moisture on their crowns or foliage.

The foregoing picture of a progression of alpine plants from the low pastures to the highest screes and crevices is a simplification. The growing conditions of alpine plants are infinitely variable.

WOODLANDS

The lowest slopes of the hills carry deciduous woodlands, and above these there are frequently coniferous woods, and in both there are beautiful flowers. The conditions of growth differ from those in lowland woods in much the same way that the conditions in an alpine pasture differ from those in a lowland meadow—the subsoil is sloping rock, so that there is little stagnant moisture, the snow cover is longer and the growing season shorter with increasing altitude.

BOGS

While fast drainage is the rule, there are nevertheless upland valleys whose bases are the catchment areas of the water from the melting snows, remaining boggy throughout the summer. These again have their characteristic flora; the plants grow in an abundance of humus, minerals and moisture, with some measure of stagnation.

ROCKY OUTCROPS

Saxatile plants (those growing upon rock) are not confined to the steepest and highest rock faces above the screes. Among and between the pastures, whether low or high, there are outcrops of rock, frequently with a thin partial covering of soil held together by wiry grasses as well as by plants of more interest to the rock gardener. True fissure plants are to be found at the low levels as well as the high, but many which *appear* to be growing in rock crevices are in reality rooted into the soil which packs the crevices, with few if any roots penetrating the rock itself. Such plants may be exposed to considerable degrees of heat and drought in high summer, and are in various ways adapted to this. They include many of the easiest as well as some of the best of rock plants, such as the stonecrops, houseleeks and silver saxifrages, which are most rewarding if exposed to full sun in situations where they are not subject to stagnant water.

A gardener walking in the hills will notice that within any one of the types of habitat just described an individual species of plant may be found within a very restricted area; and may ask himself why such a plant should not be more widely distributed throughout apparently identical conditions. No doubt there are many reasons for this: a plant colony may in fact be recently established and therefore not yet widely dispersed; there may be variations in soil conditions which are not apparent upon the surface; or it may reflect the interdependence or the antagonism between one species and another, which has led to a balance in distribution. The more closely one studies the growing conditions of alpine plants in the wild, the more does one come to realise how they can vary within quite a small area—a thicker or a thinner layer of soil over the rocks, differences in speed of drainage or in steepness of slope, and (perhaps of particular importance) variations in aspect. Obviously a south-facing slope, other things being equal, receives more sun than a north-facing one, even though the slope be not steep; what is perhaps a little less obvious, but no less important, is that when the sun does shine fully upon a north slope it does so with less heat than upon a south slope. Some plants are indeed quite fussy as to their aspect: *Ramonda myconi* (Fig 4) in the Pyrenees is a classical example of a plant which is intolerant of direct sunlight and is usually found upon a steep north face; *Phyteuma comosum* in the Dolomites and *Jankaea heldreichii* on Grecian Olympus place themselves where they will

receive a little early morning or late evening sunshine but avoid direct
sunlight in the heat of the day. In reality they do not 'place themselves'
at all: they survive and thrive where conditions are appropriate, and
where they are not their seed fails to develop into successful plants.
There is much to be learned from noting critically every detail of the
growth conditions of wild alpines, including those of dead or ailing
plants.

As would be expected, it is generally found (though there are some
interesting exceptions) that the more varied the habitat of an alpine
plant in the wild, the easier it is in cultivation.

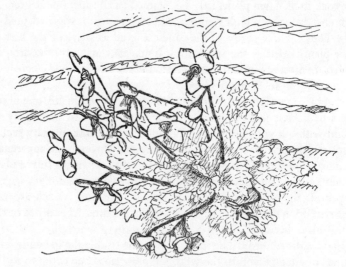

FIG 4   *Ramonda myconi*—for a north-facing crevice or wall (scale × ½)

Two

The Principles of Cultivation

It will be clear from the wide variation in growing conditions of wild alpine plants that the gardener who wishes to grow the more specialised types has to make special provision for them. However, hundreds of first-rate rock and mountain plants can be grown in the garden if just a few essential needs are met; and it is remarkable that many plants which grow in specialised habitats in the mountains are nevertheless capable of adapting themselves successfully to seemingly different conditions in the garden.

THE SOIL

The first requirement to be emphasised is adequate *drainage*. Few alpine plants will tolerate stagnant moisture or a sour soil, and even those that like abundant moisture at the roots are prone to rot at the crown if this is constantly damp. One way of avoiding stagnant surface moisture is to grow the plants upon slopes: this cannot in practice be the sole answer—it would impose unacceptable restrictions on the construction of the garden, and furthermore there are limits to the steepness of slopes in a garden compatible both with effective appearance and with soil stability. Another way to avoid stagnation is to use soil mixtures which are very porous. This principle also needs to be applied with discretion: 'soil' consisting only of chalk, sand, grit or gravel would be fast draining, but in hot weather it would dry out so rapidly that unless it were kept constantly watered the plants in it would die of drought, and if it *were* kept constantly watered from above there would be a rapid leaching-out of nutriment. It is therefore necessary to add humus in some form, both as a food and as a moisture retainer. It may sound paradoxical to speak in one breath of the need to avoid stagnant moisture and with the next to emphasise the need for moisture-retaining ingredients; nevertheless, it is the secret of the preparation of successful soil mixtures for the rock garden to secure the constant availability of a *small* amount of moisture below rather than on the surface. This is exactly what the most specialised plants manage to achieve either in scree or in crevices.

The basic ingredients of a good soil for rock garden construction are loam, leafmould, peat, grit, and sand, and with increasing skill and experience the gardener varies the proportions and to some extent the quality (eg the size of the grit) of these ingredients to meet the needs of an ever widening range of individual plants, and to suit different aspects, local rainfall, amount of tree or house shade, etc. Let us consider each of these ingredients briefly in turn.

Loam features much in gardening books, but is a very ill-defined term. For present purposes it may be taken to mean a good soil (approximating to that found among the grass roots in established pasture land), rich in humus, fibrous, somewhat spongy, crumbling when dry but reasonably cohesive when moist. It is a scarce commodity and in practice most of us have to make do with whatever soil we find ourselves gardening upon as the basis of our mixture, and modify and adapt it by use of the other ingredients mentioned; but if the decision to construct a rock garden involves the removal of a piece of lawn, it will prove a good investment to stack the turves and allow them to rot for a season or more to provide a supply of loam.

Leafmould is a most valuable additive, particularly to chalky or sandy soils, providing humus and food; but it varies greatly in texture and quality and has the disadvantage that it is likely to introduce weed seed and vermin, and few people have the facilities for sterilising it on the scale that would be required in rock garden construction.

Peat is more accessible, at least in towns, than leafmould. It is relatively sterile, usually somewhat acid (though again varying according to its source), and is best thought of as a supply of humus, assisting water-retention, rather than as readily available plant food: it is of particular value as an additive to chalky soils.

Grit is the ingredient which is peculiar to the rock garden. It is possible to grow many rock plants without it; nevertheless the addition of an appropriate quantity and quality of grit to the soil gives it an open texture which enormously increases the range of plants which can be grown. The scree, to be considered later, is essentially soil in which grit is the major component. Grit is broken-up rock, and it varies in colour, texture, chemistry and particle-size. Limestone and granite chippings are sometimes purchasable in a variety of sizes from local authorities' road-building depots. Granite would seem the more appropriate additive where the basic soil is alkaline and in areas reserved for calciphobe (lime-intolerant) plants: otherwise limestone. The yellower types of grit, such as are obtainable at some sand pits, and also the small rounded pebbles known as pea-gravel, are not to everybody's taste in colour; they may, however, be suitable if sandstone is used for the rockwork. The writer, gardening on chalk, has for many years used large quantities of ⅛in granite chippings in the preparation of soil for rock garden construction: there is, however, a tendency for this fine grit to contain a good deal of powder and to cake, and in recent years a rather coarser grit has been used, particularly on the surface.

A suggested *standard mixture* for rock garden construction is 3 parts loam, 1 part leafmould, 1 part peat, and 1 part grit—but it must be emphasised that this is a theme subject to many variations.

Sand is not included in the writer's basic mixture because the garden soil is a light calcareous marl, but it may be a useful additive on heavier or more clayey soils.

FEEDING AND TOP-DRESSING

Rock gardeners hold differing views on the subject of *feeding* their plants in the open garden. Over-rich soils are not only liable to sourness and excessive humidity, but also they tend to promote large soft leaf-formation and reduced flowering, and possibly a greater susceptibility to disease and frost damage. On the other hand it is common experience that plants do very well in a newly constructed rock garden, but that later their performance falls off and after a few years some sections of the garden need to be remade. While this might in part be due to physical factors—sinking and packing of the soil with impaired drainage and reduced aeration—it is difficult to avoid the conclusion that there is a loss of some essential soil-ingredients as well. This is to be expected, because the necessity to secure fast drainage also inevitably means leaching-out of soluble soil-constituents. Of the many specialised growing conditions in the wild, perhaps the most difficult to reproduce in the garden is the constant replacement of mineral salts washed down from the rocks above. On present knowledge it is not simply a question of adding chemicals. The usual chemical additives—phosphates, nitrates, potash, iron, etc—which are used for instance in the vegetable garden to promote lush and rapid growth are of limited use in the rock garden, where this sort of growth is seldom to be encouraged. There are some exceptions, as for instance in the feeding of bulbous and tuberous plants to be discussed later. Such chemicals are for the most part readily soluble, and so are rapidly lost from rock garden soil, and it is suggested that they be added only where definite deficiencies have been demonstrated by soil analysis. Otherwise it is more logical to use foods such as bone-meal or hoof-and-horn from which the chemical ingredients are released slowly and in small quantity.

It seems likely, though much research is still needed, that alpine plants receive and probably require traces of elements other than those provided in the chemical fertilisers normally available to the gardener. A rational approach to this problem is repeatedly to add broken stone— ie grit—as a *top-dressing*; but it must be admitted that this is a hit-or-miss affair when we really do not know what minerals the plants are requiring or what, if any, are being obtained from the stone dressing. There are, however, other reasons for periodically top-dressing the rock garden with grit. It is remarkable how ton after ton of broken stone can be added to the surface of the rock garden and disappear from sight within a few months. This steady absorption of stone into the soil improves it for growing rock plants, but unless it is frequently replaced there is lost one of the particular purposes of surfacing the soil with grit, ie to protect the crowns of the plants from excessive surface moisture. It is the writer's practice to top-dress the rock garden at least once a year with the basic mixture described above, with the addition of a small amount of bone-meal (or hoof-and-horn in beds reserved for lime-intolerant plants) and then to add a layer of coarse (up to $\frac{3}{4}$in) granite chippings over this.

PROTECTION FROM COLD

Alpine plants vary in their hardiness. Many will cheerfully survive considerable periods with temperatures around zero Fahrenheit, with the ground frozen solid around them for several inches of depth; but this is not true of all, even of the true alpine plants, and even those which are very hardy while totally at rest may be susceptible to frost damage when new growth starts in the spring. Much can be done by careful attention to the local climate of the garden as a whole, particularly to take full advantage of any available slopes which will allow cold air to drain off them provided that it is not blocked by walls or hedges at the foot of the slope. Conversely, the careful placing of trees, hedges, etc higher up the slope can contribute to the blockage and diversion of cold air currents: only the gardener who has struggled for many years in a frost pocket will realise how much can be achieved in this way. Trees and shrubs can also be used for protection from freezing winds and as overhead cover against frosts; even small leaf-losing shrubs, such for instance as the many forms of *Potentilla fruticosa*, will provide an appreciable measure of frost protection to plants growing close beneath them. With experience the rock gardener becomes skilled at placing individual plants according to their requirements, and those which are particularly susceptible to frost damage can be given some protection not only by placing them under shrubs, but also in a number of other ways. If they are placed well up on a slope they will escape the coldest air; if in addition the slope faces to the south or west they will receive some protection from the coldest winds; if the soil is fast draining it will retain less moisture near the surface, and therefore be less subject to the disruptive expansion which moist soil undergoes under frost-conditions and which breaks the roots of plants and throws them out on to the surface. Another valuable device is so to place plants that their roots and crowns are protected by large rocks placed above them. *Cyclamen repandum* has survived in the author's garden with the tuber placed under a thick flat slab round which the leaves and flowers emerge in the spring: it has not been otherwise hardy in this garden. The even more tender but wholly delightful *Convolvulus mauritanicus* (Plate, p 35) has survived in the milder winters (in which it has been subjected to twenty degrees of frost on isolated occasions) by growing it in a horizontal crevice with the upper rock several inches thick and slightly overhanging. These measures are applicable to individual plants: the question of providing special protected beds is to be considered in a later chapter.

PROTECTION FROM DROUGHT

A requirement for the optimum growth of many alpine plants is abundant moisture when they come into growth in the spring. English people are accustomed to think of springs as wet and, with thoughts of February Fill-Dyke and April showers, to discount the possibility of spring droughts. Yet such droughts occur, and a dry spell accompanied by desiccating cold winds in March or early April can be more damaging than late frosts. There is no easy answer to this problem. To advise avoiding windy gardens is a little unrealistic! In fact a good deal can be done by the skilful use of shrubs, trees and other forms of windbreak to minimise this sort of exposure. The hose or watering-can, which we tend to associate with summer evenings after hot days, has an important part to play in the spring. Shrubs, such as cistuses, which do not lose their leaves in the winter, are particularly subject to damage or death from spring droughts and so also are seedlings or rooted cuttings planted out too late in the previous autumn (or too early in the current spring) to have established deep roots.

Many, but not all, alpine plants are susceptible to damage by drought in high summer. Some—sedums, sempervivums, etc—grow with little soil and no great root depth on sun-baked rocks and are built to withstand drought. Others, such as those bulbous and tuberous rooted plants which make their flowers and growth in the spring and whose leaves die down in the summer, not only can withstand arid conditions but indeed appear to need the 'ripening' which such conditions afford in order to flower well. However, the majority of mountain plants, whether they come from meadows, screes, crevices or more obviously moist or shaded places, require a constant though limited supply of water. Watering by can or hose, or by such more complex irrigation systems as the 'moraine' to be described later, is needed in prolonged dry spells; but much may be done to reduce this need. Artificial watering takes time, and most public water supplies are adjusted to contain a measure of 'hardness' which while in no way deleterious to most plants (and possibly beneficial to those growing in a naturally acid soil) must cause some uneasiness to the gardener on chalk or limestone who is endeavouring to maintain lime-free conditions in peat-beds or otherwise. As with protection from cold, so with drought, the positioning of individual plants is important. Every gardener knows that he has drier and damper patches, and particularly is this so in the rock garden, where for instance north-facing slopes are likely to retain their moisture longer than south-facing ones. Also, the rock gardener, by varying his soil-mixture, can create areas of greater and less water-retentiveness. He can use shrubs for shade; some, such as the majority of dwarf conifers, are dense in foliage and cast heavy shadows, but for this very reason, and also because of the shape of many of them, plants cannot be satisfactorily grown close under them—and at noon in high summer the sun is nearly vertical. Some shrubs, such as cistuses, dwarf syringas, the shrubby potentilla, and some conifers, are so shaped or can be so shaped that plants grown close under them will receive shade; but again there is a snag—the shrubs themselves require moisture and may drain the soil immediately around them. However, the chief limitation is that most alpine plants, though they may be at risk in dry spells, like a good deal of sun. The main protection that these plants have against drought lies in the development of a root-system which can reach moisture even in drought conditions. In the garden as in the wild, crevices and the undersides of large stones, and the deeper layers of a scree, retain films of moisture for a long time, and the plant whose roots can reach this moisture will survive. It is the young and very shallow rooted plants that are at risk. In the main shallow rooted plants are either annuals, which complete their life-cycle very quickly and then die (and in the main are not of great interest to the rock gardener); or they are adapted to drought; or they are bog or marsh plants, which the rock gardener cannot grow unless he is prepared to provide special conditions for them. But even deep rooted plants are at risk when young. In times of drought the greatest danger is to seedlings or to other plants, whether they be rooted cuttings or fully established in pots, which have been recently planted out and have not yet so disposed their roots (which should of course be spread out and carried down as deeply as possible in planting) as to reach the deeper reserves of moisture. The matter of propagation will be considered later: for the moment it is enough to say that half the rock gardener's pleasure will be lost (and his pockets rapidly emptied) unless he undertakes regular propagation of his plants; and this means that he is constantly having to plant out young specimens. The time for doing this requires much judgement and experience, and even so, in his anxiety perhaps to avoid spring frosts, he may expose his plants to an early period of drought before they are sufficiently settled in to withstand it. Watering and temporary artificial shading are needed; in such circumstances the writer is accustomed to place pots over his young plants for perhaps 48 hours, and then for limited periods during the heat of the day for a week or more—they have the incidental advantage that they act as markers of plants needing watering.

THE POSITIONING OF PLANTS

Much of the skill in planting a rock garden lies in the placing of plants in relation to one another. In the mountain meadows they are crowded together: in the screes they are sparse and separate. The relative positioning of plants is partly a matter of taste, but also in large part it determines the success with which they are grown. The juxtaposition of different colours, different types of foliage, different habits, etc, is a matter of taste and judgement, time and thought; but the gardener must ask not only whether a grouping of plants will look well, but also whether they will grow well. There are differing opinions on this matter: some gardeners favour wide spacing, so that each plant is seen to best advantage against a background of rockwork or carefully surfaced soil, and there is no risk of the more robust plants overlying the smaller and often more precious ones. The alternative view that plants should be allowed to grow into one another also has its advocates: it is the best way of keeping down weeds; it often looks effective, in the garden as in the wild; space is always at a premium in most mature rock gardens; by interplanting a succession of flowers may be achieved throughout a longer season.

One difficulty is that the space occupied by plants does not remain constant throughout the year. Many plants—aubrietas, arabis, rockroses, veronicas, for example—need to be cut back after flowering in order to preserve them in the best condition; others, such as many campanulas, lose their leaves in the winter, and it may be late spring before they reappear. In either case there is for a time a large bare area, and if one fails to consider the later regrowth of the plant (or forgets that it is there) and occupies the space with smaller or less robust plants, these are at risk of smothering when the original occupant resumes growth. Clearly there can be no rule-of-thumb method of planting a rock garden. It is necessary to know just what growth to expect from every plant at every season, to know which plants will tolerate or even require overlying when out of flower (recall the spring gentian, soldanella, etc in the alpine meadow) and those for which it is certain death. Some spring-flowering bulbs, such as crocuses, scillas, and chionodoxas, are capable of penetrating a mat of, for instance, thyme, and will flower well above it, and the remains of their leaves can be removed before the thyme comes into flower. But not all spring-flowering bulbs are well served by this treatment: some, such as the many varieties of *Iris reticulata*, and most of the tulip species, need a summer ripening, and if they are to be left in the ground at all they are better in soil which is in full sun. Some bulbs which flower in late summer or early autumn, such as *Colchicum agrippinum* (Fig 5) and *Crocus speciosus* (Fig 6), can be grown effectively under helianthemums if their positioning is nicely judged so that they are uncovered just before they are due to come into flower when the rock-roses receive their annual haircut in late July or early August. The flowering and growth seasons of plants vary a great deal between gardens and even in one garden, and skill and careful observation are needed to achieve effective interplanting. Some of the larger mat-forming plants create

FIG 5 *Colchicum agrippinum* (scale × ¾)

a hazard for their smaller neighbours by harbouring slugs and snails in large numbers. They themselves are able to withstand the depredations of these vermin; but the latter have clear preferences in their food (broadly related to the catalogue prices of the plants!) and at night they sally forth from under the cover of the aubrietas and devour the tinier and more precious plants in the neighbourhood.

So far as any general guidance can be given in such a complex matter as the positioning of plants, it is suggested that the smaller and more vulnerable plants should be grouped together away from the more spreading and robust ones. What this tends to mean in practice is that the former are grown in screes, which are kept under especially close surveillance with regard to vermin and weeds, and from which coarser plants, not needing scree conditions, are excluded.

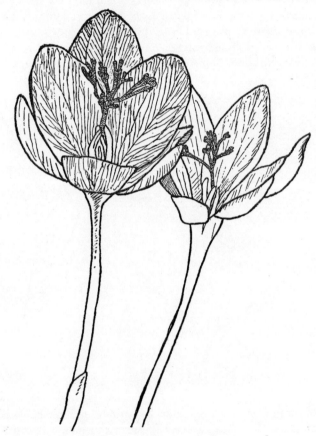

FIG 6   *Crocus speciosus* (scale × 1)

SPECIAL PROVISIONS

The wider the range of alpines to be grown, the wider must be the special provision made, and in practice this means attempting to imitate the varied habitats already described in relation to mountain plants in the wild. Few of these are perfectly reproducible, and in the garden one must deal in approximations and compromises.

Page 35 Convolvulus mauritanicus, a beautiful but somewhat tender plant from North Africa, is given a chance of survival through an English winter if its root and crown lie beneath a large boulder

Page 36 (*above*) A newly constructed peat bed in early spring. The hazel copse behind it lies to the south and shades the peat bed during the summer; (*left*) a year later in the summer, the peat bed is fully clothed

Curiously enough, the habitat which in the mountains might be regarded as the least specialised, the *alpine pasture*, is perhaps the most difficult to reproduce in the rock garden. Many people, including the author, have attempted to construct an alpine 'turf' or 'meadow', with a signal lack of success. You can assemble alpines that grow in mountain meadows and plant them close together, but the all-important missing element is the grass. You could add this too: you could go the whole hog and incorporate fine grasses (English coarse meadow grasses would rapidly smother most alpines); you could feed it with cow-dung, and scythe the whole thing two or three times a year—but few of us are either able or willing to go to these lengths, and certainly the writer would not care to guarantee the results. In practice in our rock gardens we must dispense with the grass: without it much success may be achieved with many alpines, but others remain disappointing, and

FIG 7   *Soldanella montana,* a flower of the mountain turf (scale × 1½)

C

one may wonder whether they are lacking some contribution which in their wild state the grasses would provide for them. But although this special requirement cannot be met, there are others which can— the high humus content and rich feeding, drainage which is adequate to prevent stagnation but not such as to lead to rapid drying out (using sand rather than grit), and close planting to secure the firm root-anchorage which the grasses would provide in the wild. Such parts of the garden (which can be quite small areas) can be varied as to the direction and steepness of their slope, and this in turn will materially affect their suitability for different species of plant.

Just as in the mountains there is a gradation from the high alpine meadows through more stony turf into *screes* containing less and less soil (with related changes in the flora), so in the garden one can meet the needs of a wide range of plants by providing screes of varying constitution in different situations. The term 'rich scree' is used to denote an area which has a considerable grit content and consequently is fast-draining, but nevertheless aims to be rich in plant food. *Primula halleri* (Fig 8), which in the wild grows in damp areas at the junction of high meadow and scree, is an example of plants needing rich scree conditions in the garden. 'Faster' screes (those which, draining more rapidly, have a lower moisture content and also probably more air in the surface layer) are achieved by increasing the proportion and coarseness of the grit. This means, since an increase in the grit results in a reduction in the other ingredients, that the available nourishment is reduced. This relative starvation is necessary to keep the plants in character, to encourage them to flower well, and in many cases to enable them to survive at all. But it also means that they are at risk of drying out: the faster the scree, the greater the risk of drought.

Apart from the provision of water, the risk of drought in screes can be diminished, without destroying the essential purpose of the scree, in three ways. One is to avoid a direct southerly exposure: granted that scree-plants rarely grow in full shade, it is nevertheless the case that in the mountains the richer and more varied scree flora is generally found in easterly or westerly exposures, rather than in south-facing screes. Secondly, the physical nature of the grit and stone used in the scree is important. All stone just below the surface will tend to hold a film of moisture on its surface, and this is important for the plants; but whereas some stones, particularly granite, flints and hard pebbles, contain very little absorbed moisture, others such as softer limestones may do so, and

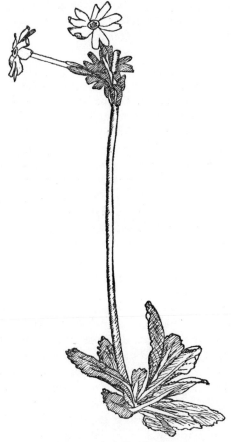

FIG 8 *Primula halleri* (scale × ¾)

even more some forms of sandstone grit. These therefore, if they are obtainable, are slower to dry out than impermeable grit. Thirdly, bearing in mind that the humus-containing elements in the mixture (peat, leafmould and to a less extent loam) hold much more water than the stone itself, there arises the important question not only of the proportion of these elements but also of the depth at which they are placed. In the construction of a scree the aim should be to secure a greater water-retaining capacity in the deeper layers than near the surface: this matter is discussed later when considering the actual building of rock gardens.

The ultimate in scree construction is the under-watered '*moraine*'. This is a fast draining scree consisting almost entirely of grit or shingle to a depth of a foot or so, overlying a shallow layer of moisture-retaining humus, on coarse stones through which water runs. It is not strictly analogous to the glacier moraine of the mountains, which tends to be more or less bound by silt. Its construction, which is considered in the next chapter, is somewhat complicated, unless you are so fortunate as to have a stream running through your garden. The number of plants which can be grown only in moraine conditions is not large, but there are some desirable and highly challenging plants, such as *Ranunculus seguieri*, *Thlaspi rotundifolium* and *Geum reptans*, for which the moraine offers some hope of success; and a large number of others, which require fast scree conditions, can be handled conveniently in a moraine without the need for frequent overhead watering. The outfall end of a moraine, which is likely to be permanently damp, though with moving rather than static moisture, provides favourable growing conditions for some plants such as *Epilobium fleischeri* (Fig 22) (the dwarf rosebay willow-herb of the Swiss moraines and river-shingles) and the alpine poppy (*Papaver sendtneri*).

Another specialised habitat is the *bog*, which in most gardens requires, like the moraine, special construction. It is in essence a bed which is very rich in humus, contains little or no coarse grit, and is always moist, preferably with slowly moving water. It provides the conditions required by such plants as the butterworts (Fig 9), grass of Parnassus, bog gentian, bog pimpernel (Figs 10, 24); and some plants of damp turf, *Primula farinosa*, *P. halleri*, and *P. rosea*, like bog conditions in the garden. Some of these bog-plants require an acid soil, and others will at least tolerate it: peat should form a large proportion of the growing mixture. The author uses about 50 per cent peat, 25 per cent leafmould, and 25 per cent fine sand. The mixture is rubbed through a ⅛in sieve and forms a smooth close soil which in its sodden condition holds the shallow roots of some of these bog-plants and the rootless winter resting buds of the butterworts. A bog of this sort can provide great interest, but there are difficulties in its management: it is particularly susceptible to invasion by reeds and pearlwort, which are not easily eradicated from the close wet soil. In drought conditions it provides moisture for birds, which seem to delight in throwing out the shallow rooted plants.

The provision of a *copse* or *woodland* in relation to the rock garden

Fig 9   The Butterwort, *Pinguicula grandiflora*—for a wet rock face or bog

caters for the needs of a large and valuable group of mountain flowers, many of which are the earliest to come into blossom in the spring. Clearly they do not of necessity have to be related to a rock garden— there are many beautiful woodland gardens with never a rock in sight. Nevertheless, the association is a natural and satisfying one. The helle- bores and hepaticas, woodland anemones, lilies-of-the-valley, some kinds of snowdrop, garlic (eg *Allium triquetrum*, Fig 11), cyclamen

FIG 10   The Bog Gentian, *Gentiana pneumonanthe* (scale × ¾)

and daphne—these are just a few of the flowers to be found in the
deciduous woods on mountain slopes. The making of such a copse,
where it does not already exist, is not such a long-term project as
might at first sight appear. An eminently suitable tree for the purpose
is the hazel, which is inexpensive, readily obtained, and capable of rapid
propagation. By constant close pruning at the base, the hazel can be
persuaded to grow up as a single trunk, and a year-by-year process of
pruning off the lower branches leads surprisingly quickly to a light and
pleasant woodland in which one can walk without stooping. It provides

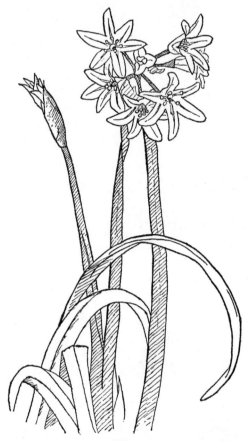

Fig 11 *Allium triquetrum*—a rare British plant for light shade or woodland
(scale⅛ × ¾)

in winter a measure of frost protection which can be used for shade-tolerant plants which would be struck down in the open garden. In early spring the catkins are a delight, and at this time the leafless branches allow enough light to encourage the growth and flowering of many plants such as the dog's tooth violet, some orchids such as the Lady's Slipper (Fig 12), and *Polygala chamaebuxus* (Fig 13) which in the mountains grow in light shade at the edges of the woodlands. In later spring the large leaves provide deeper shade, and the lilies-of-the-valley come into their own. The copse is self-feeding, gradually accumulating its own leafmould. At all seasons it is a part of the garden scenery in its own right, and a valuable setting for the rock garden.

Back in the rock garden proper, we have one other special provision to consider—the *crevice*. This is perhaps the most specialised of all habitats of mountain flowers; yet curiously enough few if any of the plants which in nature inhabit tight crevices demand such a position in the garden. The fact is that the true crevice—the fine fissure in rock with no visible space or soil-content—is practically irreproducible in the garden. A soil-packed space between rocks is quite a different

FIG 12   The Lady's Slipper Orchid, *Cypripedium calceolus*, grows in scrub or open woodland on calcareous soils (scale × ½)

FIG 13 *Polygala chamaebuxus* (scale × 1½)

matter; many plants grow and look well in such a situation, but these
are not growing as true crevice plants. Recalling the essential characteristics of a crevice—no visible soil, practically no surface water, and a
constant but minimal supply of mineral-charged water within the rock
—it is not surprising that many of the plants, such as some of the cushion
androsaces, which normally occupy such situations, are very difficult
to grow in the open garden. Their cultivation in an alpine house
depends upon growing them in pots in the equivalent of a fast scree,
with careful control of watering, and particularly of overhead watering
when they are not actively in growth: these conditions are hard to
reproduce in the open garden. *Phyteuma comosum* and *Campanula
morettiana* are two examples of interesting plants which are undoubtedly
crevice-plants in their home in the Dolomites, but which, losing their
foliage in the winter, are at less risk of rotting during hibernation than
are most cushion plants: both can be grown in well-drained scree in
the open garden. The tight compression of the roots which presumably
occurs in a fissure does not appear to be necessary for crevice plants in

cultivation. Rock gardeners in recent years have tended to make use of tufa, which is a soft rock that can be drilled so that plants grow in it in conditions which in some respects imitate natural crevices: this method of cultivation is considered in Chapter Three.

Three

The Rock Garden

The setting

The operative word is 'garden'. Alpines can be grown in various special ways—for instance in raised beds or in sinks—but a rock garden is essentially part of the garden as a whole, not a unit on its own, and the satisfaction it will give will be proportionate to the success with which it is integrated with its surroundings. This may be difficult, and usually some degree of compromise has to be accepted. The essential problem is that a rock garden is in principle a 'wild' garden, and the rest of the garden is not. Even if the garden as a whole is of an informal type the house and probably a drive and fences and possibly outbuildings are artificial and formal.

Ideally, therefore, the rock garden is away from all buildings and formal structures, so that when one is in it, or looking at it, the buildings are either invisible or are placed to give an impression of distance or separateness. This counsel of perfection cannot be achieved except in a few large gardens, and one must seek to create an *impression* of separateness by inserting as it were a barrier between the rock garden and artificial structures (the latter including formally laid-out parts of the garden) by the use of trees and shrubs or, failing this, by lawn. Trees, particularly conifers and other evergreens, make a very effective background for a rock garden, but need careful siting to avoid excessive shade on the rock garden itself and also the problems of leaf-fall. A small area of grass, where space allows, between the rockwork and the shrub or tree background, will minimise both these problems; and by keeping the grass rough not only can the sense of 'wildness' be enhanced, but also dwarf bulbs (which could not survive in a close-

cropped lawn) can be grown and make their own valuable contribution to the setting of the rock garden.

Lawn itself, without trees or shrubs, is a less effective means of breaking the continuity between the rockwork and formal or artificial
structures, but it is certainly better than nothing. A rock garden entirely
surrounded by level lawn rarely looks natural. The reason for this is
that success in rock gardening depends above all else upon creating one
great illusion—that the whole garden is built upon a bed of rock, of
which the rock garden is just an outcrop (Plate, p 18). *A garden upon
rock, not rocks upon a garden*, must be the aim; and rarely does rock
naturally outcrop from level grass.

If the site allows, it is frequently possible to create an effective break
between the rock garden and formal structures by the appropriate use
of a bank or steep slope. Here the illusion that the rock is an outcrop is
more easy to create, and the differing levels help to avoid a jarring
boundary between the 'natural' and the artificial.

Whatever the site, and however small, the effectiveness of the rock
garden will be enhanced if some sort of gradation can be achieved from
the wholly informal rock garden, via rough grass to trees and shrubs,
thence to lawn and formal beds, and finally to the buildings. Rarely
can this be done from all angles, and it is wise, before embarking upon
the construction of the rock garden, to decide upon one or two critical
positions from which the layout and structure are to be viewed. For
instance, in a very small property, it could well be that the two selected
viewing points are the garden gate and the kitchen window. By selecting
such points of view, and always bearing them in mind when the rockwork is subsequently altered and extended (as it almost certainly will
be) it is possible to retain a sense of form which is not inconsistent with
informality, and a successful unity.

Preparing to build

With the foregoing considerations in mind the situation and, no less
important, the ultimate extent of the rock garden have to be decided
upon. This may be easy. In a small garden there may be little choice:
even in a larger one the availability of a slope (perhaps the reason for
deciding to build a rock garden) may clearly determine the site.
Probably a limited and perhaps small area of rockwork is envisaged—
but it is common experience that it later grows beyond the gardener's

original intention. The number of interesting rock plants to be grown, and the need for an ever more varied range of aspects and other special provisions, are likely if space allows to lead to a series of extensions over many years. Or the gardener may envisage extending his rock garden but decide, very sensibly, to phase its construction, out of deference both to his pocket and to his muscles. Whether later extension be probable, or only a mere remote possibility, it is an excellent plan to have in one's mind's eye a clear concept of what the ultimate maximum provision could be. Unplanned piecemeal additions are likely to make for 'bittiness'—a lack of satisfying cohesion in the ultimate product.

In planning, in siting and in construction, *aim for the natural outcrop, the life-size bluff.* There are on record stupendous and costly rock gardens which have set out to imitate on a small scale a specified mountain or mountain range. You can do a lot with stone and soil to make miniature mountains, just as you can build miniature railways. You can even go a little way towards planting them in miniature by putting in a few 'Noah's Ark trees' to imitate pines—but as soon as the first real alpine is planted the whole illusion is shattered. The mountain range ceases to be convincing even as a miniature, and the rock work stands or falls by whether it does or does not look as though it belongs there—as though it is a natural outcrop. So it is far better to make this the guiding principle in construction from the start.

THE SLOPING SITE

It is much easier to do this if you have a natural slope, though the problems of effective rock construction from the level are not insuperable. Let us assume for the moment that you have a bank or slope. It need not be very high or steep; in many ways a steep bank is more difficult to handle than a gradual one. The way the bank is utilised will depend mainly upon its aspect.

Aspect is important. We have seen that in the mountains many plants are highly selective, some requiring full exposure to a southerly sun, others tolerant of little or no direct sunshine at all, and many more surviving in good health only in situations where they receive morning or afternoon rather than midday sun. These preferences are apparent in the garden as well. If your slope faces to the north (and particularly if it is additionally shaded by trees, shrubs or buildings) you will have to be selective in the plants you try to grow: on the whole you will do better with woodland plants rather than those of the alpine meadows, rocks or screes. Conversely, if your slope faces fully to the southern sun, and you do not have adequate provision for artificial watering whenever it is needed, you can grow only those plants which are adapted to stand up to drought in high summer—generally the plants of the rocky out-crops at low levels. Clearly this will depend to some extent upon factors such as the latitude, and also the rainfall, of the area in which the garden is situated: and furthermore, much may be done to create areas which face in directions other than that of the main slope, in the manner described below. Either an easterly or a westerly slope gives far greater scope, and should be chosen—if there is any possibility of choice. But it is perfectly possible so to construct the rockwork that there are slopes and bluffs facing in directions other than that of the bank as a whole. It is important to do this: even if the general slope is a favourable one, say to the west, it will still be desirable to have some north-facing areas for special purposes. The diagram (Fig 14) indicates how this can be done.

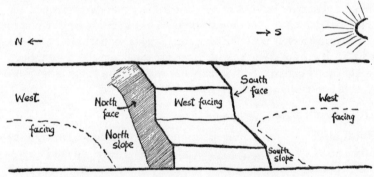

FIG 14   Diagram of construction on a west-facing bank to provide
north and south faces and slopes

If the main slope is towards the south, east and west faces and slopes can be constructed in precisely the same fashion, and it is even possible to achieve small north-facing areas as indicated in Fig 15, though this may involve some stretching of the primary rule that the bluff must look natural. This type of construction, designed to achieve varied aspects, may be carried out either by building on to the under-lying bank or by digging into it. In practice a combination of these two is likely to achieve the best results not only from the point of view of

W ←   → E

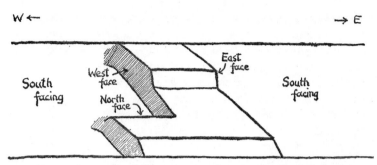

FIG 15   Even a north-facing area can be created on a south bank

appearance but also in conserving the soil and space available; and unless the bank is very small it will be more or less replaced by a series of bluffs with intervening recesses. If this is done it is important that the individual outcrops should be related to one another to give the impression that they are part of a single underlying rock-mass—and to achieve this it is necessary to follow some guidelines in the construction, particularly in the laying of the rocks.

CHOOSING THE STONE

He is a fortunate man whose garden lies upon a bedrock, near the surface, of stone suitable for the cultivation of alpine plants: most of us have to import stone, and skill is required in its placing. There are many kinds of stone, not all equally suitable, either in appearance or in their physical or chemical properties, for the building of a rock garden and the cultivation of plants. The stone must look natural—as though it belongs there—and this rules out certain kinds straight away. It rules out bricks, concrete, coke, marble, slate and flints; some of these it is true occur naturally, but not as surface stone carrying much in the way of flora. Others, such as granite, are difficult and unsatisfactory to use because they lack stratification, crevices and porosity, all of which make for success in rock gardening. The most useful kinds of stone fall under the two broad headings of limestone and sandstone. Most of the cost of stone lies in its transportation, so that in practice the choice is likely to be limited to the nearest usable rock. However, if cost is not the over-riding factor, or if there is a choice in spite of it, there are several other points to consider. The first is appearance. The actual colour of rock may vary from the almost dead-white of some limestones to a deep reddish-brown, almost black, in some sandstones; and bearing in mind the all-important need for a natural appearance, the gardener should take into account the colour of the soil in his own garden, and even the colour of the buildings, particularly if these are of natural stone. In most cases the stone will need to be set into an artificial soil-mixture, and if the appearance is to be satisfactory the grit used in the soil-mixture (and hence the colour and general appearance of the mixture) will itself be determined by the choice of rock. Apart from its colour, stone varies in appearance according to the strength and type of the stratification (that is, the appearance of natural layers and seams) and its roughness or smoothness. These factors, together with the shape and size of the blocks, affect also the ease of construction of the rockwork.

Two other considerations of importance, not so much in relation to appearance as to the suitability of the rock for growing alpines, are the porosity of the stone and its chemical constitution. Porosity means in effect the capacity to contain water, and is necessary in some measure to allow plants actually to root into rock, as well as providing on the buried surfaces a vital reserve of moisture in dry weather. Porous rock tends also to be softer and less durable: the moisture in the surface layers is subject to freezing and the expansion in the ice breaks away the outer crust. Some soft sandstones are quite unsuitable for rock garden construction for this reason.

As regards the chemistry of the rock, the most obvious distinction to be made is between calcareous (lime-containing) and non-calcareous rocks. The former (which in practice means limestones, because chalk rock is too soft and lacking in weather-resistance to be suitable even apart from its alkalinity) must be assumed to release small quantities of calcium carbonate which is favourable to a great many alpine plants but unsuitable for some others. Limestones vary in their hardness and probably in the extent to which they release calcium: it is likely that, at least in the case of hard limestones, the rate of breakdown is so slow as to be negligible—or far less important than the lime in the soil mixtures used between the rocks and in the water when public supplies are used for artificial watering. For most purposes limestone is a very satisfactory material, and some forms of it, such as water-worn Westmorland limestone, are most attractive in appearance. The adverse effects of limestone upon some plants are generally held to be due not so much to the presence of alkaline calcium carbonate as to the non-availability of

Page 53   The Sawfly Orchid (*Ophrys tenthredinifera*), and the quaint little Looking-glass Orchid (*O. speculum*) in the foreground, are relatives of our native Bee Orchid. Growing in southern Europe, they need the protection of a frost-cover in an English winter

Page 54 Plunge beds and frames for propagation and for temporarily potted plants. The plunge beds are covered to protect them from birds and animals. Slatted covers provide shade, and polythene sheeting protects from either rain or slight frost

other substances, such as iron and magnesium, which are vital to the plant's economy and whose absorption is prevented by an excess of calcium. Some limestones contain large amounts of magnesium as well as calcium, and these magnesian limestones (such as 'dolomite') support in the wild a number of plants which otherwise are found on acid or igneous rocks rather than upon limestone. Magnesian limestones are not widely available in the British Isles, though 'tufa', a form of porous limestone which sometimes has a high magnesium content, is frequently used for special purposes in rock gardening, and will be considered later.

Sandstones, no less than limestones, vary in their suitability for rock garden construction. Some are far from durable, breaking down readily into sand: others are very hard indeed. They vary also in stratification and colour, and generally speaking the deeper the colouring the greater the content of iron, which is a vital plant food.

At the Royal Horticultural Society's gardens at Wisley a special bed is set aside to demonstrate a number of different kinds of stone suitable for building rock gardens.

In order to build satisfactory rockwork, it is necessary that the stone be not only of the right kind but also in pieces of suitable size and shape. A few large pieces (2cwt is about the maximum that most of us can manipulate without special equipment) are a great asset in creating the salient bluffs, but they are somewhat uneconomical and pieces in the range $\frac{1}{4}$–1cwt will be found most generally useful. If at all possible, one should choose the pieces of stone for oneself, and try to secure those with attractive weathered surfaces.

THE SUBSOIL

Before turning to the actual placing of the rock, it is necessary to consider for a moment the subsoil upon which it will lie. This is important in two respects—its suitability as a growth medium for plants and the efficiency with which it provides or permits drainage.

Soil mixtures suitable for growing alpines were considered in the last chapter, and the stonework should be embedded in and packed with a compost such as that there suggested. It is not sufficient, however, to use the specially prepared mixture in a shallow layer or small pockets, if the underlying soil is unsuitable for alpine plant cultivation. Many alpines root deeply, and it is advisable to provide a soil which they can tolerate to a depth of at least 2ft. In some cases, for instance on a stiff clay, it may

D

pay in the long run to remove the soil totally to this depth, or alternatively to build up to this height upon it. More often the natural soil of
the garden can by suitable additives be made appropriate for the rock
garden. Light sandy or chalky soils need additional humus, which can
be provided by forking in peat and leaf mould. Clays will need sand,
grit and perhaps chalk as well as humus added to them. Peaty soils
which are excessively water-retentive will need added sand and grit. In
all these examples the aim is to modify the subsoil in the direction of
the recommended mixture for growing alpines, and the aim should be
to achieve a gradation from the unmodified subsoil to the specially
prepared mixture near the surface.

With the soil prepared in this way there are unlikely to be drainage
problems in a rock garden constructed on a bank or slope.

For several reasons, but especially in order to ensure that the subsoil
lies at an appropriate depth in all areas of the rock garden, the first step
in its actual construction should be to shape the whole area into
approximately the form which it will ultimately take—removing soil
where the gullies are to be, heaping it up where the bluffs will stand
forward from the main bank. This rough-casting of the ultimate form
of garden, crude though it must be, also permits an assessment, and if
necessary a revision, of the intended layout.

PLACING THE STONE

Let us now consider in some detail the actual placing of the stone.
However beautiful the stone itself—however well coloured, stratified,
and shapely the blocks—the overall effect will be satisfying only if the
blocks are placed in correct relationship to one another. Bear always
in mind the objective of the life-size bluff: it follows that each individual piece of stone should be placed so that it looks as though it is a
part of the same rock-mass as all the other pieces. Consequently the
layers—the strata—should lie all in the same direction. Normally this
will be horizontal when viewed from the front; the layers in rock were
originally deposited by water. But if you observe stratified rocks in
natural 'wild' formations you will see that frequently they are tilted.
This is the result of subsequent movements in the earth's crust, and it is
so common that a slight tilting or slanting of the strata in rock garden
construction certainly need not look unnatural. There is, furthermore, a
practical advantage in tilting the rocks slightly so that their strata dip a
little into the slope upon which they are built. This has the effect of

directing water which falls upon the rocks backwards into the slope
and so conserving it for use by the plants. If conversely the stratification
were to be *upwards* into the bank, water would tend to be carried away
to the surface, and to run down and be lost; and also soil from between
the rocks would tend to be washed down.

It is not sufficient that the strata should all lie in the same direction. If
the rocks are to appear as though they are all one the strata must furthermore be continuous; that is to say the major lines of cleavage
should appear to continue from one stone into the next. In practice
these cleavage lines, as they will appear in a rock garden, are not the
strata in the stones but rather the clefts or crevices *between* the stones;
and to retain an effect of continuity in horizontal strata it is therefore
necessary to choose very carefully each individual stone so that it is of
the right vertical thickness to place its upper surface at the same level
as that of its neighbours. In fact, quite the most satisfactory method is
to build up the stonework of each bluff, and indeed of the whole rock
garden, in a series of layers.

So far we have considered stratification (the horizontal or near-
horizontal cleavages) only; but you will have vertical cleavages too.
This must be so because stone comes in blocks. This does not mean
that they have been cut like cubes of butter in the quarry; on the contrary it reflects the fact that most rocks have in nature vertical as well
as horizontal fissures, and indeed the quarryman takes advantage of
these in gaining his material. These vertical lines tend to be at right
angles to one another, as well as to the horizontal stratification; in other
words the rock tends to come out in cuboid lumps. In many natural
formations this is plainly visible: the Dolomites provide a classical
example. These vertical clefts run for great distances, cutting right
across the lines of stratification; they are not 'staggered' as are the joints
between bricks in house building. So in the garden the blocks should
be placed with the gaps between them running vertically for the whole
height of the bluff—otherwise you will tend to get an appearance
rather like a rough stone wall.

Carried to its logical conclusion, this placing of stones so that both
their horizontal and their vertical faces are aligned has the effect of
making the rock garden appear as though it were derived from one
great cuboid mass. This has been advocated as the primary rule to
follow, and there is much in its favour. It involves just a little more than
what has already been said, in that a rigid adherence to this principle

means not only that all the stone within each individual bluff is composed in this rectangular way, but also that the separate bluffs are so related to one another that they appear to be part of one great whole—which is the effect one is seeking to create. To achieve this, it is helpful to mark out on the ground, before the first rock is placed, the lines of cleavage which are to be followed. Probably the general direction of alignment of our bank will determine the direction in which the fronts of the rocks are to face: the second plane, that is the line of the vertical faces running back into the bank, will be at right-angles to the first. The third plane—the 'horizontal' one—will not automatically follow: the gardener must decide upon the extent to which he is going to tilt his rocks backwards into the bank, but having decided this he should aim to keep the tilt much the same throughout the whole structure.

Rockwork built in this manner might sound to the reader to be very square and formal. In practice this is not so. Stones do not come in clean and perfect cubes; furthermore, unless your pocket is very deep, you will not be buying such an excess of stone that you can pick and choose every individual piece to suit your exact needs. So, in the garden as in the wild, the ultimate appearance is of worn, broken and defective surfaces which nevertheless are satisfying. A stone may have broken down so that one or more of its surfaces ceases to comply with the original rectangular pattern, but it still will not look 'skew'. A stone which is *placed* 'skew' will stick out like a sore thumb.

Rockwork in nature is weather-worn. The attrition is likely to be more marked at the exposed upper surfaces, with the result that rock faces are only rarely quite vertical. They tend to slope back a little, even where there is not an actual tilting of the strata. This effect is used in the garden. For appearance, and indeed for the cultivation of a few kinds of plant, a truly vertical surface, or even an overhang, may occasionally be of value, but in general the faces will slope slightly backwards, and this is achieved by insetting each level of construction very slightly as compared with the one below. It has the additional effect already mentioned, particularly if the strata are sloped slightly into the bank, of ensuring that water running down the face tends to flow back between the layers. This insetting should be slight, otherwise it will contravene the rectangular principle of construction and will not look natural or satisfactory. Assuming the slope of the bank to be fairly shallow—let us say at 15 degrees to the horizontal—there are three alternative methods of construction, shown in Fig 16, of which the first two are far more satisfactory than the third. Method (a), where the vertical height required is gained all in one face, is appropriate for the main bluffs. In the 'gullies' between the bluffs more height will be gained at the back than at the front (b). The step-like appearance produced in (c), while it may conform with the rectangular principle, is unlikely to be seen in nature (since it represents an improbable form of attrition of the original cuboid block), and will appear formless and unsatisfying in the garden.

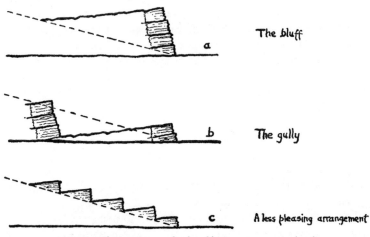

FIG 16   Alternative methods of laying stone on a bank

THE LEVEL SITE

Many an effective rock garden has been built upon a flat site. The principles of construction are the same as upon a slope. The aim is to create one or more life-size bluffs: the rock must look as though it belongs there: the strata and the vertical planes of the rock should be aligned.

These objectives are attained by tilting the strata, so that the rockwork presents as a steep escarpment with a very long shallow slope behind it; this is the only manner in which natural rock is likely to erupt from a level surface. The escarpment could be produced simply by building upon the pre-existing level ground, but this would require a large quantity of made-up soil, and unless the area to be built upon is large, the escarpments would need to be very shallow to avoid creating unnaturally steep slopes behind them. Both these difficulties can be overcome by digging down as well as building up. This method of construction (see Fig 17) has some advantages over building upon a preexisting slope. A series of escarpments can be made in the manner illustrated, which can impart a quality of 'depth' to the rock garden. But the major advantage is that there is greater scope for choosing the main aspect. The choice is not likely to be entirely free: the need to take account of the setting, the background, and the main viewpoints remains, but within these limits the escarpments can be set in a favourable direction. Several factors, such as the prevailing wind, protection from trees, etc, will influence the choice of main aspect in any particular garden. Having made the choice, the gardener can then create areas with different aspects in the same way as if he were building upon a bank.

FIG 17   Building a rock garden on a level site

Perhaps the worst mistake one can make in creating a rock garden on the level is that of attempting to achieve too much height. This cannot be done without excessive and unnatural tilting of the rocks, and apart from this it is exceedingly difficult to make a ridge of more than about two feet in height appear natural in perfectly level surroundings. On the other hand, by going down for a similar distance below ground level, one can create a four foot escarpment, which is sufficiently impressive in any but a very large rock garden.

One special difficulty in building upon a level site is the problem of drainage. If the soil is not naturally fast draining, water will accumulate in the lowest areas, that is to say those below ground level. There are two ways of dealing with this. One is to improve the drainage: this must be done in much the same way as one would set about improving an ill-drained lawn. It involves digging deeply and replacing the soil by a layer of coarse flints, crocks or other suitable drainage material, adding progressively finer layers of stone and grit above this, and then a layer of turves to prevent clogging of the drainage: only above this does the construction of the rock garden proper commence. On really difficult sites it may be necessary to spread the drainage more widely by laying land drains.

The alternative is to accept that the lowest levels will be water-logged at times, and to dig in peat and leafmould and use these lower levels for moisture-loving plants.

Building the rock garden

Before we really set to work with soil and stone, let us just recapitulate, and make as it were a check-list of the preparatory steps.

The site has been decided upon, with particular regard to the setting, and the main viewpoints have been determined.

The rock garden has been roughly shaped (Fig 18a), removing the turf, heaping up the main bluffs, hollowing out the gullies, and forking into the soil any additives necessary to make it suitable as a subsoil for rock gardening. Adequate drainage has been ensured.

A line has been marked, 'toe-ed' by one or more of the main bluffs, to ensure that the forward faces of the rocks are aligned; and the approximate tilt of the strata has been decided upon.

So now to work with the stone. Place the largest and best blocks first—partly in order to avoid having to manipulate large blocks up to higher levels, partly to show off the best stone to the greatest advantage. Obviously the stones should be placed so that their best faces are exposed to view, so far as this is compatible with the rectangular principle of construction; but although a newly cut rock face may have a raw

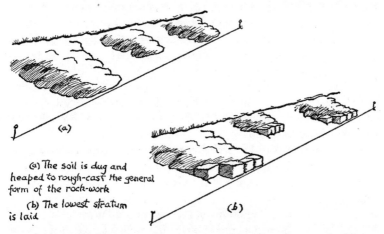

(a) The soil is dug and heaped to rough-cast the general form of the rock-work

(b) The lowest stratum is laid

FIG 18   The first stages of construction of a rock garden on a bank

and ugly look about it, it will very soon weather and tone down to its surroundings. The first step is to place the bottom layer in position throughout the whole area to be built. Because of the tilting of the strata, this bottom layer will not be continuous: it will disappear into the hillside (Fig 18b). (In fact, the more steeply the strata are tilted into the bank or the escarpment, the less stone will be required; so steeper tilting is an economy, but it should not be overdone.) The blocks must be completely firm. They will be walked upon, both by yourself and your visitors, and they will have to carry the weight of other rocks above them. Some settlement is to be expected: ideally the subsoil should so have settled before building commences, and the made-up soil should be so firm under and between the stones, that there is no appreciable settlement. In practice, most of us are too anxious to get on with the job for this to happen; consequently some adjustment of rock positions later on is usually needed, somewhat to the detriment of the plants. To ensure stability it is obviously advisable to lay the blocks upon their biggest surfaces. Usually this means that the strata run correctly, but occasionally this is not the case, and to get the strata right the block must be placed on end: this should be done rather than destroy the stratification—but a better course may be to split such a rock into two or more pieces along its seams. The rocks, especially the lower ones, should be deeply embedded: this goes against the grain when rock is so costly, but it is essential not only for stability but also to give the plants the maximum advantage from running their roots against the underground faces of the rocks where moisture is retained. The rocks are not laid directly upon the subsoil: the prepared compost is laid both below and between the stones, and rammed tightly. Air spaces below ground are not only damaging to the growth of plants in a direct way but also they diminish stability, allow sinkage, and provide homes for a wide range of vermin from millipedes to rats. The close packing of soil between the stones will be facilitated if it is put through a ¼in sieve for this purpose.

Some planting may be carried out as the work progresses—indeed this is usually advocated, on the ground that it is easier to place plants in crevices as the rocks are laid than later on. This is true; but on the other hand few plants are permanent, and there will undoubtedly be need for a great many additions and replacements. Furthermore, plants inserted at the earliest stages of construction are liable to damage as the work proceeds. There are other reasons for *not* planting as you go along. Success depends upon the correct placing of every stone; the work must be continuously and critically reappraised; one should be prepared to dismantle unsatisfactory work and begin again: planting as one goes is certainly a discouragement from doing this. Planting-out should be done in appropriate weather, when both the soil and the air are damp and warm: building the rockwork is easier when the soil is fairly dry, and pleasanter when the weather is fine. On the whole then it is better to build without planting, allow time for some of the inevitable settlement, and then plant when conditions are favourable.

So, then, we can proceed to our second layer, untrammelled by plants. The procedure is the same. The vertical thickness of the second layer does not have to be the same as that of the first—in general the bigger stones will be at the bottom, and the layers will get shallower as the work proceeds upwards. But the stones of the second layer should all be of approximately the same thickness as one another, so that the continuity of the horizontal strata is preserved. The second layer is likely to be more difficult than the first; the choice of suitable pieces of stone diminishes as the work goes on, and it becomes increasingly hard to find pieces of just the right size to keep the vertical fissures continuous. This problem can be mitigated by reducing the size of the bluffs as one works upwards. Only in a few selected places is it necessary so to fit the blocks one above the other as to provide a near-vertical face. A possible type of construction is shown in Fig 19: the rectangular concept is retained, and indicated by the ruled lines, but its angularity is diminished by the natural wear on the stones. In practice few of the rocks are likely to be truly rectangular, and those which are not can be utilised to advantage in various ways. For instance the stones marked 'a' and 'b' have irregular faces buried underground: similarly stone 'c' is of a thickness greater than that of the other stones in the bottom stratum in which it is used, but rather than splitting it up it has been buried more deeply, and will give greater stability. Stones 'b' and 'd' have irregular upper and inner surfaces; these will be covered with soil, and the irregularity of the stones will provide a useful pocket.

The laying of the upper strata follows similar principles. Less rock will be needed, and more irregular and rounded pieces can be used on the upper surfaces of the bluffs without creating any unnatural effect. Perhaps the biggest danger at this stage is that of using too much rock: there is a tendency to feel that because one is building a rock

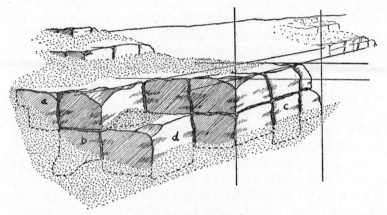

FIG 19 The utilisation of stone

garden the whole surface should be stone-faced. It is a common experience of rock gardeners that once it is really established, and more
and more planting space is needed, they are continually removing
superfluous stone!

The rock garden need not be one continuous structure, particularly
if it is on a slope. The construction of a series of separate bluffs, with
turf in between, can be very effective and mimics a formation seen
commonly enough in the mountains. Bearing in mind the overall aim of
attempting to represent that the whole garden lies upon rock, an
effective device is to create small outlying bluffs on any slope or bank
where this can be done conveniently. For instance, in the author's
garden the entry drive is banked on one side, and a few outcrops of
stone are placed along it to 'set the scene', although the main rock
garden is well away. It is, however, important that such isolated outcrops should conform to the same pattern and direction of stratification
and aspect as the main rock garden.

It has so far been assumed that the rockwork is to be built in stone
which is roughly cuboid and has a clear stratification. Not all stone
which is suitable for plant cultivation has these properties: an example
of an amorphous stone which is particularly valuable is tufa, which is
considered below. In general, however, it may be said that the use of
amorphous stone is easier in the sense that one is not restricted by the
need to regulate the strata, and indeed the whole principle of rectangular construction ceases to apply. On the other hand it is far more diffi-

cult to produce an aesthetically satisfactory result: formless stone means a formless garden, and one is far more dependent upon really skilled planting. The same basic criterion, that it must look natural, still applies.

In the last chapter we discussed how the range of rock plants that can be grown successfully depends upon preparing areas especially adapted to their needs. The principles of cultivation in such special beds as screes were considered: such areas need care in their construction, which is the subject of the following paragraphs. The amount of space allocated to special requirements will depend very much upon the total space available and the extent to which the gardener is interested in, and able to acquire, plants needing such special provision. It may well be that he will decide to start with a 'straight' rock garden, and meet the more specialised needs later as they arise. There is, however, much to be said for having at least a scree area from the beginning, since this is so favourable a medium for so many alpines.

Lists of plants suitable for growing in special conditions will be found in Chapter Nine.

SCREES

The scree is essentially an area in which the amount of grit and stone in the mixture is greatly increased. It will look best and flourish best if it is on a slope, but it should not be continually exposed to full sunlight, and this means that in warm gardens it should not face to the south. If space allows, small areas of scree, with different aspects—east, north, west—should be provided. Place them in hollows rather than upon the tops of bluffs or crests, so that they fall away from the rock faces. An area to be constructed as a scree should be prepared to a depth of a foot or more, and this assumes that the subsoil for at least a further foot is suitable for alpine plants. The scree should be prepared so that there is a gradation from a fairly high humus content at the lowest levels to pure grit on the surface. On the author's chalky soil 2in of peat are laid at the base to reduce some of the alkalinity in the soil and as a moisture-retainer. Above this place a layer of 2 or 3in of a mixture of equal parts of loam, leafmould, peat and grit; then 6in of a scree mixture of 50 per cent grit and the remainder equal parts of loam, leafmould and peat. Finally, a layer of 2in of pure grit is used for surfacing. This provides a fairly 'rich' scree: it is to be emphasised that there is nothing magical in these proportions, and the gardener as he gains experience will vary them considerably to suit his local conditions and the particular plants he intends to grow.

FIG 20   *Edraianthus serpyllifolius*—for the scree (scale × $\frac{7}{8}$)

THE 'MORAINE'

A 'moraine' is a more ambitious undertaking, requiring as it does a running water supply and usually a concrete base. Unless you are fortunate enough to have a stream running through your garden, or

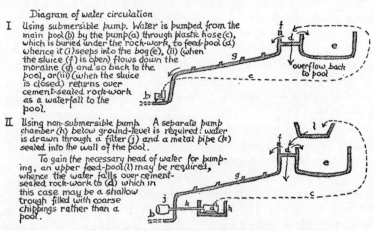

Diagram of water circulation

I Using submersible pump. Water is pumped from the main pool (b) by the pump (a) through plastic hose (c), which is buried under the rock-work, to feed-pool (d) whence it (i) seeps into the bog (e), (ii) (when the sluice (f) is open) flows down the moraine (g) and so back to the pool, or (iii) (when the sluice is closed) returns over cement-sealed rock-work as a waterfall to the pool.

II Using non-submersible pump. A separate pump chamber (h) below ground-level is required: water is drawn through a filter (j) and a metal pipe (k) sealed into the wall of the pool.

To gain the necessary head of water for pumping, an upper feed-pool (l) may be required, whence the water falls over cement-sealed rock-work to (d) which in this case may be a shallow trough filled with coarse chippings rather than a pool.

FIG 21 Moraine and bog construction

are prepared to allow piped water to run to waste, you will need a continuous circulation system using an electric pump. For this reason it is useful and effective to combine the provision of a moraine with additional water features such as a pool, with or without a stream or waterfall. In the author's garden water is pumped through a buried hose-pipe from an ornamental pool up into a small inconspicuous feed-pool near the top of the highest part of the rockwork. From this feed-pool it overflows to serve three distinct purposes: it keeps a small bog continuously sodden; it flows down through the moraine back into

FIG 22   *Epilobium fleischeri*—for the moraine (scale × 1¼)

the main pool; and it also discharges directly back into the pool as a small waterfall. A very simple sluice controls the allocation of water as between the moraine and the waterfall (Fig 21). The construction and planting of the pool will not be considered here: there are many excellent books on the subject, and it is sufficient to say that if space allows the provision of water can greatly enhance the beauty of a rock garden as well as permitting the cultivation of a number of aquatic and waterside plants such as may be found in and around pools and lakes in the mountains.

The moraine itself is a concrete tray at least 12 to 15in deep, sloping, and with water entering at its highest point and leaving at its lowest. It should be strongly constructed because it will carry a considerable weight of soil and stone; furthermore, unless it is very small, it is likely to contain a path or stepping stones and will therefore have to carry the weight of people walking upon it. If it cracks it will lose its efficiency and involve a constant wastage of water, and its repair is a major operation liable to result in the loss of plants. The base should be

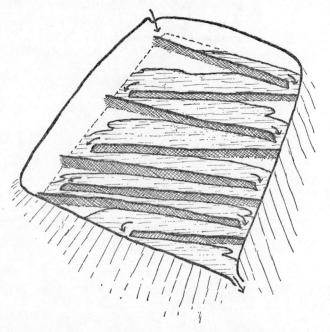

FIG 23   The cement tray for a moraine

level (not dished) from side to side. Upon this base a series of cement barriers is built, about 2½in high, which starts immediately below the entry point of the water and zigzags the full width of the tray right down to the bottom: so that when water is run in the whole, or nearly the whole, of the base is covered by a series of slow-moving pools. There is a small gap between the lower end of each barrier and the side wall of the moraine to allow entry of water into the next pool (Fig 23). A layer of broken crocks placed with their concave sides downwards is laid along the upper side of the barriers to keep the water channels open, and over this a layer 2 or 3in deep of coarse (¾in) grit or pebbles; above the pebbles a 2in layer of peat is laid and thereafter the construction is on the same lines as for an ordinary scree, as already described. Because the moraine can be kept continuously moist from below, it can be made more fast-draining (with 60 per cent or more of grit) in its upper layers, and also can be placed in full sunshine, facing south: this presupposes that there will always be someone to switch on the water-supply in high summer! The supply of water should not be continuous: it is unnecessary and it will leach out minerals and humus too quickly. Furthermore, the water-supply should be cut off during the winter months; at this time most of the plants are resting, and their biggest enemy is damp round the crowns of the plants, which the moraine is expressly designed to prevent. Usually this is simply a matter of not using the electric pump, but if the moraine is fed by natural running water it is essential to be able to divert this when it is not required. Needless to say, the concrete structure of the moraine is not apparent upon the surface: the rockwork is constructed over and around it, and the scree mixture is carried 2 or 3in or more above the level of the side walls of the tray to form a scree on either side of the moraine. This means that some water is lost by seepage into surrounding areas, to the benefit of the latter: it also means that in a circulating system additional water must from time to time be added either to the feedpool or to the main pool. Because of the leaching effect of running water, frequent top dressing (see Chapter Two) is required.

THE BOG

The provision of a bog presents no great difficulties in a garden which already contains water, whether as a stream or as a pool. As a somewhat arbitrary distinction the word 'bog' is here used to indicate

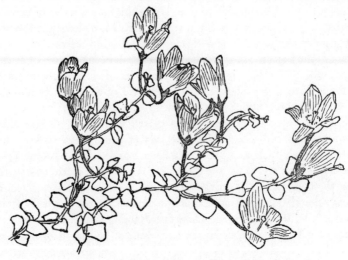

FIG 24   The Bog Pimpernel, *Anagallis tenella* (scale × 1¼)

a humus-rich and waterlogged area which is acid, as opposed to 'marsh' for a similar area which is alkaline. Therefore, except in gardens which contain continuously sodden areas of lime-free soil the construction of a bog involves making a concrete basin which does not lose water except by overflow or slow seepage. In the author's garden this is combined with the feed into a moraine, and works satisfactorily. It can with advantage be in full sun. Probably a slow movement of water through it is better than complete stagnation. The bottom is covered with some fairly open medium such as pea-gravel to a depth of 2 or 3in: the whole thing is then filled up with the fine rich mixture described in the last chapter. The purpose of the gravel is to assist in an even dispersal of moisture throughout the whole bed; the bog-mixture permits only very slow movement of water and without the drainage layer would tend to be always much wetter at the point of inlet of water. As with the moraine, the concrete structure is hidden by carrying the bog-mixture 1 or 2in above the rim and out over the surrounding area.

THE PEAT BED (Plates, p 36)

The gardener on lime or chalk, with many hundreds of plants which he can grow, will probably wish sooner or later to try his hand

Page 71 (*above*) A pair of raised frames, used both for propagation and for summer 'baking'. The slatted cover over the left-hand frame provides light shade; (*below*) the same frames, the nearer one boxed in for full frost protection

Page 72 (*above*) A raised bed for rock plants is sufficiently formal in outline to associate closely with the house; (*below*) a more formal raised bed for rock plants in a town garden

Fig 25 *Sisyrinchium douglasii*—for rich peaty soil (scale × ⅝)

at some of the 'calciphobes'—the heathers and heaths, dwarf rhododendrons and azaleas, asiatic gentians, meconopses, and many others—which are intolerant of lime. This can be done by constructing raised beds of lime-free soil.

A satisfactory example of this is the peat-bed. Such beds are now to be seen in association with the rock garden at Wisley, at the Royal Botanical Gardens in Edinburgh, and in many public gardens. They can be large or small, and present no great problems in construction. Because a peat-bed differs in appearance from most types of rock-

E

work it is probably better built separately, in association with the rock garden rather than as an integral part of it. Many of the plants which are suitable for a peat-bed will tolerate, or even demand, a certain amount of shade, and one satisfactory arrangement is to place it between the rock garden proper and a hedge, copse or woodland area. Another alternative, if there is an ornamental pool, is to separate the peat and the rockwork by water. The area on which the peat-bed is to be built should be cleaned, and one or two layers of heavy-duty polythene laid; this will prevent worms from carrying calcareous soil up into the peat-bed. In a garden where moles are troublesome an additional safeguard would be to lay wire netting, with a mesh not exceeding 1in, under the polythene. The walls of the bed are built of peat-blocks. These are obtainable in varying degrees of dryness, and blocks which are fully dried out are remarkably tough and resistant to weather, and are recommended for this purpose. Not only will they wear much better than fresher, softer peat-blocks, but also they will shrink much less: if soft blocks are used the initial appearance is better but the whole structure will steadily sink and shrink. The shape of the bed is outlined to suit the gardener's taste and to adapt as far as may be possible to the general layout of the garden. The peat blocks are used in effect as walling stones, successive layers being built up, leaning slightly inwards for strength. The whole of the inner part of the bed and the spaces between the blocks are filled with a mixture of three parts peat, and one part each of soil, leafmould and sand, all the ingredients being lime-free. They should be well mixed, sifted through a 1in sieve, and very firmly trodden down: even so there will be some sinkage, and it is advisable to heap up the soil mixture rather above the level of the walls. The latter are likely to appear open jointed, particularly if they are curved, and the appearance can be improved by sifting some of the soil mixture more finely, soaking it into a paste and using it like cement between the peat-blocks; it endures surprisingly well.

A bed thus constructed can be most rewarding and remain lime-free for many years. One of the problems is watering. The bed must not be allowed to dry out, and despite the fact that the mixture contains a great deal of moisture-retaining humus the upper layers do tend to become dry because of the raised construction. Public water supplies nearly always contain lime, and it is well to use rain water whenever possible. Care should be taken also in planting to remove lime-containing soil from the roots of the plants: not all plants which are suitable for and look well in the peat-bed are strict calciphobes, and the nursery-man may well have grown them in a mixture containing some lime.

It is possible to make provision for lime-hating plants within the structure of the rock garden itself. Attempts to produce more or less level lime-free beds by sinking concrete basins and filling them with a lime-free mix have not, in the author's experience, been very satisfactory. Good drainage is essential, and this permits the entry from the surrounding soil not only of lime-soaked moisture but also of worms, which are enthusiastic soil-mixers. Such a bed is likely to be suitable for calciphobes for no more than two or three years. On the other hand a *sloping* lime-free bed is a possibility, using either polythene or concrete for the base and sides: provided that the slope is adequate no perforation of the polythene or concrete is necessary for drainage, so that contamination from the surrounding soil can be minimal. This implies that there is no limy soil above the topmost edge of the bed. Watering can be a problem. Nevertheless the author has found that a millstone grit scree constructed in this way, using polythene, has remained satisfactory for at least four years.

Fig 26   *Selliera radicans*—for moist peaty soil (scale × $\frac{3}{4}$)

TUFA

A specialised method of cultivation which has become popular in recent years involves the use of tufa. This is a light, porous rock somewhat like pumice, formed by the deposition under water of carbonates upon organic matter. Chemically it is mainly a mixture of calcium and magnesium carbonates in varying proportions; and in some cases it consists almost entirely of the former and is thus a softish porous limestone. Its special features from a gardening point of view are that it is light, that it lacks stratification, that it contains air spaces and is easily bored or chiselled, and that it absorbs and holds moisture to a marked degree. It varies in its hardness, and newly quarried tufa has a soft surface which rapidly weathers; it is usually recommended that such tufa should be hosed down and left for the surface to harden for some months.

Many plants grow remarkably well in tufa. Of particular interest is the fact that many plants which in the wild show a preference for the non-calcareous formations and are normally regarded as lime-haters will flourish in tufa. This is perhaps not so surprising where the tufa contains significant quantities of magnesian limestone, since one of the reasons why calciphobes cannot flourish in lime is that they cannot absorb enough magnesium in the presence of an excess of calcium. What *is* surprising is that calciphobes will frequently do well in tufa that consists almost entirely of calcium carbonate. One can only assume that other qualities of the tufa—its porosity and its capacity to retain moisture without being water-logged—are very much to the plants' advantage and outweigh the deleterious effect of the lime; indeed it raises the whole interesting question of just what it is that goes wrong when a calciphobe attempts to grow in chalk or lime.

Tufa, as a rock for use in the open garden, has some limitations. First, it is expensive if there is no local source of supply—though perhaps rather less so than the list price might suggest because it is light and you get a lot to the ton. Secondly, as with peat, there is a problem of integrating it with the rest of the rock garden: it is usually rounded, has no stratification and is very white when new. It is frequently soft, and tends to break away even after initial weathering. For these reasons tufa is more often used in pot culture and under cover than in the open garden.

However, despite its disadvantages, tufa *can* provide in the rock garden for the cultivation of some plants whose needs would otherwise be very difficult to meet. It is best used as a near-vertical wall or face. If large pieces are available this is not difficult to achieve; with smaller material, which is more likely to break away, it is better built into a bank sloping backwards rather than as a wall. It is likely that there will be a lot of small broken tufa, down to powder, available with the rock, and this can be wetted into a sludge and packed between the blocks in the same manner as was suggested with peat, but it is not very durable. The space behind, above and between the blocks should be packed with a lime-free mixture—otherwise one of the main advantages of tufa will be lost. For this purpose all the tufa, down to the dust, which remains over from building the wall or bank, can be used together with finely sifted peat, a small quantity of lime-free soil, and sand in sufficient quantity to give a well-drained mixture. The wall can be planted either by placing plants between the stones or by drilling holes into them, inserting the plants, preferably small seedlings or rooted cuttings, and packing them with moist tufa dust. This is the easiest way of achieving something which really approaches a true crevice, and it is remarkable how plants force their roots right into the substance of the tufa; indeed, not only their roots but stems as well in some cases—for instance *Campanula zoysii*, planted into a hole on one side of a piece of tufa, so permeated the block that it appeared and flourished on its other faces.

It has been said that you can grow almost any alpine in tufa. This is an exaggeration, but what is more important is that assuming the tufa to be a small section of the rock garden the obvious thing is to use it for those plants which cannot be equally successfully cultivated elsewhere. This applies to a number of the highest alpines, of true crevice plants, and of plants whose natural habitat is dolomite limestone. This is a magnesian limestone, and it is interesting to note that, tufa apart, dolomite plants are frequently best treated as lime-haters in English gardens. *Campanula zoysii* has already been mentioned; *C. morettiana* and *C. caespitosa*, two other difficult and beautiful bellflowers of the dolomite, are obvious candidates for the tufa wall; *Phyteuma comosum* will grow quite well in an ordinary scree but looks far better on a vertical face (as almost always in the wild) and is a suitable tufa plant. Some of the crevice primulas, such as *P. tyrolensis* and *P. hirsuta (rubra)*; the more difficult drabas such as *D. mollissima* and *D. imbricata*; *Petrocallis pyrenaica*; the aretian androsaces, such as *A. vandellii (imbricata)* and *A. wulfeniana*, which are not too intolerant of winter wet; *Asperula suberosa*; the lewisias—all these are examples of plants which, in some gardens at least, are difficult to accommodate and are well worth a trial in the tufa. Experience with this medium is still fairly recent, and reports are varied; and I think we are still in a stage where it is fair to say, 'If you are anxious to grow a plant, and can't manage it anywhere else in the open garden, try it in tufa!'

Our rock garden is built. The stones are in position, packed tight with the right soil mixture below, between, above and behind them. Probably we have included one or two areas of scree, and perhaps some other more specialised features. There are extensive areas, both level and sloping, where no rock shows—and indeed where no rock *is*, though if the construction has been effective it will *appear* to the observer that there is rock everywhere a little way down. It is in these areas that most of the planting will be done. In the next chapter we will turn from the setting to the plants themselves—their planting, protection, propagation, and care.

Four
Plant Care

Because of their special characteristics, the cultivation of alpine plants differs in some respects from that of other garden plants. They tend to be small, and so at greater risk from vermin and from overlying, and they are easily lost sight of; they are of numerous kinds, competing with one another; it is unlikely that even in a small area of a square foot or two all the plants will be identical in their needs.

Planting

Purchased plants are usually pot-grown, and this permits planting at any time of the year when the soil conditions and weather are suitable. Nevertheless it is well to remember that some root disturbance is unavoidable (indeed it is usually *necessary*) so that there is likely to be a check or setback in the growth of the plant. Ideally, therefore, planting out should be done only when conditions are favourable to growth—when the ground is reasonably warm and moist but not waterlogged, and there is no threat of drought or desiccating winds. This calls both for space and for patience. If conditions are not favourable for planting into the rock garden potted plants are best plunged in a sand bed until they are. Plants which are not received in pots, such as gifts in polythene bags from friends, unless they are very fresh and well rooted and planting conditions are ideal, are best potted up and plunged in the sand bed for a few weeks. Indeed this applies to many plants received in pots: frequently the roots are packed tightly and directed upwards on the inner surface of the pot; such roots must be disentangled and well separated, and unless conditions for planting out are right temporary repotting into a larger pot is the best immediate treatment.

The positioning of plants was considered in Chapter Two. The ground should be loosened to an ample depth and the plant placed with its roots extending down deeply into the soil, against the lower side of a rock whenever possible. It should be planted *firmly*, and the soil well trodden around it. If the plant is a 'piece' from a friend or if there has been much root loss in removal from a pot it may be desirable to trim away much of the foliage, leaving a few healthy young leaves, so that there is not excessive water loss before the roots are re-established: in such circumstances flower buds should also be sacrificed.

If there is any danger of drought, plants should be well soaked before they are put out; because rock garden soil mixtures are fast draining drought is always a major risk to unestablished plants. If weather conditions turn unfavourable (particularly if there are drying winds) shortly after planting, protection with inverted pots should be given.

LABELLING AND RECORDING

It is not easy to keep track of plants in the rock garden. In no other part of the garden are there so many kinds of plant in so small an area, and their identity can very readily be lost. It is easy to say, as many a beginner does, 'I am a gardener, not a plant-collector: I don't worry about their names and I can remember where I put them, and I don't want my garden cluttered up with labels!' This is all right for perhaps the first 200 plants, particularly if some sort of list is kept of plants bought and received. But then problems begin to arise. You can easily have a thousand kinds of plant in quite a small rock garden, and this begins to tax the best of memories. There are some excellent reasons for wanting to know what plants you possess—to avoid buying duplicates, to avoid looking too much of a fool when your friends ask you the names of your plants and particularly when you are giving pieces away, to be able to link your plants with your reading, to be able to identify the ones that need special care, and as an essential part of a propagation programme.

Labelling is especially necessary for plants such as bulbs, which die down completely, and above all for those which, like the Shooting Stars (Fig 27), reduce to an inconspicuous and vulnerable resting root quite early in the year.

One of the problems is to find the ideal *label*, which should be legible, permanent, inexpensive, readily found, inconspicuous and proof against removal by blackbirds! After many trials, and much

FIG 27   Shooting Stars, *Dodecatheon pauciflorum* (scale × $\frac{3}{8}$)

advice from friends, the writer uses plastic labels inscribed in water-proof black ink with a fine felt-tipped pen. They are embedded as firmly as possible with only about $1\frac{1}{2}$in showing. They have to be hunted for, and are mainly for the gardener's personal use rather than for the benefit of visitors.

There is much to be said for keeping *records* of one's plants. It is not everyone who will want to go to the trouble of maintaining a card index, which can be time-consuming. Nevertheless there are many advantages in doing so. If a rough plan is drawn of the rock garden, dividing it into numbered areas, you can enter upon the card for each newly acquired plant the appropriate number to indicate whereabouts in the garden it has been planted. This greatly facilitates tracing it, and can be a partial substitute for labelling. The writer has kept a card-index for many years, and has come to regard this entry of the position of the plant in the garden as the most useful information that the card provides. It is in addition an *aide-mémoire* to the name and synonyms of the plant, and contains information as to the date and source of its acquisition, the date of its coming into flower each year (a check that it still exists), and information as to seed sowing, cuttings, division, etc. This may seem a cumbersome, complicated and perhaps un-necessary procedure; but in fact such a card-index probably saves more time than it takes in the long run, and becomes an increasingly valuable source of information as the years go by.

Photographing one's plants is an additional and valuable method of recording them. The making of good colour transparencies is a relatively easy and increasingly popular sideline for the alpine gardener. A coloured picture is a pleasanter record of a dead plant than a card or label! Plant photography is outside the scope of this book, and I will only add that if a photographic record is kept of one's plants (whether black or white or in colour) it is useful to enter on the plant index card a record of photographs taken: this means that when the plant comes into flower each year, and you turn up the card to enter the date, you can see at a glance if you do not yet have a satisfactory picture.

Trimming and pruning

Many rock plants form neat, slow growing mats or cushions and need no trimming of any sort until they begin to encroach upon one another. When this happens there are three alternatives—to remove one or more of the plants to a new situation, to let them grow into one another, or to trim them back annually. The choice will be determined by the plant's tolerance of trimming or invasion, by the availability of space, and by personal preference. Some degree of interweaving of plants looks attractive, helps to keep down weeds, and accords with the growth of many of them in the wild; but care is needed to ensure that the stronger grower does not overpower the weaker.

There are many rock plants which need shearing back either to improve their own appearance or that of the rock garden or both.

First there are the bulbs, especially those that flower in early spring—such as crocus, iris, chionodoxa, scilla, narcissus, snowdrop and snowflake. The better the spring show (and there is no lovelier time in the rock garden) the greater the quantity of untidy foliage in May and June. Fortunately the majority of readily grown spring bulbs suitable for the rock garden appear to tolerate an early loss of foliage—indeed, seeing how they are regularly close-chewed by sheep or goats in the Mediterranean area one wonders whether they are biologically adapted to having most of their foliage removed in this way! Perhaps a more realistic assumption is that in the wild (since so many of our spring bulbs come from warm climates) their foliage is dried off more rapidly than in temperate gardens. If time allows, it is probably better to do the shearing in two stages, cutting the leaves back to about 3 or 4in when they become too unsightly, and then back to ground level when most of the foliage is either dried or rotting. There are some spring bulbs, for instance some of the forms of *Iris reticulata*, which have a tendency to 'go back' in the open garden, and one may speculate as to whether they are less tolerant of losing their foliage while it is still green: but it is more likely that their greater need is for a thorough baking in the summer, and clearance of the ground above them, including their own foliage, may be of greater value. In this as in so much else in alpine gardening there is room for individual experiment. Later flowering bulbs, for instance many of the alliums and brodiaeas, likewise need trimming back while still green for the sake of the general appearance of the rock garden and to avoid smothering neighbouring plants.

Perhaps the most important group of plants to prune annually are those which make a great deal of new growth each year and left to themselves will soon cover vast areas, smothering their neighbours. The 'type-plant' of this group is aubrieta, that magnificent mainstay of the colourful rock garden. The growth comes initially from a central tuft, which gets thicker year by year, and the crowded leafy stems flower at their tips, spreading in all directions. After flowering, if left to themselves, these stems make further growth, several inches of it, and tend to root down, so that a single plant may come to cover upwards of a square yard. It may indeed look very fine, though untrimmed plants do tend to become bare in patches and to flower less well. In the ordinary smallish rock garden space cannot be spared for these great plants, but fortunately they respond very well to a close cut-back after flowering to the central rooting mass, which will then make new growth and flower well the following year: by repeating this annually the plant can be kept down to almost the same size. If the shearing is left too late, for instance till the autumn, the following year's flowering may be less satisfactory—and other plants may have been smothered in the meantime. At the time of cutting back it is well to make an attack upon the slugs and snails which abound under these mats. There is one other point to be noted: when the plant is shorn there is a bare area round it, and a temptation to put other plants there—don't forget that the aubrieta will be just as big again next spring! There are a good many of the commoner, robust, valuable rock plants which need the same sort of treatment, though some of them differ from the aubrieta in that they die back to ground level each winter: some of the arabis (particularly *Arabis caucasica (albida)*), campanulas, *Veronica rupestris*, geraniums such as G. *sanguineum*, *Gentiana septemfida* and its allies, the many forms of *Phlox subulata* and *P. douglasii*—these are all examples of plants which will benefit from trimming back hard after flowering.

Then there are the shrubs. Many of the larger rock garden shrubs, such as the forms of *Potentilla fruticosa*, the dwarf lilacs *Syringa palibiniana* and *S. microphylla*, the cistuses, and some of the dwarf rhododendrons, need an annual trimming to limit their size and improve their shape, and to preserve their health. The best season for this varies with the shrub, and indeed a certain amount of snipping and pruning can usefully go on throughout the year. The cistuses are subject to die-back in the late spring, possibly a result of overdrying winds, and apart from removing dead wood, any necessary trimming is best done in the summer after flowering. *Potentilla fruticosa* can be trimmed to shape in the autumn before it loses its leaves, and this is the time to remove any weak and spindly growth as well as any which has become very old and woody. The taller forms of this shrub are particularly useful to give shade to smaller plants if the lowest branches are removed as well as much of the new growth around the base. These procedures can be carried out as necessary through the year. Some of the dwarf conifers (which are really slow-growing conifers, and sometimes not so very slow) can to some degree be kept down to shape and size by a constant light trimming throughout the year.

There are some really dwarf shrubs, such as rockroses (*Helianthemum*), heaths and heathers, which need annual trimming to keep them free-flowering and in good shape. The many garden forms of the rockrose vary a good deal in their manner of growth, but the majority of them tend to become large and straggly if left to themselves: they should be cut back hard after the peak of their flowering, usually in July, and they will then make good new growth and flower well the following year. This new growth provides easy cutting material, and it is as well to put up a few cuttings of any good form of rockrose because the old plants slowly become more woody and the time comes when they fail to make adequate new growth after trimming back. The winter heathers, forms of *Erica carnea*, similarly benefit from trimming at the end of their very long flowering season: this needs care, particularly as regards timing—if it is left too late new growth will have been formed, and if this is removed next year's flowering will be spoiled and the plant may die back. The summer-flowering heaths, such as *Erica vagans*, and heathers (*Calluna*) need similar treatment after their flowering period. In all these instances—rockroses, heaths and heathers—a practical problem is to decide when the plant has finished flowering! They go on for a long time, and there is a natural reluctance to cut them back while they are still making a worthwhile show—nevertheless if it is left too late next year's growth will suffer.

This is not a complete list of plants that need trimming or pruning in the rock garden; it should be read as a series of examples. The trimming away of untidy growth, and even more of dead leaves and branches, is a continuous process, not only to maintain a fresh and healthy appearance in the rock garden but also to discourage pests such as millepedes and woodlice which feed upon decayed material, and also invasion by fungi.

Feeding

In Chapter Two some consideration was given to the question of feeding plants by the use of additives to the soil-mixtures used in rock garden construction and top-dressing. Some plants are 'greedy feeders', and in general these are the larger, lusher, more rapidly growing plants and those with storage systems such as bulbs and tubers. Most of the former and some of the latter come from the lower, richer mountain meadows, and if they are grown in the rock garden they are best kept together in deeply dug, well-manured areas. They include plants such as the larger gentians, phyteumas and geraniums, pulsatillas, *Anemone narcissiflora*, *Ranunculus aconitifolius*, and *Trollius europaeus*. Some of them are suitable only for larger gardens.

It is mainly in relation to bulbous and tuberous rooted plants that the question of individual feeding arises; particularly those which, either because their overground stature is small or because they need fast drainage or summer ripening, are unsuitable for growing in richer beds with coarser plants. They include many of the crocus species, the smaller irises such as *I. reticulata* and *I. danfordiae*, tulips and some fritillaries. These plants usually grow in conditions providing an abundance of soluble minerals but not a great deal of humus. The late E. B. Anderson, a most expert grower of these small bulbous plants, recommended that they be dressed in December or January every year with bone-meal to which is added about 5 per cent by weight of sulphate of potash. Bone-meal is a most valuable food for all but lime-hating plants, consisting as it does largely of calcium phosphate with a small organic content. It is, however, a variable product according to the manner in which it has been prepared, and in particular this affects the organic (nitrogen-containing) content and the solubility and rate of release of the phosphates. The writer uses it as an ingredient of a general top-dressing (see Chapter Two) as well as for the individual feeding of bulbous and tuberous plants, including orchids, the hardy cyclamen and the mountain lilies.

With the exception of the kinds of plant just mentioned, the rock gardener is recommended to think in terms of maintaining his soil in good condition rather than of individual plant feeding.

FIG 28   The Lady Tulip, *Tulipa clusiana* (scale × ⅜)

Weeding and soil care

Weeds can be a major problem in a rock garden, especially in the country. They can be kept down to some extent by keeping the ground well covered with plants, but the necessity to hold the big spreading rock plants in check so that they do not damage the small alpines, of course, lets in the weeds. So weeding is needed, and obviously the aim is to remove them each year before they set seed: small annual weeds are the main problem in an established and well-kept garden. They cannot be dealt with by hoeing—the smallest of hoes is far too destructive in the rock garden: they must be lifted individually with a fine-pointed trowel: if they are scraped to death *en masse*, and particularly if this is done while the seedlings are still very small, you are likely to deprive yourself of one of the rock garden's pleasantest bonuses—self-sown seedlings from your alpines. It is a galling feature of rock gardening experience that some plants are reluctant to germinate their seed in pots but will seed themselves spontaneously round the garden! So there is much to be said for learning to recognise the early seedlings both of your weeds and of your plants.

Large, deep-rooted weeds such as docks and dandelions can be awkward in the rock garden if they are not removed while still small. Their uprooting is very disturbing to neighbouring plants, and pieces of root left behind are liable to re-sprout. One treatment which is frequently effective is to paint the leaves with a hormone weed-killer: another is to cut off the plant cleanly just below the crown and paint the cut root with creosote; but neither method is wholly reliable.

Protection from vermin

Many alpine plants, because of their small size, are highly vulnerable to the attacks of plant pests. The rockwork, particularly if badly constructed, provides harbourage for vermin, and so also do the larger mat-forming plants. Eradication of some kinds involves dismantling the rockwork; prevention should be the aim, and so far as possible the garden should be constructed to avoid holes and crevices where vermin may lodge. Most of the smaller creatures multiply very rapidly if left undisturbed, and it is important to keep a sharp look out for them and tackle them early.

Slugs and snails are always with us and are the major enemy. There are several preparations combining bait and poison which are effective if used regularly. Pellets and granules scattered on the surface are taken better by slugs than by snails, but, at least in damp weather, a proportion of the slugs recover if not picked up. To be effective, baiting must be an almost continuous process, but in damp situations the bait if left *in situ* is liable to grow moulds. A highly effective, though admittedly onerous, method of treating a heavily infested rock garden is to place bait under small pieces of glass a foot or so apart, leaving them in position for about three days and collecting up the slugs and snails each day. On the third day the spent bait is also collected and the glass is moved on to a new area—until the whole rock garden has been covered. Snails under, for instance, aubrieta plants do not seem to take the bait, or else they recover: as mentioned earlier, these plants should be cleaned up as far as possible when they are trimmed hard back after flowering.

Ants nest in the soil between the faces of rocks, and even between peat blocks. They break down the soil into a very fine powder which drains rapidly, and probably some of the damage that they do to plants is a result of local drought. However, they can be more specifically destructive: a plant, for instance a dwarf dianthus, is seen to turn yellow—not all over but in a localised patch—and then that part of the plant dies. Dig it up and you find an ants' nest, and extensive root destruction: try to re-establish the green parts, or to take cuttings from them, and you *may* be lucky, but sometimes the plant seems to have lost all vitality. So watch for the early signs, scrape the soil, and if ants are seen dig for the nest and be prepared to remove rocks in all directions until no more grubs or runs are seen. Provided that they are laid bare, the destruction of the ants is not difficult: powdered insecticide applied with a 'puffer' or a liquid from a pressure spray are quicker and easier (but more expensive) than the traditional kettle of boiling water. There are available preparations of poisoned liquid bait which are claimed to attract ants, which then take the poison back and feed their grubs with it, so destroying the nest without the necessity of dismantling the rockwork: I have found that 'black' ants (but not 'red' ones) take the bait on occasions but not consistently.

Cutworms (the caterpillars of the Yellow Underwing and some other moths) live in the soil and feed by night. They devour foliage, but are particularly destructive in eating through the main stems of small

Page 89 A trough garden for small alpines associates satisfactorily with buildings

Page 90 (*above*) An alpine house with associated frame and, at the rear, plunge beds. The shading is lowered on the west side against the afternoon sun; (*below*) a corner of the alpine house in April. The pots are shallowly plunged in $\frac{1}{8}$in granite chippings

plants at ground level. Their work is plain to see. Dig in the soil round the plant and you will probably find the caterpillar an inch or so below the surface: if you do not, dust the plant and the soil with insecticide powder.

Millepedes will similarly mow down small plants. They also feed upon the rotting stems and roots of dead or dying plants, and are one of many reasons for keeping the rock garden clean. They occasionally take slug-bait, but are best dealt with by prevention and by destroying them whenever they are seen. They feed at night and seem to enjoy climbing up vertical rock faces where they are easily spotted with a torch. (*Woodlice* occur in similar conditions, but their preference is for rotting material, and damage to live plants is probably slight and incidental.) Millepedes should be clearly distinguished from centipedes, which are carnivorous and beneficial in the garden. The former are grey-black, cylindrical, and coil up when disturbed: the latter are of two main kinds (the one very thin and yellowish, the other broader, shorter and shining brown) but both are flattened, their legs project sideways, and they do not go into a coil when disturbed but move actively away.

Leaf-eating insects such as *caterpillars* are not a major problem in the rock garden. Their work is there to be seen, and they can be sought and destroyed. If they do become a serious nuisance, it is likely to be on shrubs or larger plants, and these can be treated by spraying with a systemic insecticide which is absorbed into the plant and kills creatures feeding upon it.

The major use of systemic insecticides, however, is in relation to *aphis* and *spit-fly*. The former particularly, in some years and weather conditions, can be a serious nuisance, damaging the plants by direct attack and also by introducing virus diseases. Aphis cause the leaves to curl over, which protects the insects against spraying or dusting with contact insecticides, but they can be reached by the systemics. Aphis are a problem not only in the open rock garden but also in frames and plunge beds where one may be reluctant to spray indiscriminately with systemic insecticides because some plants and small seedlings appear to be damaged by it. The only thing to do is to carry out a pot-by-pot inspection and remove those that are affected from the frame and spray them.

In some years *weevils* cause a good deal of damage in the late spring to the foliage of daffodils and of some rock plants, for instance dode-

F

catheons. They live in the soil near the plants by day and can be dug up like cutworms, but are more difficult to find; at night they are found feeding on the leaves, and a search by torchlight will reveal them and they can be picked off and destroyed. They also cause underground damage in the larval stage.

Turning to larger vermin, *mice* can do a lot of damage to crocus bulbs and perhaps other bulbs and tubers in the open garden, as well as devouring seed in pots. The alternative methods of destruction are poisoning by warfarin or the use of spring traps: in either case care should be taken to avoid killing birds.

Moles can be a serious nuisance in the rock garden. They do not directly attack plants—they are carnivores—but in their search for worms they can wreck a bed and throw the plants out on to the soil. Their burrows are both deep and shallow, and the former are almost impossible to abolish among rockwork and provide homes for other vermin. The best hope is to trap them in their main runs before their points of entry into the rock garden.

Special protection

The varying needs of special groups of rock plants, and the manner in which the rock garden can be constructed to meet these, were discussed in Chapters Two and Three. Some plants, however, need additional protection against one or more of the following—frost, winter damp, summer damp. The measures to be briefly described involve some detriment to the general appearance of the garden for the sake of a few precious plants—the old problem of the garden versus the plants. I can understand the gardener who eschews them, but he deprives himself of the means of growing some very beautiful plants.

Many lovely mountain plants are at the borderline of frost-hardiness, surviving in some temperate gardens but not in others. It is possible to give useful protection to such plants by covering them individually. Until recently, this meant the use of glass cloches—ugly, expensive, easily broken, difficult to handle, and not very good heat-insulators. The coming of transparent polythene sheeting has provided an alternative which does away with most of these disadvantages. In single thickness it is certainly no better an insulator than glass, but two sheets of polythene with an air space of an inch or so between them are a highly effective insulator. To use this material to the best advantage, plants requiring frost protection should be grouped together. For example, the writer has two beds, constructed in the same manner as the rest of the rock garden and a part of it, which contain respectively plants from Greece and from central Spain. For each of these beds a lightweight portable double-thickness polythene cover has been made, in the one case about a yard square and in the other about 1 × 2yd. They are ugly, though not more so than glass; but they are only *in situ* during cold spells in the winter or overnight in frosty weather in the spring, and they take only a minute or two to assemble or dismantle. The smaller consists of five pieces—back, front, top and two sides: the larger has two tops. Each piece (d) consists of two layers of polythene, 1in apart, mounted on light (1 × ½in) deal battens, except that the uprights (b) of back and front are stouter (1in square oak) and extend downwards as legs: these drop into metal sockets (a), made of galvanised-iron sheeting, in the ground. The top is fixed to the back and front by nails (e) slid loosely into drilled holes, and side-pieces which are only used in more severe weather, are fixed by simple catches (g). The whole thing is easily made (Fig 29), and the pieces are light to handle: storage is the main problem, but not a serious one as the pieces lie flat. Except in very severe weather, the back, front and sides are held off the ground by small wood pieces (c) which permit ventilation and prevent damage to small plants which may have spread across the lines of the frame. In really severe weather on the

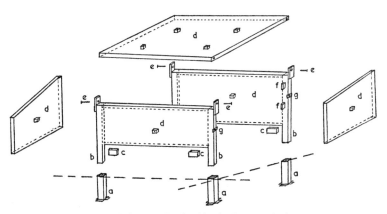

Fɪɢ 29 A light-weight double-thickness polythene cover
for frost protection

contrary, particularly when there are freezing winds, the frames rest upon the ground and soil or sand is heaped against the lower edges. Examples of plants which have withstood several winters in these beds are *Ranunculus asiaticus, Erodium gruinum, Cyclamen repandum* (Fig 30) and *C. cyprium,* and a number of Mediterranean ophrys and other orchids (Plate, p 53).

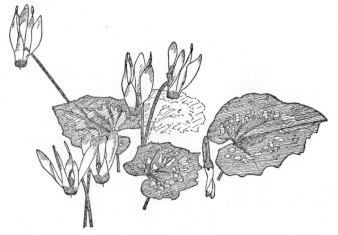

FIG 30   *Cyclamen repandum* (scale × ½)

Many plants, especially some of the most difficult high alpines, are more at risk from wet than from cold in the winter. If they are grown in the open garden at all they are usually best in screes, where the surface grit holds a minimum of moisture. Overhead protection for individual plants or small groups is an added advantage, and here again polythene is adequate and much more manageable than glass sheeting. For this purpose top rather than side cover is needed, and indeed free circulation of air over the plants is important. So polythene, preferably double thickness, is stretched over a light wooden frame, with stout legs which drop into sunken sockets to prevent it from blowing away. Such protection offers the best hope of survival for such plants as *Asperula suberosa, Draba mollissima, Eritrichium nanum,* and the cushion androsaces.

Many mountain plants, particularly from the southern sides of hills that do not carry permanent snow, dry out completely or nearly so in the summer. Such plants are adapted to survive such conditions: they form bulbs, corms or rhizomes and become dormant. Not only do they survive summer heat and drought: they actually need it, and will flower poorly if at all without it. A great many of the plant introductions from expeditions in recent years to the Near and Middle East are of this kind—irises, tulips, crocuses, colchicums, aroids and many more.

One way to grow these plants is to put them into special frames (see Chapter Six). It is, however, possible to go a good deal of the way towards providing the conditions they require within the rock garden itself by the construction of a raised bed, facing south and unshaded, and composed to a depth of about 9in of very fast draining sandy grit. Such a bed is for bulbs and tubers alone: it would indeed be suitable for a few specialised plants which though retaining their top growth during the summer are specially adapted to drought conditions; but their foliage would defeat the object of the bed, which is to secure maximum heating of the sand during the summer. To achieve its purpose it must be both hot and dry for several weeks: in areas with variable summer rain, such as the British Isles, this means covering it to keep out rain—in effect, therefore, a bulb frame is introduced into the garden. Such a bed, with or without its cover, is inevitably unsightly for the greater part of the year, and it is probably better, if one is going to grow these plants (which while in flower may be very beautiful), to use a special bulb frame away from the rock garden.

The care of plants in pots

The rock gardener always has plenty of plants in pots in various stages of propagation or awaiting planting out, and it is worth making proper provision for them. This means plunge beds and frames.

Plunge beds (Plate, p 54) should be large enough to be economical but small enough to allow ready access to the middle: $3\frac{1}{2} \times 4\frac{1}{2}$ft is a practical size. It is helpful to have at least two, one in full sun and one in light shade. They are prepared by levelling and cleaning the ground, digging it out to a depth of 10 to 12in, placing a 2in layer of crocks, flints or other coarse stone at the bottom for drainage, over this a layer of peat, and filling up with the plunge material. This assumes that the bed is in fast draining soil, not subject to flooding; if this risk exists more elaborate drainage is necessary, or alternatively the plunge bed may be raised, using pre-cast concrete slabs or railway sleepers for the retaining walls. The main component of the plunge material is sand or fine grit, and if plastic pots are used this is all that is needed. If clay post are used, sand alone is not an ideal plunge because it dries out very quickly and water is lost through the porous walled pots. In this case a plunge of two parts of sand and one part finely sifted peat is better. (Vermiculite instead of peat is better still in that it is cleaner and less supportive of weeds and pests: but it is more expensive and becoming hard to get). Creosoted $3 \times \frac{1}{2}$in timber set on edge and sunk to a depth of 2in makes a convenient edging, which improves appearance, defines the positioning of pots, and prevents the contamination of the plunge by soil.

A light frame should be made to fit over the plunge bed. In most gardens and certainly in the country, this is necessary to keep out birds, which can be destructive of young plants in pots. It should be covered with netting of a mesh not exceeding 1in. Plastic strawberry netting is light and clean, but fairly easily torn and inclined to sag when the polythene covers (see below) are on, allowing pooling of rainwater. Wire netting is heavier but stronger: 'Netlon' is better still but expensive. The cover should be sufficiently high, and strongly sloping from 15in at the back to 9in at the front.

Provision should be made for protection against both sun and rain. For the former a cover is made, slightly larger than the plunge bed, of $1 \times \frac{1}{2}$in slatting nailed across light battens, with 1in spacing between the slats. These should run from back to front of the plunge bed, so that there is less risk of rain-drip. Protection from rain is particularly important in the winter: polythene sheeting is effective, and provides some frost protection as well. It is nailed on to broomhandles so that it can be readily rolled, and should reach ground level both at the back and the front of the plunge bed, and also extend for 3in or so beyond the cover at each side to avoid drip on the pots. The polythene sheeting is easily lifted by wind, and should be fixed down by brass screws and wing nuts to the bottom edge of the plunge bed cover both at the front and the back.

The skilled use of the shading and the polythene cover throughout the year is an important part of plunge bed management. Remember that in dry spells in the spring and autumn plants are dependent upon night dews: at such times there may also be frost risk, and nice judgement is needed in deciding whether or not to leave on the polythene covers!

Frames are only to a limited extent interchangeable with plunge beds. The type of construction depends upon the uses to which the frame is to be put: in the present context it is assumed that it is to hold plants in containers (pots, pans or trays) not as a propagation frame into which cuttings or growing plants are directly placed in the soil. Such a frame should be thought of as a means of providing more complete frost protection and also greater warmth than the plunge beds can provide. It cannot replace the plunge beds, partly because it is, area for area, much more expensive, and partly because the majority of alpines do not need the additional protection that the frame can give and will remain tougher and more in character growing in a plunge bed.

A useful type of frame is the one illustrated (Plates, p 71). It is raised on breeze blocks to minimise stooping. It is glass sided, so that the plants do not become drawn. About 6in of drainage was placed at the bottom, starting with coarse flints and adding progressively finer layers up to $\frac{1}{8}$in grit. Over this a thick layer—about 6in—of peat was laid; and above this 9in of a mixture of sand and vermiculite. A 1in hole was drilled on each side 2in above groundlevel to drain away excessive water, and a small gully was built round each drainage hole to a height of $2\frac{1}{2}$in above the ground to enable this depth of water to be retained at the bottom of the frame. Most of the year the plants in pots are not plunged, but just rest upon the sand: they are protected from winds by the side glass and are mostly in polythene pots anyway. In the winter, however, they are plunged, to give greater frost protection. The whole of the glass can be boxed over with effective frost covers. These consist of 1in thick expanded polystyrene sheeting boxed in (because otherwise it is too light and easily damaged) with hardboard. The side covers are held in place by spring wires stretched across between hooks: the top covers lie on the glass lights, fitting closely into the framework. The whole gives efficient protection against severe winter cold.

A high standard of cleanliness in the plunge beds and frames will amply repay itself. Most of the plants, because they are small or incompletely established, are more than ordinarily vulnerable to pests and diseases. Keep a small supply of slug-bait and a spray, loaded with a dilute insecticide, always to hand in this, the 'workshop' of the rock garden.

Five
Propagation

Rock plants are mostly perennial, but this does not mean that they are immortal: in the rock garden as in the wild there is a considerable fatality rate, some dying of old age, some from neglect or ill-treatment, some perhaps from over-coddling, some from the attacks of plant or animal parasites, and some it would seem from sheer cussedness. So a continuous programme of propagation is needed. There is far more satisfaction, as well as economy, in maintaining one's own stock of plants than in letting them die and buying new ones. It should be remembered, too, that most of the plants that grow in our rock gardens are the wild flowers of somewhere or other. Failure to propagate means in the long run reducing the wild sources, and an important contribution to conservation lies in the careful cultivation and perpetuation of garden stocks.

The propagation of alpine plants is a large subject in itself, and there are useful specialist books about it. All the usual methods of propagation are applicable to alpines, and they are considered here under the three broad headings of division, cuttings and seed sowing. The first two are 'vegetative' methods which ensure that the original stock ('clone') is continued unchanged, so that they are particularly useful for keeping going a good form of a plant. Propagation by seed on the other hand provides plants which may vary from the original stock, as well as permitting hybridisation, intentional or otherwise.

Division

Many plants can be broken apart, and this is a useful method of securing a *small* number of additional plants. The aim is to divide the plant into pieces each of which has adequate roots and foliage, and new plants obtained in this way proceed more rapidly to flowering size than is usually the case with plants from cuttings or seed. If the divided plants are going straight back into the garden, the division should be carried out when planting conditions are suitable. Many plants can be divided in open weather in the winter, while they are dormant, and will grow away in the spring, but the writer's preference is wherever possible to divide a plant while it is in active growth. This usually means in early spring well before flowering, or after flowering in the summer. To divide a plant while it is in full flower is obviously destructive of the appearance of the plant and the garden, though in some instances it may be the most reliable way of ensuring that you propagate the right plant!

Division is in some cases a forcible procedure, involving damage to the roots, in which case excess foliage should be trimmed away and the plant nursed back to health by careful watching and watering if necessary after planting. On the other hand a number of rock garden plants in effect divide themselves. For instance, the autumn-flowering *Gentiana sino-ornata* if it is dug up in the spring will be found to have separated into a number of small plants, each with several thong-like roots, which fall apart undamaged when the plant is lifted: these are then replanted, spaced apart. Many plants behave in this way, though not all of them separate so easily; they frequently need carefully easing apart to avoid root-destruction. In general, such plants are very much the better for dividing and separating, and indeed the division of alpines is sometimes necessary not simply for propagation but also to maintain the health of the plants. Especially is this true of many kinds of primula, which appear to need dividing after flowering so that they may make new roots before the following winter: if they are not so divided new roots do not form, and the old roots tend to rot away and the plants are thrown up by frost in the winter.

Apart from dividing in order to propagate, it is good practice to break up one's plants if they cease to flower well or if they show signs of ageing in the centres of the clumps or mats. Rhizomatous irises are another group which seem specially to need this treatment, and it is frequently recommended also for that puzzle among alpine plants *Gentiana* 'acaulis'—the big blue trumpet gentian which flowers so well in some gardens and not at all in others. Part of the value of division (for the purposes of plant-health rather than propagation) lies in introducing fresh soil; this should always be done—do not plant the pieces back into their own spent soil, but work in a fresh mixture appropriate to the plant.

Division is a method of propagation appropriate to most alpines with multiple fibrous roots, as well as to those forming bulbs, tubers or rhizomes which naturally multiply underground by division or offsets. It is not applicable to those coming from a single root-stock; and there are some other plants with which this method, although it can be used, calls for considerable care. In general these are plants which have the reputation that they 'do not like moving', and what this really means is that they are intolerant of root-damage: you can move any plant successfully if you can manage to do it without any root-destruction. Plants such as pulsatillas form a dense mass of closely adherent crowns, each of which may have a small amount of fibrous root of its own but in the main is dependent upon a thick root-trunk which is a branch of the root-mass. Such plants *can* be divided, but this involves cutting (rather than breaking) through the main roots, which are then liable to rot. The cut surface should be treated with a fungicide such as captan or quintozene, and the division should be made with great care to minimise bruising or bending of the root-system. The cuts should be made in such a way as to preserve as much fibrous root as possible with each division of the plant. This can best be done by lifting the entire plant; but it is liable to be a major operation, and there is a natural reluctance to risk destroying an established plant of say *Pulsatilla alpina* by lifting it in this way.

It is frequently possible to cut away rooted pieces without lifting the main plant, but the procedure is not without risk to it as well as to the divisions. If a divided-off piece shows much evidence of damage, it is wise to treat it rather as though it were a cutting, removing excess foliage and all damaged root, dusting the surfaces with fungicide, and potting it into sand in the manner described below for cuttings. It is particularly with regard to these rather more difficult subjects which cannot be divided without root-damage that it is better to carry out this procedure just as the plants are coming into growth in the spring.

Many of the smaller scree plants can be propagated by division, but direct replanting into scree always involves a drought-risk until the plant is re-established. With the smaller, more difficult and more precious plants is is better to pot up the divisions and plant them out when they are fully recovered. For most of the small scree plants, however, cuttings or seed are better methods of propagation.

Cuttings

Many alpine plants can be successfully propagated by means of cuttings, mainly from the stems. The techniques employed are essentially similar to those applicable to plants other than alpines, and include soft tip cuttings as well as the use of maturer (half-ripened) branches taken with or without a heel, and young growths taken directly from their point of emergence from the root-stock. Which of these methods is used for a particular plant depends partly upon the growth of the plant and partly upon the season at which the cuttings are taken. With cuttings as with division, the author prefers whenever possible to take cuttings of material which is actively growing. Many alpine plants make new stem and leaf growth after flowering, and so June or early July is the time when good cutting material normally becomes available. However, this by no means represents the whole range of season through which cuttings can be taken. For example, summer-flowering gentians such as *Gentiana septemfida* come into growth early in the year with an abundance of soft shoots springing straight from the crown of the root-stock: these, if taken while still very small, make excellent cutting material, despite the fact that left to themselves they would have borne flowers later in the year.

Generally, shoots with visible flower-buds make unsatisfactory cuttings, but a shoot taken well in advance of its flowering time, before there are apparent buds, seems to be able to redirect its energies to root and leaf formation. Many plants present alternative types of cutting material at different seasons. For instance, *Potentilla fruticosa* not only provides suitable half-ripened wood during the summer but also young non-flowering growth from the base of the plant much earlier in the year: the latter will root rapidly and make good plants well in advance of the former. Growths springing directly from the crown of a plant can sometimes be obtained with a root or two attached—'Irishman's cuttings' which should strictly be regarded as divisions but in fact are best treated as cuttings. Some cuttings, particularly soft tips, if treated by the methods to be described, will root very rapidly: other, and particularly older and woodier, growths appear to respond quite differently—the cut end, instead of rooting immediately, becomes sealed off by the formation of callus (scar tissue). The formation of roots through the callus is then a slow business, sometimes taking many months, and in the meantime the cutting usually sheds its leaves and remains dormant. This behaviour means that the season at which cuttings can be taken extends into the autumn. Some plants appear always to react in this way, but others such as cistuses will provide soft cuttings immediately after flowering which will root quickly, and partially ripened wood a little later which will very likely callous over and not root until the following spring.

There is much to be said, if you are particularly anxious to propagate a plant and do not know its behaviour, for taking cuttings of varying degrees of ripeness at any time of the year when they are available in the hope that sooner or later you will find a time when they will root. The kabschia saxifrages provide another example of plants from which cuttings can be satisfactorily taken in the autumn. For the most part they will not root till the spring: by the following autumn they will be soundly rooted, but are probably best left until the next spring (eighteen months after taking the cuttings) before potting up. This is a slow business, but it gives good plants and the cuttings are taken at a season when time can be better spared.

It is wise to assume that cuttings, before they have made new roots or callus, are vulnerable to attack by fungi which enter through cut or damaged surfaces. For this reason some care is needed in 'making' (ie preparing) cuttings. The material should be cleanly cut with a razor blade rather than torn. With most types of cutting the stems will be inserted into the rooting-medium to such a depth that at least one node (the point at which a leaf is attached) is buried: this is because some plants will root from the nodes in preference to the cut tip. In preparing the cutting the leaf or leaves arising at nodes which will be buried are cut cleanly away. Rooting can sometimes be promoted by hormones, which are available in either liquid or powder form. For a number of years I made a practice of dipping half the cuttings of each plant in hormone, leaving the others untreated; some plants undoubtedly responded favourably and rooted more quickly and abundantly, with others very little difference was to be seen, and in a few cases the cut-tings treated with hormone appeared to rot and die whereas untreated cuttings survived. It is now my practice not to use hormones routinely but to try them if I do not get satisfactory rooting without. If they are used, the prepared cutting is dipped or soaked in the hormone accord-ing to the instructions provided with it.

The preparation of a cutting needs less time than it takes to describe. It should in fact be done as quickly as possible after the cutting is removed from the plant, and wilting should not be allowed to occur. If the cuttings cannot be 'made' immediately after they are gathered, they should be kept in a sealed polythene bag. After preparation they are placed without delay in a rooting medium, either in a specially prepared bed or in pots, pans, boxes or trays. They root at varying rates (even cuttings of the same species) so that a position is rapidly reached when cuttings all made at the same time come to need different treatment in terms of air-exclusion, watering and potting up. For this reason there is much to be said for putting all the cuttings of a single type into a small unit such as a pot. On the other hand this involves more space, time and cost than does putting a large number of cuttings of different kinds into a single container. If these containers are prepared in the manner about to be described, they permit the cuttings to remain in them for a long time—months if necessary—after they have rooted: by this time the cuttings will all be either well rooted, dead, or firmly callused, and they can be handled easily.

It is the author's practice to put the cuttings of specially precious or difficult plants into pots (one kind to a pot), but otherwise to use plastic trays with fitted transparent lids which can be bought specially for the purpose. There are considerable advantages in having portable containers which can for example be transferred to a shady or a sunny position as required and brought on to the kitchen table for potting up; and although many cuttings will root perfectly well in open, prepared beds, on the whole this method is not recommended for alpines on a domestic scale. Whether pots, pans, trays or boxes be used, they are prepared in the same way, as follows:

First a layer to ensure good drainage: ¼in chippings are suitable for this. The depth of this layer will depend upon the container: it is preferable to allow 1in, but the one disadvantage of the plastic trays made specially for the purpose is that they are mostly rather shallow, and ½in of drainage material is all that can be allowed. Over the drainage is placed a thin layer, about a ¼in thick, of sifted peat, packed down: this is a safeguard against drying at the roots. Above this again is placed about 1in of potting mixture of a type appropriate to the plants: the purpose of this is to ensure that when the cuttings have made roots they will be able to feed and grow on. As already indicated, this provides greatly increased latitude in potting up the plants: it does, however, impose one limitation—cuttings of plants with very different soil-requirements cannot be mixed. Over the soil-layer is placed the rooting medium, the main ingredient of which is sand, which must be coarse and as 'sharp' as can be obtained. This quality of sharpness, which can be felt by rubbing it between the fingers, appears to be important, possibly to ensure aeration of the mixture, and perhaps, as has been suggested by some growers, as a direct irritant to the cutting, provoking root-formation. Good, sharp sand is unfortunately no longer very easy to obtain in some districts. Used alone, it is, of course, fast draining, and is suitable for cuttings only when it is possible to ensure, either by constant supervision or by some such means as an automatic mist-spray (see below) that the medium does not dry out. For most of us it is better to mix the sand with an equal quantity of peat which has been rubbed through a fine sieve such as a flour sieve. This mixture is far more retentive of water than pure sand. The rooting medium must be sufficiently deep (at least 2in) to enable the cuttings to be placed in it to such a depth that the cleaned nodes are covered by it but the bottom of the cutting does not reach through it. The prepared tray is thoroughly wetted, preferably by plunging in water, and allowed to drain. The cuttings are then dibbled into the rooting medium, and made firm; they should be well spaced out or there will be difficulty later in separating them for potting up. They should be labelled and dated, with a note as to whether hormone has been used.

The subsequent handling of the cuttings depends upon the time of year and the facilities and time available. With many kinds it is possible to secure rapid root development by 'forcing' the cuttings—that is, by keeping them warm (70-75° F) and in a continuously humid atmosphere. This involves providing them with a transparent airtight cover: in the case of single pots, polythene bags held by rubber bands are suitable, plastic trays can be bought with fitting covers, and a wooden box can be covered with a sheet of glass. The container is placed in a warm position, preferably in direct sunlight though with shading from hot midday sun, and is frequently watered. After two or three days, when the cut ends will have sealed over and they will be less prone to flagging, a little air is admitted. The more frequently they can be watered the more rapidly can air be given: flagging is the indication that they still need to be kept in a humid atmosphere.

Two artificial means are available to aid the 'forcing' of root formation—bottom heat and mist-spray. Propagation frames can be bought or made which enable the soil to be heated to a controlled temperature. This makes one independent of the weather, it extends the season during which cuttings may be expected to root, and it permits the frames to be placed in light shade without the constant reliance on movable shading necessary when one is relying upon the sun for heat. The use of an intermittent mechanical mist-spray (which must be in an enclosed space, such as a greenhouse) means that the containers are not individually covered, and solves what is perhaps the most difficult problem in the initial stages of establishing cuttings—how quickly to admit air. A combination of bottom heat and mist-spray can produce very rapid rooting. The roots, however, are soft, and the whole root mass can easily break away from the base of the cutting, so that they require great care in handling.

Cuttings can be rooted successfully by a less intensive process, without special apparatus such as is necessary for bottom heating or mist-spray, and with less expenditure of time and constant attention. The containers, prepared as described and provided with close-fitting transparent covers, are placed in light shade. In most weather conditions this means that they will be at a lower temperature than the 70° F recommended for 'forcing' cuttings, and root formation will be slower. Care is otherwise the same. Air is admitted cautiously, and they are watered from above if there are signs of flagging or if the surface of the rooting medium appears dry. Leaf-growth is an indication that rooting has occurred, and the covers should then be totally removed and the plants brought into full light, otherwise they may become drawn. It is at this stage that difficulties can arise when there are several kinds of plant in a container.

Once rooting is fully established the plants can be transferred to individual pots. There are two stages at which this can be done. The new roots are at first soft, white and fragile, and are contained in the rooting medium: they require care in handling at this stage, but on the other hand the texture of the rooting medium is such that it should be possible to remove them without damage. They are then transferred into pots. These are prepared in the usual way, with drainage at the bottom, a thin humus layer over it, and then a soil mixture appropriate to the plant. However, the cutting itself should not be placed directly into the soil: it should be planted into a 'pocket' of the same rooting medium in which it has been growing. This is a critical stage of propagation by cuttings, and a great many cuttings produce roots successfully but die at this transplanting stage. The potted plants should be 'nursed' for a few days, carefully watering them and protecting them from full sun.

Alternatively, the cuttings can be left in their containers to root through into the soil below the rooting medium. They will form harder, more fibrous roots, more firmly attached. They can be potted up (or even directly planted out if conditions are suitable) with less risk than at the earlier stage. There are, however, two disadvantages: one is that it is difficult to deal with individual plants—the whole tray must be planted out at the same time; the other is that, particularly if the cuttings have been put in close together, there is considerable root entanglement and some damage is unavoidable.

It should be added that some plants, particularly the more woody and slow growing types of cutting, will not respond to the intensive treatment, and must be kept, sometimes for many months, in the shade, without covers, and prevented from drying off.

Not surprisingly, some of the alpines which are the most difficult to grow are also difficult to propagate. The hairy cushion plants, such as *Eritrichium nanum*, aretian androsaces, and *Draba mollissima*, rot away rapidly in a humid atmosphere, and cuttings of these plants must not be covered over but kept in shade until they are rooted.

There are many variations, based on personal preferences and experience, in the techniques of raising stem cuttings, much depending on the time and facilities available. Most kinds of rock and alpine plants can be satisfactorily propagated by cuttings raised non-intensively in trays in the manner just described. Specially precious or difficult kinds are best dealt with in pots, with only one species to a pot, and in this case clay pots are recommended, and the cuttings are placed round the edge of the pot. It is generally found that cuttings so placed will root better than those nearer the centre of the pot: this is presumably due to the porosity of the clay (it does not apply to plastic pots) permitting a small continuous supply of moisture, or possibly of air.

Seed

Propagation by seed has particular attractions in the cultivation of alpines. It is the quickest way of getting many plants of a kind; it makes for healthier stock (the indefinite propagation of a plant vegetatively frequently seems to lead to a loss of vigour); and it is the *only* way of getting hold of a great many of the more interesting alpine plants. Seed of many alpines can be purchased, but a wider scope yet is available through numerous Seed Exchanges throughout the world. The

Page 107 The American Erythroniums are beautiful spring flowers for peaty soil in half-shade. On the left is the rose-pink *E. revolutum* and on the right pale yellow *E. californicum*

Page 108 One of the prettiest of all irises for the rock garden, *Iris cristata lacustris* produces its brightly coloured two-inch flowers over a long period in a variety of situations

main *dis*advantage of propagation by seed is that the material may not always come true, particularly when the seed has been collected in the garden rather than in the wild—but there is always a gambler's chance of getting something better than you hoped for!

When to sow? One tends to associate seed-sowing with the spring, and in the case of alpines with the early spring (February in England). The obvious advantage of this is that seed germinating early in the year can be kept growing actively, pricked out and potted up or even planted out during the ensuing growing season. There is a great deal to be said for sowing seed of any kind of alpine or rock plant as soon as it is obtained, and in the case of seed from one's own plants this means as soon as it is ripe. The most obvious reason for this is that seed loses its viability, sometimes slowly but sometimes very rapidly. Many kinds of seed, collected and sown during the summer, will germinate well—much better than in the following spring. The snag is that seedlings from late summer or autumn germination have to be nursed through the winter—easy for many plants in many winters, but not always so. The solution is obvious: sow most of your seed as soon as you can, but save a little for the following spring as an insurance. Some kinds of seed are remarkably consistent in the time of year at which they germinate, but others are not so, and will germinate in favourable weather at any time. In particular, the seed of monocotyledonous plants (the flowering bulbs) tends to germinate in the winter: if it is sown in the spring a year may be lost.

Not all seed germinates better when fresh: some kinds need a period of ripening, and others a process of 'vernalisation'. The essence of the latter seems to be that the coat of the seed needs to become stratified (split into layers) as a preliminary to germination. Particularly does this apply to high alpines, and it is assisted by exposure to frost; or possibly frost itself is not needed, but a wide range of temperature as between day and night—such as might be expected in the spring in the mountains immediately after the melting of the snow. It is possible to 'vernalise' seed in the packet by mixing it with moist sand and giving it several days and nights of alternate warming and freezing; and the writer has found this successful in experiments upon seed obtained late in the spring. This is not necessary in the British Isles if the seed is available during the winter: it can be sown and exposed to the vicissitudes of the winter weather. For seed that does not germinate immediately on sowing, one has to consider the pros and cons of letting it

G

ripen in the packet or sown in pots. The latter is probably advantageous for most seed provided that one can give the pots the care and protection mentioned below. Some alpine seed is slow to germinate, particularly if it is not fresh, and may go through two or three seasons, perhaps putting up a seedling or two in each.

It is worth going to some trouble in sowing one's seed. Most alpines are small and only small quantities of seedlings are needed, so that pots are preferable to trays or boxes. Because they may have to be kept for a long time, and be exposed at intervals to frost action, plastic pots are better than clays. The seed should never be allowed to dry out, nor to become waterlogged; the seedlings of alpines often root deeply, while top-growth is still very small; and these considerations determine the way that the pots should be prepared. Drainage material and a layer of peat are placed in the pot as described for cuttings, and the pot is filled above this with the appropriate seed mixture. The writer uses two seed mixtures only—one for lime-hating plants and the other for the rest—and these are the same as those described already for the general cultivation of alpines, with the difference that some of the ingredients are sterilised and they are sifted finer. The leafmould and loam are sterilised—not the peat, grit and sand. The purpose of sterilisation is to kill weed-seed (which can cause much confusion in a seed pot) and vermin: it is *not* sterilisation in a surgical sense, and indeed the more soil bacteria that survive the better. A satisfactory way of doing it is to put the materials into a biscuit tin in the oven and use a sugar thermometer, and it is adequate to bring the temperature up to 200° F in the centre of the material. This sterilisation upsets the balance of bacterial and protozoal life in the soil, and it is theoretically desirable to inoculate the mixture, after it has cooled down, with a tiny quantity of unsterilised loam and leave it for a fortnight or so before use: I have not always done the latter, and have not observed the seedlings to suffer—there is rarely less than a fortnight before germination is apparent. The ingredients should be passed through a $\frac{1}{8}$in sieve before mixing. The pots are filled to within $\frac{1}{2}$in of the top and then, particularly with smaller seed, it is helpful to add a layer of the same mixture passed through a $\frac{1}{16}$in kitchen sieve. The seed is then sown thinly and as evenly as possible. Covering the seed poses a problem, because some seed appears to germinate better in the light and other in the dark. A satisfactoy compromise is as follows. A little more of the finely sifted soil is added, approximately to a depth corresponding with the thickness of the seed, which in the case of the finest seed means practically none. The soil is lightly pressed down, and then a layer of coarse grit or, better still, coal-grit, is added: this should pass through a $\frac{1}{8}$in but not a $\frac{1}{16}$in sieve, and should be just deep enough to hide the soil. It has several purposes: it stabilises the surface and prevents the seed from being washed out by rain; it helps to prevent drying out of the surface; it probably excludes most but not all light without excluding air; it helps to fix the germinating seedlings into the soil; and it discourages the formation of moss and liverwort on the surface. For the last of these purposes coal-grit seems to be preferable to other forms of grit.

The pots should be labelled with the name and date of sowing, and in choosing the type of label bear in mind that it may have to remain legible for two or three years.

The pots of ungerminated seed need protection from desiccation, from heavy rain if a grit facing has not been used, and from birds and mice. They are suitably placed in a frame covered with wire netting in partial shade, unless immediate germination is expected or desired. In the latter case, as for instance with spring-sown seed of annuals or plants of doubtful hardiness, it is preferable to place them in a covered frame for frost protection, and also quicker germination may be expected if they are placed in full sun, ensuring, however, that the surface of the pots is not allowed to dry out. A bottom-heated frame, as described for cuttings, can be used to accelerate germination in the early spring.

Germination can be very slow and erratic with some alpines. If the seed is precious, and particularly in the case of high alpines (as these are most prone to slow germination) it is worth keeping the pots for at least three springs.

When the seed germinates it is important to keep the seedlings growing as fast as possible, and at the same time to keep them in character. They should be exposed to air and light from an early stage and thinned out as necessary so that they form hard stems and do not become drawn. Such problems as 'damping off' are rare among alpine seedlings grown in this way. Because many of them make a root-system disproportionately large to the top growth, pricking out should be done as soon as they are big enough to handle. Usually one has more seedlings than one requires, and the writer's practice is to pot up half a dozen of a kind (more if it is especially precious or a useful gift or exchange plant) in separate pots. The remaining seedlings are then planted out in little clumps into the rock garden, where they may or may not survive—but one is spared the pain of deliberately throwing baby alpines on to the rubbish heap! Even if you only keep six of a kind, once the seed-sowing 'bug' has bitten you you may very easily find that you have some hundreds of seedlings on your hands in the early summer. If ordinary pots are used they take a lot of space and a lot of soil: excellent for the purpose are the thin plastic mugs supplied for use in tea-vending machines, pierced with five or six holes in the bottom by means of an electric soldering iron. If you do not mind going to the trouble of washing them, you can probably obtain these, used, free of charge from a local firm or office. In shape they are comparable with the clay 'long Tom', a favourite type of pot (when it could be obtained) for growing alpines because of their long roots.

Pricked-out seedlings should be protected from full sun for a few days. They will quickly become established plants and can be planted out into the garden as soon as they are big enough and the weather is suitable.

Other methods of propagation, such as *layering, root cuttings* and *leaf cuttings*, are applicable to a few alpines which are unsuitable for division or stem cuttings. They will usually produce flowering plants (in small numbers) more quickly than from seed, and being vegetative methods, they are especially applicable when it is desired to propagate a particular clone. The methods are described in general books on gardening and call for no special modification for alpine plants.

One final point. Do not wait till you have nearly lost a plant before deciding to propagate it. On the contrary, as soon as you obtain any new plant, ask yourself how best and how quickly you can increase your stock of it.

Six

The Cultivation of Alpines Otherwise Than in the Rock Garden

A rock garden is the most satisfying setting for alpines, but it is not essential. They have been successfully grown in windowboxes and upon rooftops, in sandbeds and ashbeds, in paths (where they sometimes successfully plant themselves), in walls, in raised beds, troughs and sinks, frames and in special alpine houses. Much has been learned about the growth requirements of alpine plants from their behaviour in such unusual situations. Coke-ash, readily and cheaply obtainable until the coming of oil- or gas-fired central heating, was not only an excellent plunge material, but also proved to be a first rate pabulum for many high alpines, perhaps owing to a high mineral content combined with good drainage. *Viola eizanensis* has been described as requiring 'sheltered woodland conditions': by far the most robust and floriferous plant I have ever seen was self-sown in one of my frames, where its 'soil' was sand plus vermiculite to a depth of 9 or 10in and then peat—nothing else—and its companions were Mediterranean bulbs having their summer baking!

In this chapter we shall consider the cultivation of alpine plants in raised beds, in troughs, in the alpine house and in frames. The first two of these are, or can be, a part of the garden: not so the alpine house, which is in effect a giant 'frame' in which the plants for the most part are grown in pots.

Emphasis has been laid in this book upon the rock garden as essentially a *wild* garden, isolated so far as possible from formal structures.

Troughs and raised beds on the contrary are frankly formal and artificial in construction, which means that they can be brought into close proximity to the house, rising perhaps from a patio or terrace. They are eminently suitable therefore for growing a limited number of alpine plants in a small plot dominated by the house.

The raised bed (Plates, p 72)

CONSTRUCTION

The raised bed for alpines, because it is essentially formal, should be rectangular. If it is curved or irregular in outline it is in danger of looking like a piece of thoroughly bad and ill-placed rock garden. The walls should be of stone: other materials such as brick, railway sleepers or breeze blocks can be functionally efficient but will usually look unsatisfactory, though in some settings what is in effect a hollow brick wall, integrated with the house buildings, can form an effective raised bed. The stone used should be suitable for the purpose, bearing in mind that one is building walls and not rock faces. Purbeck or Cotswold limestone, and also sandstone, is obtainable as 'walling-stone' (in rather thicker and considerably smaller slabs than those used for paving), and these are suitable materials for the purpose. The stones can be used with or without cement: the writer's preference is for the latter, on grounds both of appearance and ease of planting, but cementing makes for greater stability and is necessary if a totally structured appearance is desired—as when bricks are used. As a compromise when stone is employed, some cement may be used, but in any case gaps should be left for planting. If lime-hating plants are to be grown, any cement used may with advantage be made with an admixture of peat and only a low proportion of cement: the peat tends to neutralise the alkalinity of the cement. This mixture, which has been called 'hypertufa' because it has some of the characteristics of tufa and has been used as a substitute for it, will be considered in the next section, dealing with troughs. The walls should slope very slightly inwards (unless they are solidly cemented) as they rise, in order to increase their stability, and as in building the rock garden each stone should be tilted very slightly inwards so that rain tends to be carried into the structure and also to retain the soil between the stones.

The 'filling' of the bed is essentially the same as that of the rock garden—adequate drainage at the bottom, a humus layer as a moisture-retainer, and above this a well-drained soil mixture suitable for alpines; but because this is a *raised* bed it will drain fast and be subject to drought. It should therefore contain a higher proportion of humus, such as peat, and rather less grit, than are used in the ordinary rock garden mixtures. The soil can be varied to suit the kinds of plant which it is proposed to grow. It can for instance perfectly well be a peat-bed; but if its walls are made of peat-blocks rather than stone it is liable to wear into a formless heap which would be acceptable if carefully placed in the rock garden but not as a more formal bed.

The building of the walls of the raised bed should proceed *pari passu* with the filling in with soil, pressing the latter down hard and carrying it between the stones of the wall, assuming that they are not to be cemented. There is much to be said for sifting some of the soil through a ⅛in sieve for filling between the stones: this results in a more effective packing of the interspace. Plants which will hang down the walls and are suitable for planting in the interstices can with advantage be planted as building proceeds: they are not at the same risk of damage from being trodden on or by subsequent moving of stones as are plants put in during the construction of a rock garden. In spite of packing down there will be sinkage: the counsel of perfection is to delay the planting for some months, but most of us will prefer to allow for some sinkage by taking the soil level a little above the stones.

The dimensions of the bed need careful consideration. As to its height, the more you bring it up the less you will have to stoop to see your small plants but the greater will be the risk of excessive drying out at the surface. Also the height should be related to the area of the bed, both for appearance and because a high ratio of height to area means more rapid desiccation. A height of 2ft is generally enough, rising perhaps to 30in if the bed is large. The horizontal dimensions may well be determined by the space available, the cost, and the appearance of the bed in relation to neighbouring structures. Bear in mind that you want to be able to get at the middle of it without damaging plants near the edge by leaning on them: 4ft is an adequate width, assuming access from both sides.

Whether or not to use rocks on the surface is a matter of personal taste: there is always the danger of turning a good bed into a bad rockery. If stones are used they should be unobtrusive, rising very little above the level of the soil, and carefully placed. A grit dressing at the surface (choosing the material to suit the walling stone and other neighbouring structures) enhances the appearance and has the advantages already mentioned in relation to the rock garden.

Planting needs care. Almost certainly the raised bed will soon be too small, so avoid rampant spreaders or carpeters and shrubs which cannot be kept strictly limited in size both vertically and laterally. Because space will be limited, careful inter-planting will be needed, for instance with spring bulbs under and between carpeting plants and summer-flowering herbaceous plants—and this means careful labelling.

The raised bed, like the rock garden, is subject to invasion by vermin, but the major enemies, slugs and snails, are limited in their mountaineering propensities. In fact, the care and supervision of individual plants is in general easier in a raised bed than in the open rock garden. Top dressing is needed periodically, partly to replace soil-loss and sinkage, but also because such a bed is liable to lose soluble soil-nutrients rapidly by washing-out. The principles of plant feeding are the same as in the rock garden, but the frequency and quantity may need to be relatively greater.

The bulb frame

The introduction in recent years of many kinds of bulbous and rhizomatous plants, mainly from the Near and Middle East, has led to much experimenting with their cultivation. Most of these plants come from mountainous areas (and so are appropriate material for the grower of alpines) and are frost-hardy, and their chief special requirement is a prolonged period of summer ripening. While this can be achieved sometimes in the open garden (see Chapter Four) the specialist grower of such plants will probably use one or more bulb frames. Such a frame associates better with the alpine house and plunge beds than it does with the rock garden.

A bulb frame should be raised, to ensure perfect drainage, and the construction can be either on the lines of a raised bed or of a propagating frame (Chapter Five). It differs from other raised beds in having a glass frame over it, and from other frames in containing suitable soil into which the bulbs are planted directly.

Bulbs, corms, tubers and rhizomes are, or contain, food storage systems. The food stores are accumulated during a relatively short growing period, and for this reason such plants generally demand a fairly rich soil. The basis is a good loam, which should contain no more grit or sand than is necessary to ensure that it does not become waterlogged. It should contain plant food such as bone-meal, and the surface should be dressed as for bulbs in the open garden (see p 86). The glass covers should be designed to ensure that rain is excluded, while permitting some degree of ventilation during the ripening period and ample ventilation during growth.

The optimum ripening period is not the same for all bulbous plants. If, as is usually recommended, water is excluded from May onwards, there will be many plants which are still in full green growth at the beginning of this period. Some such plants retain their leaves for a long while if watering is continued: the withdrawal of water hastens the withering of their leaves, and it may be that this is exactly what happens in their natural growing conditions and is an essential part of the ripening process. The duration of the ripening period must be in the nature of a compromise, and the lights should be kept on from late May till early September. Watering presents no problem, because for the rest of the year the frames can be open to the rain; however, many bulbs make root growth before their leaves appear on the surface, and do so as early as September, and if there is a dry spell at this time, the watering-can must be used.

It is not unusual to include in the bulb frame such plants as some orchids, or some of the South African bulbous plants, which need the conditions that the frame provides but may not be fully frost-hardy. In this case the lights will be kept on in cold weather, and it is then necessary to ensure that the soil does not become too dry.

One problem of the bulb frame is that of keeping the different kinds identified. Some 'stay put' and multiply very little; others make many offsets or even travel underground by means of stolons. There are various ways of marking the surface of the bed to indicate where bulbs have been placed, but it is best to try to ensure that closely similar bulbs are not planted in juxtaposition.

The bulb frame is essentially a collector's display box. The plants are there for their individual interest and beauty. The overall effect is not, in the writer's view, particularly attractive. During the resting period there is nothing to see: during the growing period the plants which are in flower do not always display to advantage among the foliage of others.

Troughs and sinks (Plate, p 89)

These have become very popular in recent years: the two words relate to the original function of the utensil and are interchangeable in the present context. They are now expensive and difficult to obtain, and there is much to be said for making one's own.

A trough garden, well sited, well proportioned and well planted can be a very attractive feature in its own right, sharing with the raised bed the advantage of fitting in with formal structures—even against a house wall—but much more self-contained and independent of its surroundings. Troughs are usually raised up on stone supports for access, for easy vision, and with the advantage of being less accessible to vermin. The height to which they can be raised is limited only by the stability of the supports.

Stone troughs come in a variety of shapes and sizes. The depth internally should be not less than 6in—9in is better—and some shallow troughs have to be built up at the sides to secure this depth. The thickness of the walls should be adequate both for strength and to limit frost penetration at root level. This last point is important: the trough is rather like a large unplunged pot, and severe winter cold can reach it from the sides and the bottom as well as the top. There must be an adequate drainage hole near one or both ends, covered with a piece of perforated zinc to prevent the drainage material from dropping through. In the bottom of the trough is placed coarse grit for drainage and over it a layer of peat as already described for cutting trays and pots; and the trough is then filled with a suitable compost for the plants to be grown. For most plants suitable for a trough a 'rich scree' mixture is appropriate. There is no reason in principle why troughs should not be used for any appropriately small and neat plants, for instance bog plants or those requiring peat and shade, provided that the trough is suitably positioned and adequate provision is made for watering, and the drainage and compost adapted to the plants to be grown.

However, a trough is more than just a large pot for growing plants in. It is at its best a work of art. The skill lies in the appropriate selection, placing and control of the plants, and the use of carefully selected stone to form a miniature rock garden. On its small scale, let the trough look natural—a tiny piece of caged mountain rock; so that the principles of placing the stone are the same as in the rock garden itself. If the stone is stratified the strata must be aligned—indeed with more care than in the rock garden since the trough is viewed more closely and critically. The stone should rise above the level of the top of the trough; partly this is to gain extra height, but also it facilitates planting in such a way that the plants cover and fall over the rim.

Although the choice of plants suitable for troughs is wide, the choice appropriate to any particular trough is more limited and calls for much skill and some experimentation. The limitations are imposed by the size, depth and siting of the trough, by the soil mixture chosen, but above all by the compatibility of the plants with one another; so that the first plant selected may go far towards determining the remainder. Perhaps the most important consideration is that in a trough no plant can be effectively hidden at any time. Consequently the plants chosen must look attractive in leaf as well as in flower, and at all seasons of the year. For this reason there is a tendency to choose plants which are neat and effective in foliage rather than brilliant in flower—rosetted silver saxifrages, sempervivums, and the smaller and neater sedums. Many of these plants have the added advantage that they need relatively little attention—perhaps the pulling off of a few rosettes here and there and repacking with grit. However, it would be quite wrong to convey the impression that a trough is suitable only for 'foliage plants'. There are many neat alpine plants, some easy, some difficult, which are beautiful in flower and leaf, and eminently suitable for a trough. The spring gentian (*Gentiana verna*), the moss campion (*Silene acaulis*), the purple saxifrage (*Saxifraga oppositifolia*), many of the Kabschia saxifrages, *Saxifraga cochlearis minor*, *Helichrysum milfordiae*—these are just a few of the many plants, beautiful alike in foliage and in flower, that are neat and small enough for cultivation in troughs.

The trough presents one major problem—that of replenishing the soil. Obviously one does not want to have to turn out and reconstruct a trough at frequent intervals, in the way that one re-pots plants. Nevertheless, in the confined space of a trough, particularly if it is shallow, the soil becomes exhausted of nutrients. Some plants are adapted to a sparse diet, and sempervivums, sedums, etc, may flourish in the arid soil of an old trough. However, it must not be assumed that because plants are small in stature they can flourish without food—turf plants such as the spring gentian for instance certainly seem to need plenty of humus. So frequent small additions of finely sifted leafmould and bone-meal should be worked in among the plants, with perhaps a little liquid plant-feed for selected individual plants.

Troughs and sinks are now hard to get. They can be made from 'hypertufa' (or 'hypertupha'), which is a modified concrete made of cement, sand and peat. This mixture is lighter, more porous and pleasanter in appearance than ordinary concrete. Its appearance varies according to the proportions used, and so also does its strength and weight. Unless the trough is to be very small and is unlikely to need to be moved, the cement should constitute not less than one part in five by volume. In making my own troughs I used cement, sand and grit (that is, an ordinary fine-textured concrete) without peat for the base, and built up the sides with a 1 : 2 : 2 mix of cement, sand and peat. The trough is made by pouring the mixture between an inner and an outer mould, and these may be of wood, cardboard or hardboard. The last of these, tacked on to light wood laths, provides a good compromise as regards rigidity. The outer mould is assembled, and four or five short lengths of broomhandle are stood on end in the bottom to provide drainage holes. The length of these must be the thickness of the floor of the trough: this will vary with the size of trough, but (unless metal reinforcement of the mixture is used) should be not less than 2½in. The mixture is then poured into the bottom of the mould to the level of the tops of the pieces of broomhandle, and the inner mould positioned upon it; and the space between the walls is filled in. It will be found necessary to strut the inner mould—one or two pieces of wood are all that are needed for this—and to support the walls of the outer mould with bricks, stone or whatever is handy, because even hardboard tends to sag under the pressure of the cement. It is neither necessary nor desirable to be too fussy in securing precise rectangularity of the finished trough. It is then left to set, and will be stronger if this process is delayed by covering it over with damp sacking. The outer mould is removed first, and at this point the surface can be worked or roughened to suit the maker's fancy. A few hours later the inner mould is removed, and the plugs are knocked or drilled out. The appearance of the trough will improve with time.

The alpine house (Plates, p 90)

Modified greenhouses for the cultivation of alpines are probably as old in concept as the rock garden. Nevertheless the view that the proper place for alpines is the rock garden was little disputed until the early 1930s, by which time the alpine house was becoming popular, and even so recently as the Third International Rock Garden Conference in London and Edinburgh in 1961 there were those who seemed to consider that the alpine house needed defending. It is nowadays in common use among serious growers of alpines. There is a considerable literature on the subject, which will be treated here only in its essentials.

The alpine house is used (1) for difficult alpines, which rarely flourish in the open garden; (2) for those which flower during the winter or early spring when their blossoms, though perhaps freely produced in the rock garden, are rapidly destroyed by the weather; (3) for plants whose frost-hardiness is in question; (4) for growing plants for exhibition; and (5) for protection against industrial air pollution.

These purposes are not wholly consistent with one another and are not quite identical in the special provision they need: this accounts to some extent for the diversity of opinion as to the manner in which an alpine house should be managed.

(1) A 'difficult' alpine is one which will not readily survive in the open garden. The key questions in the writer's view are why they are difficult out of doors and why they flourish (if indeed they do) in the alpine house. Wherein lies the essential difference? An important group of these difficult alpines are those that grow at high altitudes. They include such species as *Ranunculus glacialis*, *Geum reptans*, *Eritrichium nanum* and the American *E. howardii*, *Campanula cenisia*, and the aretian Androsaces. All these plants are snow-covered for six to eight months of the year. Under the snow they are cold but not hard-frozen, exposed to low humidity, and more or less deprived of light and air, so that growth ceases or nearly so. When the snow melts the sun is already hot by day and there is abundant moisture; but the air, even when humid, is not stagnant. Growth is rapid. The conditions do not favour the development of moulds and fungi. These conditions cannot be reproduced in a garden in a temperate climate where the winters are on the whole wet and mild, and cold spells, often unaccompanied by snow, are unpredictable in timing and duration. Can the alpine house offer anything better? The answer seems to be that it can, though it certainly cannot in all respects reproduce alpine conditions. First, and probably most important, it can eliminate overhead moisture: the foliage of the plants can be kept totally dry. Secondly, with adequate and properly used ventilation, possibly supplemented by fans, it can eliminate stagnation of the air. Thirdly, it can prevent the freezing of the plants at their roots, either by incorporating a heating system or,

short of this, by plunging the pots: only in a very exceptional winter in England are there cold enough spells to freeze down to the roots of plunged pots in a house which provides overhead cover from descending cold air. In these three ways, then, the alpine house is a better proposition than the open garden for the *winter* care of high alpine plants. Nevertheless, there is at least one important respect in which the alpine house cannot reproduce alpine conditions: it cannot keep the temperature *down* to the constant level, just below freezing point, that plants under snow experience. Consequently the growth of these plants does not cease during the winter in the alpine house, and this profoundly affects their management. Let us take an example. *Eritrichium nanum*, a particularly difficult plant that takes one's breath away (if one has any left after struggling up there) on the high alpine acidic rocks, can be over-wintered in a plunge bed with a pane of glass over it to protect it from overhead moisture: thus managed, each of its tiny rosettes will die down to a dry brown bud in which the eye of faith, aided by a lens, may discern a minute green living point. It is nearly at total rest until the first warm spell in spring. In the alpine house, if it is kept frost-free, the story is different: some of the Eritrichium leaves will turn brown, to be assiduously picked off with forceps, but the plant remains green. It must therefore be watered, only from below and with the greatest circumspection—but nevertheless the aim is clear, to maintain the plant not at total rest but at an extremely low level of growth; and this principle applies to all the difficult high alpines. Some of them, such as *Ranunculus glacialis*, may lose their leaves during the winter, but it is doubtful if the plant is really in total hibernation, which is perhaps the reason why the Ranunculus is even harder to grow than Eritrichium, because of the difficulty of knowing just how much or how little water to give.

It is not in the winter alone that the alpine house can offer advantages over the open garden for the highest scree alpines. Most of them come into active growth and flower in the mountains as soon as the snow melts: and in temperate lowlands they will do so very early in the spring. In the mountains the change-over from winter to summer is likely to be rapid and well defined, and any cold spell is likely to lead to fresh snow protection. Not so in the garden, where hard frosts without snow may assault the young growth at any time into May. In the alpine house the plant is protected against these extremes. But there is another side. Plants grown constantly in the alpine house, and particularly during their season of most rapid growth, are liable to get 'out of character', their foliage becoming taller, softer, lusher, laxer than is characteristic of the plant in the wild. Also, unless special precautions are taken, there is a greater risk of disease, especially associated with infestation by aphis, than in the open garden; but on the other hand the depredations of slugs and snails, birds, etc, are largely eliminated in the alpine house. It is not surprising that, while those who maintain that all alpine plants should be grown in the open have probably lost their battle, there still remains a difference of opinion as to whether they should be kept constantly in the alpine house or whether they should be grown outside in plunge beds and brought in only when special protection is required.

There is one other point to be made—possibly it is the most important of all. The alpine house permits, and indeed demands, a high standard of individual care for every plant—far more than is possible in the open garden. A plant out of doors may perish unnoticed, from disease, vermin or accident: in the alpine house it is under daily review, and any signs of sickness can be observed and treated at an early stage.

'Difficult' plants for the alpine house are not confined to the high alpines of temperate zones. There are other plants, suitable for the rock garden could they but be grown there, which are difficult or impossible out of doors in temperate climates in the northern hemisphere for various reasons. There are plants of equatorial Africa and South America which grow at high altitudes and are subjected to nightly freezing alternating with intense heat by day. There are plants of the mountains of the southern hemisphere, for instance in South Africa and New Zealand, whose growing conditions may not be dissimilar from those of the European mountains, but which have to be adapted to a change in annual growth-cycle before they can be established in the northern hemisphere. Some of these can be managed in the alpine house though not in the open garden, because the former permits a greater manipulation of their growing conditions. Then there are the plants, particularly bulbous and rhizomatous plants, from the eastern Mediterranean and the Near and Middle East, and other comparable areas of the world, which even though they be winter-hardy are difficult to accommodate satisfactorily in the garden because of their need for summer baking. Some of them *can* be grown outside if special provision is made such as has been described; but for the more demanding of them the alpine house offers the better hope of success.

(2) Some of the most enchanting rock and alpine plants come into flower very early in the year in England—at the end of January or early in February. One thinks particularly of the wide range of Kabschia and Engleria saxifrages—neat, free-flowering, beautiful and varied. With them come some of the early spring crocuses (though these indeed are *late*-comers in the succession of crocus species that flower from September till March), irises and many more; and the alpine house in January and February can be a delightful place. Many of these plants will flower in the open, but the blossoms are pathetically damaged by winter winds, frosts and rains: in the alpine house the individual flowers last much longer, and the overall duration is likewise extended.

(3) The alpine purist eschews plants which are not frost-hardy, and will have no heating in the alpine house—which is a counsel difficult to apply in practice because of the impossibility of defining hardiness. A plant may be hardy in one garden but not in another, even in the same vicinity; in one season but not another; at one stage of growth but not another; its roots may be frost-resistant but its foliage or buds or flowers tender; the same species may be hardy or not so according to the way it has been grown. It is therefore not surprising that a great many plants have been accepted on the show benches of the Alpine Garden Society as 'alpine' which would not survive in the open in most English gardens but are amenable to cultivation in the alpine house. If one can say of a plant 'I wish that plant were hardy in the open —it would look well in the rock garden' and if, furthermore, it is a plant that in the wild grows in rocky or hilly places (and these two criteria amount to very much the same thing) then it is a fair contender for a place in the alpine house. Such plants are legion. They come from the Mediterranean, South Africa, California, southern China, Japan, Burma, New Zealand, the Andes.

(4) Those who exhibit their plants, competitively or otherwise, generally grow them in pots, and usually in alpine houses or with similar protection. It has often been said that this is not necessary—that plants can perfectly well be lifted from the open garden and potted up for exhibition; but the comparative infrequency with which this is done testifies to the practical difficulties. It is certainly possible with many plants to lift them, exhibit them and replant them without any serious setback to the plant: what is not so easy is to prepare such plants really satisfactorily for exhibition.

Page 125 The Blue Gromwell, *Lithospernum purpureo-coeruleum*, a rare British native, produces brilliant blue, purple-budded, flowers in sun or shade, and propagates itself by rooting down at the tips of its non-flowering shoots

Page 126 The hanging tubular flowers of *Onosma albo-roseum* open white and 'fade' to a delicate rose-pink. It shows to best advantage hanging from a rock-face or crevice

(5) The writer has no experience of gardening in an industrial city; but one eminent grower in a large English city where the air is (or was) heavily polluted, has said that he took to growing his plants in an alpine house primarily to protect them against industrial deposits.

CONSTRUCTION AND EQUIPMENT

In the preceding paragraphs the different purposes which an alpine house can serve have been discussed at some length because they indicate the kind of construction and equipment needed, and also partly explain why expert growers differ in the manner of managing their alpine houses.

Certain requirements are beyond dispute. The alpine house must be so sited and constructed that there is full control over the lighting and shading and the ventilation. It should be in the open (not under trees) and preferably it should run from north to south. The roof-pitch should be low, and there should be ventilating windows along the whole length on either side of the ridge and on both sides: all windows should be separately controllable. Air-circulation is important: normally it is ensured by giving the maximum ventilation that the weather conditions permit, but in specially difficult conditions, such as still fog, an electric fan is a valuable adjunct. Draughts are to be avoided, and it cannot be too strongly emphasised that in the alpine house as in the dwelling house draughts result from too *little* ventilation, not too much: a draught is a jet of fast-moving air coming through a small aperture; it is abolished by opening the windows. There is some difference of opinion as to whether there should be ventilators below the staging, just above the flooring. This depends partly on how the floor-space is to be used. Provided that they can be efficiently sealed by sliding covers when they are not wanted there is good reason for having them: they permit ventilation under various combinations of weather-conditions when the windows are insufficient or cannot be kept open. If the door is at the south end (which means that the crossbench is at the north end) less shading is needed and, in the northern hemisphere, there is less risk of draught from the coldest winter winds. In practice the choice is probably determined by the position of the alpine house vis-à-vis the dwelling house. Shading is important—surprisingly so, when one considers that many of the plants which are grown in the alpine house are in the wild exposed to hot clear sunlight; it is inescapably true that under alpine house conditions a great many plants wilt or

H

scorch unless they are adequately shaded. The main kinds of shading, in diminishing order both of efficiency and of cost, are slatted blinds, curtaining, and white or green colour wash on the glass. Slatted blinds which will roll up and are controllable by ropes certainly are expensive, but they have a long life and are easily controlled to provide the necessary variations in shading according to weather conditions: they can be fitted to roll up over curved metal struts which hold them clear of the windows alongside the ridge, so that these can be opened: split-reed blinds used in similar fashion are cheaper but less durable. Rigid slatted panels, homemade to fit, and fixed by hooks or catches to the outsides of the windows, are less expensive and are effective; but they are awkward to take up and down and they interfere with window opening. Gauze curtaining on the outside of the windows is unsightly and awkward to control and has a short life: on the inside of the windows it can be more readily slid on wires and has a longer life, but since the sun still falls on to the glass it does not do much to prevent overheating: PVC roller blinds can be used in the same way, and, at increased cost, have some advantages in convenience and durability. Colour wash on the glass has little except cheapness to commend it for the alpine house, since it cannot be varied to suit the weather.

The question of heating has already been mentioned. Electric tubular heating, set just above the level of the staging and thermostatically controlled to operate when the temperature drops to 34° F, is a necessity if slightly tender plants are to be grown and is a safeguard against frost damage to the roots even of high alpine plants in really cold spells, particularly if the pots are not fully plunged. A more recent introduction which may well prove to have advantages over tubular heating combines air-heating with a slow moving fan. Heating by paraffin stoves is not to be recommended: it is more difficult to obtain evenly dispersed heating and, more serious still, the combustion of paraffin produces substantial quantities of water in the air.

The installation of an electricity supply in the alpine house can in some circumstances pose a problem: nevertheless it is very desirable, not only to provide heating but also for lighting, which greatly extends the hours during which the owner can work in his alpine house during the winter. It is also necessary if a fan is to be used, or an electrically heated aerosol. Not least, it can provide comforting warmth for the gardener, even if he spurns it for his plants! This need for an electricity supply may be a determining factor in the siting of the alpine house.

In most alpine houses the plants are grown in pots, the majority of which, at least while the plants are in flower, are placed upon staging. This is usually set between 30 and 36in high and (like the kitchen sink) should be set to suit the height of the owner if backaches are to be avoided. The width of the staging is about the same, and this too should be suited to the length and strength of the owner's arms. The staging, which normally runs down both sides of the house and across the end farthest from the door, may consist either of (a) wooden slats, (b) a base such as asbestos sheeting on a supporting framework, or (c) water-tight trays. The first of these is suitable only if the plants are brought in briefly for display, not for cultivation: this use is not further considered here. Asbestos sheeting and wooden sides can be sufficiently sealed with a proprietary sealing tape to retain the moisture from a wet plunge mixture: it is not really suitable for standing water, and should have an outlet hole over the water tank. Really water-tight staging is required only if a method of watering is employed which involves flooding the trays: galvanised iron is strong and long-lasting, but is heavy and necessitates strong supports; an alternative is a lighter construction, eg of timber with a plastic lining.

The staging is covered with a material into which the pots are plunged, and this necessitates retaining walls. The height of these will depend upon the depth of plunge used, and in this respect there are two rather different methods of cultivation. In the first, the staging is covered to a depth of 2–3in only with some such material as $\frac{1}{8}$in granite chippings, and the pots are pressed lightly into this. Watering of all plants is individual, either overhead or by standing the pots in a water-trough, and is not via the chippings: the latter act as a stabiliser, give a good appearance, and are kept just sufficiently moist to prevent the pots from drying out at the bottoms. The plunge material gives no frost protection, and the method therefore is unsuitable for an alpine house which is not kept frost-free. It is appropriate for use with either plastic or clay pots. It is a method which can be highly successful, but it is demanding in watering time. In the second method the plunge material is water-retentive, is deeper, and is used as a major (though not the sole) source of the plants' water supply. The plunge material is usually sand plus a moisture retainer such as peat or vermiculite. The pots are plunged deeply so that the walls are always kept moist by the plunge. This method gives a considerable degree of frost-protection. It is not applicable to plastic pots. Time is saved in watering, as this is via the plunge, but it cannot totally replace individual watering; and indeed a major criticism of the method is that it makes for uniform watering of plants whose needs in this respect are highly individual. The time saved in watering is largely offset by the time spent in making new holes for the pots every time they are moved. In principle, this method involves plunging the pots to their rims, but it would be quite impracticable to do this with the largest pots, and a depth of about 6in of plunge is a reasonable compromise. Deeply plunged pots are more likely to root through into the plunge material, with a risk of root damage when they are moved.

Both these methods of cultivation in different ways permit the installation of equipment to enable the plants to be watered by flooding or irrigating the plunge material, provided that the staging and its rims are water-tight. If deep plunging is used, it is possible to irrigate the staging by bringing a piped water supply (for instance, electrically pumped from the rainwater tank) to a position where by turning the tap one or more sections of the staging can be flooded: by unplugging the drainage holes water is allowed to return to the tank. In the alternative method the plunge material, which is shallow, is kept continuously wet: the pots are pressed lightly into it and the soil is kept moist by capillary action. To secure this the soil must be packed right down to the bottom of the pot—there is no drainage layer: either plastic or clay pots can be used, and with the latter a refinement (or complication) is the insertion of capillary wicks into the drainage holes. These methods are liable to create a high general humidity in the alpine house, and while they may be suitable for some plants they are inclined to make for soft leafiness so that cushion plants in particular tend to become out of character. Mosses and liverworts are liable to develop on the surface of the plunge mixture, which needs to be periodically scraped and cleaned.

The flooring of the alpine house needs some consideration. The central area, which is walked upon, is best made of concrete, which is durable and easily cleaned. With regard to the areas under the staging, there is variation in the uses to which they are put: if they are to be used only for standing plants in pots (and the cool shade under the staging is an excellent place for many plants to spend their resting period) the flooring can be satisfactorily prepared by levelling the ground, treating it with weedkiller, laying polythene sheeting, and spreading 2in or so of gravel on the polythene. This makes a clean and satisfactory stand for the pots, and also is suitable for storage of bins of soil mixture, etc. Some growers have a series of trays under the staging into which resting plants are plunged, and a few (a very few) plants grow and thrive wholly in these shaded positions.

An important item in the construction of the alpine house is the rain-water storage tank. Main water supplies nearly always contain some lime, natural or added, so rainwater is precious. Some alpine houses have sunken tanks outside the walls, some inside, and some partly in and partly out; while others have an inside tank standing on the floor. An outside tank simplifies the plumbing and conserves space but means trotting in and out to fill the can. Inside fully sunken tanks are more accessible but involve a good deal of stooping and lifting and are difficult to clean out. An inside lightweight fibreglass tank sunken to only half its depth under the end staging occupies space but otherwise has all the advantages.

The remaining matter to be considered is the exclusion of vermin. Flying insects, particularly aphis, are always a potential danger to pot plants, and involve keeping a constant close watch and spraying with appropriate insecticides. An alternative method, rather more expensive but effective and convenient, is the use of an apparatus such as 'Aerovap' in which an electrically heated container is charged with a chemical insecticide which evaporates to maintain an effective concentration of the chemical in the atmosphere of the alpine house. It is open to the criticism that it produces a decided smell in the vicinity of the burner, but it is claimed to be harmless to the alpine house user. It has also been criticised as inefficient when the alpine house is at full ventilation, because of the rapid displacement of air; but it can nevertheless be highly effective. The same apparatus can be used to provide a fungicide vapour. The exclusion of creeping vermin, from woodlice to mice, is largely a matter of efficient construction of the alpine house combined with a high standard of care and cleanliness.

THE USE AND MANAGEMENT OF THE ALPINE HOUSE

It is assumed here that the alpine house is used for growing plants not simply for displaying them.

Most growers do not keep their plants all the time in the alpine house. There is a continuous in-and-out flow, and when a plant is not in the house it is normally in a plunge bed or frame. The alpine house itself, therefore, is the central element in an assembly of equipment for growing alpines in pots. The frames and plunge beds serve the purposes of (i) providing suitable growing conditions and storage space for the plants while they are not in the alpine house and (ii) providing for the summer baking of resting plants that need it. The first of these two functions will be more efficiently served if provision is made for protection from winter wet and some degree of winter cold: this can be provided by plunge beds (see Chapter Four). The summer ripening of bulbs and tubers requires a glass covered frame, in which the pots are protected from rain: the greater the area of glass covering the frame the more heat can be conserved in a temperamental summer—but it must be remembered that it is possible to over-heat if ventilation is totally eliminated. It is not possible to give any precise assessment of the amount of frame and plunge bed space needed in relation to an alpine house, since this depends so much upon personal choice as to the number and type of plants to be grown; certainly an area twice as great as that of the alpine house staging (implying that on average a pot spends twice as long outside the alpine house as in it) is not excessive.

Plants are placed on the alpine house staging when they are on display: with many plants this means when they are in flower, but others present an attractive show even when they are not. Many of the latter are cushion plants or otherwise interesting in form or foliage, and are worth looking at all the year round; and the grower has to use judgement in deciding whether and when they should nevertheless be put outside in order to keep them in good condition. Plants are also brought inside when they need protection from weather beyond that which the plunge beds can give, and in general such plants will be placed on the staging if they are in active growth and below it if they are dormant. These are no more than guiding principles—in practice the placing of plants at any particular point of time may well be determined by the relative pressures on space on and below the staging, and outside. In this method of alpine house control there is an underlying assumption—that a plant is better outside unless there is some good reason for its being inside. However, this view is not universally held, and some growers keep their plants constantly inside the alpine house, maintaining that with proper control, particularly of lighting, ventilation and watering, the plants can be kept in character. Such a procedure limits stringently the number of plants that can be grown in a given area of alpine house. A hazard of the more usual (and in the writer's opinion more commendable) method of 'rotating' the pots is that of importing vermin—slugs, snails, earthworms, earwigs, woodlice, etc —into the house. The preventive is strict care and cleanliness in the management of the plunge beds, and careful examination of all pots when they are brought indoors.

Alpine house cultivation not only permits individual care for each plant—it requires it. In the rock garden plants requiring similar conditions of cultivation are in general planted together. In the alpine house, plants with widely differing requirements are on the same staging under the same roof. Each plant must be in a pot of the right shape and size for its own stage of growth and type of root system. The soil in the pot must be appropriate to the plant, and the drainage material under the soil suited both to the plant and to the method of watering employed. Some plants require starvation, some feeding. Some require regular and frequent repotting; some are best disturbed as little as possible. All require watering (at least while they are inside the alpine house) but the frequency and method must be suited to the plant and the season. Some require frequent division or pruning to keep them to shape and size: others resent or do not need such treatment. Some, if they are to remain healthy and free from risk of fungus attack, must have every spent flower and every dead leaf removed. These are just some of the many facets of alpine house care, and it follows that a really comprehensive treatment of this subject needs plant-by-plant consideration—a matter for a specialist work.

A few general principles can be mentioned, which are really an application to alpine house conditions of the methods of care of rock plants already discussed in relation to the open garden.

The choice of pot is important. Under-potting (ie using too small a pot) is likely to mean under-feeding, and an under-potted plant rapidly becomes 'pot-bound', with a great mass of root packed into a small quantity of soil and the roots commonly directed upwards against the wall of the pot. Such plants, apart from being starved of nutriment, also rapidly exhaust the water in the soil and so need more watering than would the same plant in a larger pot. Some plants, however, flower better when they are pot-bound in this way. Over-potting on the other hand (placing a small plant in too large a pot) appears to be unfavourable to many plants, and the explanation usually adduced is that the soil round the outside of the pot, containing no roots, becomes stagnant and sour. The *depth* of the pot should be suited to the plant. Some plants are taprooted or have many long deep roots, while others are shallow-rooted. The former are likely to do better in the normal deep pot, or even in the exceptionally long narrow type known as 'long Toms'. Shallow-rooted plants in such pots do not utilise the lower soil, so that the pot is of unnecessary bulk and weight, and in watering from below it is more difficult to ensure that the water reaches up to the right level. Consequently alpines are frequently grown in 'half-pots', which are shallower in relation to their height than the ordinary type. A more extreme version of this is the 'pan', a much shallower pot which is useful for seed-sowing where a large quantity of one kind is to be sown, but is not suited to the majority of alpines.

The question of plastic versus clay pots calls for consideration, since the former are coming progressively into use. The essential differences between the two are as follows:

(a) Clays are porous, allowing retention and slow passage of water and, to a limited degree, when dry, of air. This means that when they are plunged in a moist medium they will not dry out totally—probably the reason why plants in clay pots tend to produce a mass of fine roots against the wall of the pot. It also means that if they are not plunged, and particularly if they are exposed to dry winds, the soil is liable to dry out. Neither of these effects occurs with plastic pots.

(b) Clays vary in thickness, but plastics even more so. Thin plastic pots, unplunged, probably allow more variation in the soil temperature and a greater risk of freezing at the roots than clays.

(c) Clays are usually drained by a single large hole and plastics by a number of smaller ones. The latter (which do not usually require covering with perforated zinc) are sometimes inadequate and easily clogged: the holes of some makes need enlarging (use heat, not force), and even so a deeper layer of coarser drainage material is required with plastics than with clays. The plastics appear to hold their moisture longer and to require less watering, but, perhaps because they contain less soil, are at greater risk of suddenly and unexpectedly becoming very dry. A moisture-retaining humus layer over the grit is therefore more important with plastic than with clay pots.

The effect of these differences is that plants grown in the two types of pot call for rather different handling, especially as regards watering methods. There is a natural tendency for experienced gardeners to stick to the methods they know, and this accounts for some of the considerable prejudice against plastic pots. Their use is at present exceptional in the alpine house.

The soil mixtures to be used are essentially those which have already been discussed, but under alpine house conditions it is necessary to take into account not only any special requirements of the individual plant, but also the watering methods used. Other things being equal, a deeply plunged pot will need a somewhat faster draining soil than an unplunged one. Because the watering is individual and under constant surveillance, the bottom drainage layer and the humus layer above it (which jointly are a device to ensure the constant availability of only a small amount of moisture) become less important, and some alpine house growers dispense with them altogether.

Alpine house plants are grown for display. They are to be looked at and admired. So it is not quite enough that a plant should be in the right soil in the right pot, and be looked after so that it grows and flowers well. It must be kept groomed for appearance. Those who exhibit their plants competitively know the need for this, and become skilful at it; but it applies to alpine house plants whether they are exhibited or not. It requires cleanliness—of the pot, of the soil surface, of the plant. Dead or dying leaves, flowers or stems must be removed, and the plant pruned to be shapely without destroying its natural method of growth. For instance a cushion plant should be neat and compact, but it need not have the symmetry of a pudding basin. The surface of the soil should be kept dressed with clean grit or chippings: the colour and form of these is to some extent a matter of taste, suited to the type of pot and the style of the plant—but the result is more satisfying if the plant appears to be growing in a material similar to that in which it may be found in the wild. As an example *Campanula cenisia* growing in clean and neat pea-gravel or sandstone chippings must jar upon the observer who has seen it in the high black schists. Pieces of stone, skilfully used, can do much to enhance the appearance of a plant in a pot: a specimen (or two or three) of *Androsace vandellii* (*imbricata*), growing over and among pieces of carefully chosen and placed stone, may not achieve the symmetry of a single cushion in the middle of a pot faced with nothing but chippings, but the result will probably be much more pleasing. Pieces of stone skilfully inserted into the gaps can go far to redeem a plant which has died off in patches. Small pieces of tufa have achieved recent popularity for the facing of pots, not only for their appearance but also as an aid to growth. They have, however, some disadvantages, and need using with discretion: they readily grow mosses, which are not easy to remove, and because of their capacity to retain moisture they may lead to rotting at the neck of the plants—the very negation of what they are intended to do.

Finally, a word on propagation. This is no less important with alpine house plants than with others. Indeed, since some plants are in the alpine house precisely because they are difficult to grow, it becomes the more important to ensure against loss by timely and efficient propagation, and also to have sufficient stock to be able to experiment with different methods of growing. They are propagated in the same way as plants in the open, but there is one matter that needs watching. Alpine house plants which depend upon insects for pollination are at a disadvantage, particularly if insecticides are in use; and if seed is required hand fertilisation is likely to be needed.

ROCKWORK IN THE ALPINE HOUSE

The 'normal' use of the alpine house has been described, with some indication of the variations in practice. In addition some growers have been experimenting with the use of rock inside the alpine house to create protected miniature rock gardens. Tufa provides a convenient stone for this purpose: it is easier to use effectively on a small scale than stratified stone. Such indoor rock gardens can be very satisfying indeed. It may be objected that because the plants are permanently positioned here they are at the same risk of growing out of character as potted plants kept permanently in the alpine house; but this risk can be minimised by careful control of lighting and ventilation.

In the Cambridge University Botanic Garden, the alpine house is maintained as an indoor rock garden in which plants *in pots* are skilfully 'planted' so as to appear to be growing in the rock: they are kept constantly changed as new plants come into flower in the plunge beds, and the method is highly effective for this special purpose of public display.

Frames

The use of frames for the care of plants in pots has already been discussed in Chapter Four in relation to plants *temporarily* in pots for propagation or awaiting planting out. It is perfectly possible to use a frame just as one uses an alpine house. Preferably the frame (like the alpine house) should be used in conjunction with plunge beds, partly because, area for area, the latter are cheaper, and partly because for much of the time there will be some plants that need the additional protection that the frame can give and others that do not. Indeed there is no reason why the rotation of plants as between frame and plunge beds should not follow exactly the same pattern as that already described for the alpine house.

The reasons for growing potted plants in frames are essentially the same as for growing them in an alpine house, where either cost or lack of space rules out the latter. In particular, a number of alpine enthusiasts who exhibit their plants and who do not have alpine houses grow them successfully in frames. There are obvious limitations vis-à-vis the alpine house. The plants cannot be seen or displayed as satisfactorily, and you cannot work in a frame as you can in an alpine house; so that in practice it is really only in relation to exhibiting plants that the frame (as a permanent milieu of cultivation) comes into its own.

There is little that need be added with regard to the management of frames for this purpose. The principles which are applicable in the alpine house also hold good for the frame, but the needs cannot be so well met. The lack of electricity, with all that this means, and the limited 'head-room' over the plants and hence the diminished ventilatable space, are disadvantages; ground level frames are scarcely less vulnerable to vermin than are plunge beds: but (a most important consideration) the plants can receive the same individual care and supervision as they do in the alpine house.

Seven
A Note on Nomenclature

It is not surprising that many people, when they first become interested in rock gardening, find the Latin names a stumbling block. Alpines are wild flowers, and few have English names: it is the Latin name or nothing.

For those to whom Latin is a closed book, the names may indeed upon first acquaintance seem alarming. Nevertheless the principles of scientific naming are fairly simple, and the names themselves frequently informative and helpful to the gardener. Furthermore, because so much of English is derived from Latin the meaning of the words is often readily guessed, and there are not really so many of them. As with everything else, the problem is at the beginning: the more names one learns the easier does it become to learn the rest.

Latin names are necessary not only because there are no English ones for most alpine plants but also because they are *scientific*—that is to say they are planned, meaningful, and they represent one internationally agreed name per plant. At least, that is the aim. It must be admitted that the aim is not wholly achieved, and to the annoyance of gardeners plant names are liable to change. There are two main reasons for this. The first is that botanists in many countries have been giving Latin names to plants for centuries, and not surprisingly they have given different names to the same plant or called different plants by the same name. By international agreement the 'priority rule' has been adopted, and the name *first* given (after 1753) to a plant is the correct one. It still occasionally happens that an old work comes to light necessitating a change of plant names in accordance with the priority rule; however, this will happen with decreasing frequency. The far more important reason why plant names change is because as more and more is learned about plants the botanists change their ideas about classification. Two plants previously thought to be different are found to be the same; two plants previously thought to be the same are found to be different; plants previously thought to belong to the same genus are classified in separate genera; plants previously separated are brought together into the same genus: these and other considerations all represent attempts to achieve a really sound and orderly plant classification, but they all require changes in names.

All the same, these changes are exceptional. By far the majority of scientific names are firm and internationally agreed, and this is their great merit.

The Latin name of a plant consists usually of two words. The first, spelt with an initial capital letter, is the GENERIC NAME—that is to say it indicates the genus, or group, into which the plant falls; eg *Primula, Linaria, Saxifraga,* etc. All the plants in a genus have some common characteristics, so that to know that a plant is a primula, for instance, is to know quite a lot about it. This assumes that one already knows something about primulas, and the more plants one already knows the more meaningful do the Latin names become. The second name is the SPECIFIC NAME, usually spelt without an initial capital, eg *fragrans, alpinus, minor.* These two names together really pin down the plant: they tell you what kind (genus) of plant it is and which one (species) of the kind. Furthermore, as the three examples just given show, the meaning of the specific names is often clear enough even if you don't know any Latin. The specific name is usually an adjective—it is descriptive, either of the plant itself (*Allium roseum, Crocus purpureus*) or of its place of origin (*Scilla italica, Petrocoptis pyrenaica*) or its habitat (*Aster alpinus, Dianthus glacialis*), or some other characteristic, frequently giving valuable information to the gardener. A minor complication with specific names is that their endings vary: this is because in Latin there are three genders—masculine, feminine and neuter—and the specific name has to 'agree' in gender with the generic name. The words *alpinus, alpina* and *alpinum* all mean the same thing; so do *perennis* and *perenne.* These examples cover the endings most commonly met with: masculine endings are usually *-us* or *-is*; feminine *-a* or *-is* (but a catch is that generic names ending in *-ma* are usually neuter); and neuter *-um* or *-e.*

The aim of having only one name for one plant has not yet been fully achieved. When a plant's name is changed the old name may well persist in use for many years, and it continues to be accepted, not as the 'correct' name but as a SYNONYM, an acceptable alternative. Often indeed there are several synonyms for the same plant.

A plant may have a THIRD NAME in addition to the generic and specific names. The reason for this is that plants are so variable. *Saxifraga oppositifolia,* for instance, varies so much that two individual plants may look quite different from one another; but because they are connected by a range of intermediate forms they are all accepted as the same species. Nevertheless it is convenient and useful to divide them up, and this is done by using a third name, eg *S. oppositifolia latina* or *S. oppositifolia rudolphiana.* The third name may represent a subspecies or a variety or a form—but these distinctions need not worry the gardener: in all cases they represent subdivisions of the *wild* plant and the third name is in Latin. A third name may also be used to indicate a garden variety, or 'CULTIVAR'. Such a name may be in Latin, but the more recent and preferred practice is to have it in a modern language, usually that of the country where the cultivar was produced. Cultivar names, even if in Latin, can be recognised by being written between inverted commas, eg *Phlox douglasii* 'Rose Queen'. Sometimes a cultivar is of such mixed (or unknown) parentage that its species cannot be stated: in this case the specific epithet may well be omitted, eg *Dianthus* 'Whitehills'.

Many garden plants, even some alpines, are HYBRIDS. This is indicated by the use of '×' before the specific name. This '×' is used in two slightly different ways. *Moltkia × intermedia* is a hybrid but the name tells you nothing about its parentage. *Moltkia petraea × M. suffruticosa* (which is in fact the same plant) indicates the parentage.

The *pronunciation* of scientific names can be a source of confusion. They are Latin, and should be pronounced as such; but the problem is lack of agreement as to how Latin should be pronounced. There are in fact two main methods in general use, and this is the reason why there is disagreement and inconsistency: it cannot be said (at least, not without incurring much wrath!) that either is 'wrong'. Apart from the differences between the two main methods of pronunciation (which were exemplified by 'Mr Chips' ' objection to pronouncing *vicissim* as 'We kiss'im' instead of 'vice-issim'!) there is the problem of knowing where the stress should fall, and frequently there is a discrepancy between what has become accepted practice and what the classicists regard as correct. The only realistic attitude towards the pronunciation of plant names at present seems to be one of tolerant acceptance of wide differences. In Latin, whichever of the two methods of pronunciation is preferred, every vowel is separately and fully pronounced. There is no mute 'e'. It is particularly the 'e' which comes at the end of the neuter form of specific names that is liable to be mispronounced, especially as such words frequently look the same as English words and there is a natural tendency to give them an English pronunciation. There may be grounds for argument as to whether *saxatile* should rhyme with 'silly' or 'highly', and where the stress should come; but never can it rhyme with 'Nile': *hortense* cannot rhyme with 'pence': *vulgare* may rhyme with 'starry' or 'hairy' but never with 'stair': *viride* cannot rhyme with 'hide' nor *perenne* with 'hen'. And so on—that last 'e' must be sounded.

The MEANINGS of Latin names, especially the specific names, can be helpful to the gardener, giving information as to what the plant looks like or how to grow it. Many are obvious as in the examples already given. Some others, while less obvious, are in common use and are particularly helpful, and a short list of these follows. In each case the masculine form is given. There are just a few instances where the specific names are liable to confuse. For instance *insignis* means the reverse of insignificant; *formosus* means handsome but *formosanus* means from Formosa; *calcareus* or *calcicola* means that the plant grows in chalk or lime, *calceolus* means like a little slipper and *calcaratus* means spurred. Specifics indicating place names may vary in form, eg *pyrenaeus*, *pyrenaicus*; *sinensis*, *chinensis*; *asturicus*, *asturiensis*. In general, however, the scientific names are altogether helpful and well worth the trouble of learning.

Some common and useful specific names

(A) DESCRIPTIVE

acaulis	stemless	*latifolius*	broad leaved
aestivalis	summer flowering	*luteus*	yellow
albus	white	*macranthus*	large flowered
angustifolius	narrow leaved	*microphyllus*	small leaved
argenteus	silver	*nanus*	dwarf
aureus	golden	*niger*	black
biflorus	two flowered	*officinalis*	medicinal
bifolius	two leaved	*parviflorus*	small flowered

caespitosus	tufted	*plumosus*	feathery
chrysanthus	golden flowered	*polyphyllus*	many leaved
coccineus	deep red	*pulchellus*	beautiful and little
coelestis	heavenly blue	*pumilus*	dwarf
coeruleus	blue	*pygmaeus*	dwarf
cyaneus	dark blue	*radicans*	rooting from stems
flavus	pale yellow, tawny	*repens, reptans*	creeping
fruticosus	shrubby, bushy	*ruber*	red
glaber	} smooth, hairless	*sempervirens*	evergreen
glabellus		*simplicifolius*	simple (undivided) leaves
gramineus	grass-like		
guttatus	spotted	*speciosus*	showy, splendid
humilis	low growing	*striatus*	streaked or lined
laciniatus	cut petals	*tenellus*	delicate
laevigatus	smooth, polished	*tenuifolius*	slender leaved
lanatus	woolly	*viridis*	green

(B) INDICATING HABITAT

alpinus	} in alps—ie in mountain pastures	*nivalis*	among snow
alpestris		*palustris*	in marshes
†*alpicola*		*petraeus*	among rocks
aquatilis	} in water	*pratensis*	in meadows
aquaticus		*rivalis*	} by brooks
arenarius	in sand	*rivularis*	
calcareus	in chalk or lime	*rupestris*	} among rocks or cliffs
†*cauticola*	on rough rocks	†*rupicola*	
collinus	on hills	*saxatilis*	} among rocks or stones
glacialis	by glaciers	†*saxicola*	
maritimus	by the sea	*saxosus*	
montanus	on mountains	*segetum*	of cornfields
muralis	on walls	*sylvaticus	} in woods; or, wild
nemorosus	in woods	*sylvestris*	

* Also spelt 'silvaticus', 'silvestris'.
† Words ending in -*cola* are nouns and always in the feminine form.

Viola papilionacea. This lovely North American violet, with abundant clear white rounded flowers, seeds freely around in sun or shade

Page 144 If a plant that seeds itself everywhere is a 'weed' then *Viola curtisii alba* is as charming a weed as you could have in the rock garden

Eight

Selected Plants for the Rock Garden and Alpine House

The purpose of this chapter is to enable the reader who is not yet deeply versed in the subject to visualise plants which he may be buying or growing from seed, and to help him in their cultivation. It is a limited selection but I hope balanced and representative. Both 'easy' and 'difficult' plants are included, but in general the more difficult a plant is to grow the more attractive it has to be to warrant inclusion.

Exactly the same applies in respect of the ease or difficulty of obtaining the plant. While the majority appear in nurserymen's lists, there is a substantial number which are usually obtainable only as seed. Some of these are listed by commercial firms specialising in seed, and others can be obtained through the seed exchanges of the various alpine plant societies (see p 225). A few (particularly alpine house plants) are very hard to come by: they are obtained by gift or exchange between members of the alpine plant societies, among whom there is much generosity and camaraderie.

I have deliberately included a proportion of plants suitable for each of the specialised types of habitat described elsewhere in the book—eg woodland, bog—which are not in the narrower sense 'alpine'. A larger number of such plants will be found in the following chapter, which contains lists, without descriptions, of plants suitable for specialised habitats.

The plants included as suitable for the alpine house differ a little in the criteria of selection, in that they tend to be scarcer and more specialised in their cultural requirements.

The following notes will help the reader to use the list.

I

To avoid repetition, as much information as possible is included under the GENERIC name; but it is to be emphasised that *the information given applies only to those species listed.*

So far as possible the botanically correct NAME is used (see Chapter Seven). In the case of those European plants in the first two volumes of *Flora Europaea* (see p 242) the name there given is accepted as correct: in other cases the main source of reference has been the Royal Horticultural Society's *Dictionary of Gardening*. For most plants only the generic and specific names are used: where a THIRD NAME (which may indicate a sub-species, variety or cultivar) is employed, the description refers only to this form of the plant. SYNONYMS are given without botanical precision. A 'synonym' in this list may be a correct botanical alternative; or it may be a subspecific name, so that it refers only to a part of the species; or a variety or cultivar; or even a totally incorrect name in common use: the aim is to alert the reader to alternative names he may meet for what are, from a gardening point of view, practically identical plants.

HEIGHT indicates the tallest part of the plant, usually the flowers. Heights vary a lot, and the measurement given only indicates a typical average height in my own garden. The SIZE OF LEAVES given is usually that seen at flowering time: in some plants they enlarge later.

Plants are PERENNIAL unless otherwise stated. They keep their leaves during the winter unless described as HERBACEOUS (or in the case of shrubs DECIDUOUS); but the information is imprecise in that the shedding of old leaves is often accompanied by the first appearance of the next season's growth, more or less at ground level; and this may vary with season and local climate. Bulbous plants though not described as herbaceous lose their leaves during their resting stage. 'MONOCARPIC' plants die after flowering.

The descriptions of leaves and flowers are given briefly and in non-technical terms. This inevitably means a lack of precision, but it is hoped that enough information is given to enable the reader to picture the plant. 'ENTIRE' leaves are undivided and smooth-edged. Petal-like structures (eg in Ranunculaceae) are called petals though this is not always strictly correct, and the compound flower heads of Compositae are treated as single flowers.

The SEASON of flowering (in rare instances, of fruiting, where the seed-head is more important than the flower) aims to indicate when it commences and the duration of main flowering: the latter varies with season, climate and latitude, and many rock plants will produce an odd flower at any time of the year. Flowering is likely to be earlier in the alpine house, and only in the case of plants definitely recommended for alpine house cultivation is this the season given. Flowering times in the wild may be very different from those in the garden. The times given are based upon an early season in southern England. It is not practical to indicate the probable flowering times in different countries; but gardeners in countries other than the United Kingdom, and particularly those in the southern hemisphere, will appreciate that there is a very big adjustment to be made.

The following generalisations may assist in this adjustment:

Plants listed as flowering in *January–March* are likely to be 'snow-melt flowers', with pre-formed flower buds that open in advance of leaf growth on cessation of snow cover, at a season of heavy rainfall, occasional warm spells and short day-length.

April–May flowerers are 'spring flowers' producing simultaneous leaf and flower growth as the moist soil warms up and day-length increases.

June–July flowerers produce maximum leaf growth before flowering, which occurs when the soil is hot, day-length maximal and the soil frequently drying.

August–November flowerers are naturally aestivating (ie they rest during the summer) and produce preformed flowers upon resumption of rainfall after their summer rest.

Notes on CULTIVATION are given only when the plant has special needs: otherwise it should be assumed that 'ordinary rock garden soil' (see Chapter Two) is appropriate, and that the plant is not especially demanding as regards aspect and situation. Plants should be assumed to be lime-tolerant unless described as 'calciphobe'. In the absence of an indication to the contrary, the plants have withstood winter or spring temperatures of 10–15° F (often much lower) without snow protection, showing no significant damage or impairment of flowering. A recommendation for alpine house cultivation is included where the plant cannot be effectively grown out of doors, or is subject to severe flower-damage because of its season of flowering: many others can be included effectively in the alpine house, but in general if a plant is fully tolerant of cultivation in the rock garden it is not included in the list as an alpine house plant.

The indications as to PROPAGATION are given in order of choice, but this choice will be influenced by eg the need to obtain large numbers or to perpetuate a particular clone (see Chapter Five).

As regards the COUNTRY OR AREA OF ORIGIN, this is only an approximation. The word 'Alps', unless qualified, means the main central European mountain range, running from the French Maritime Alps through Switzerland and northern Italy to Austria and northern Yugoslavia.

Abbreviations

AH = Alpine House
c = (Stem) cuttings
C = Central
D = Division
FL = Flower(s)
L = Leaf, leaves
LC = Leaf cuttings
S = Seed

ACAENA (*Rosaceae*)
A. microphylla   4in. Spreading loose mat. L in ¼in, round, toothed, pairs of leaflets. FL inconspicuous. Crimson spiny seed heads in July–Aug. Part-shade. D, S. New Zealand.

ACANTHOLIMON (*Plumbaginaceae*)   Mats of thin, pointed L. FL in narrow spikes, ½in, funnel shaped.
A. glumaceum   6in. L green. FL pink. June. Light soil; sun. D, C. Armenia.
A. venustum   8in. L grey, hard, sharp. FL vivid rose. July. Hot position, very sharp drainage. LAYERING (difficult). Cilicia.

ACHILLEA (*Compositae*)   Low clumps. L usually toothed or divided. FL daisy-shaped, usually in flat multiple heads. Light soil; sun. D.
A. ageratifolia. Syn *Anthemis aizoon*   6in. L silvery. FL ¾in, white, solitary. May. N Greece.
A. × kellereri   Natural hybrid. L very feathery. FL white. Bulgaria.
A. rupestris   4in. Tufted mats of green almost entire L. FL ¾in, white. May. Italy.
A. tomentosa   12in. Dense mats. L narrow, very finely cut, woolly. FL small in 2in flat heads, yellow (deeper in var *aurea*). May–July. Europe, N Asia.

ADONIS (*Ranunculaceae*)
A. vernalis   10in. Herbaceous. Clumps of feathery 10in L, smaller at flowering time. FL 2in, solitary, many-petalled, greenish yellow, showy. April. Good soil; sun or half-shade. S (sow fresh; slow), D. Europe.

AETHIONEMA (*Cruciferae*)   Small sub-shrubs, 6–12in. L small, narrow, bluish. FL small in crowded heads or spikes. C, S.

A. *armenum*   L ¾in, glaucous. 'Warley Rose' is a good deep-coloured form. April–May. Armenia.

A. *grandiflorum*. Syn *pulchellum*   Looser, larger, paler-flowered. Lebanon.

A. *saxatile*. Syns *creticum, gracile, graecum, ovalifolium, pyrenaicum*   6in. Scarcely shrubby. L oval. FL deep pink in good forms. April–Sept. Short-lived but seeds itself around. Light soil; sun. S Europe.

A. *schistosum*, A. *speciosum* and A. *stylosum* are all generally similar to *grandiflorum*. Turkey to Iran.

ALBUCA (*Liliaceae*)
A. *humilis*   3in. Bulbous. L 9in, thin spreading. FL 1in, white, green-striped. June. S. Basutoland.

ALLIUM (*Liliaceae*)   Bulbs or fleshy roots. Garlic smell. L usually very narrow or cylindrical. FL usually in umbels. Some form bulbils among FL. D, S, BULBILS.

A. *callimischon*   6in. FL ½in, white, speckled dark red; red buds. FL-stems appear withered. Sept. Protection or AH. Greece.

A. *cyathophorum* var *farreri*. Syn A. *farreri*   10in. FL ¼in, reddish-purple. May–July. China.   ·

A. *flavum*   8in. FL ¼in, yellow (pink in 'A. *flavum roseum*'). July. S Europe.

A. *kansuense*. Syn *cyaneum brachystemon*   9in. L very narrow. FL ¼in, abundant, good blue. July–Aug. Kansu.

A. *moly*   To 12in. L broad, glaucous. FL ¾in, yellow, in large umbels. Usually rather coarse and spreading, but there are neater forms. June. Mediterranean.

A. *narcissiflorum*. Syn *pedemontanum*   9in. FL ½in, bell-shaped, deep rose. June. Good drainage. Alps.

A. *oreophilum*. Syn *ostrowskianum*   6in. FL ½in, rose. June. Good drainage. Caucasus, C Asia.

A. *pulchellum*   18in. FL rose red, ¼in in large loose tufts with long bracts, showy. July, Aug. Mediterranean.

A. *roseum*   To 15in. FL ½–¾in, pale to good rose, with bulbils (spreads freely) or without. Can be good or bad. May, June. Mediterranean.

A. *sikkimense*   Similar to *kansuense*, slightly larger. June–July. N India.

A. *triquetrum*   12in. L keeled. FL ¾in crystalline white, tubular. May. Shade, woodland. Can be invasive on acid soils in mild gardens. Europe incl Britain. (Fig 11, see p 43.)

ALYSSUM (*Cruciferae*)   L entire. FL ¼in yellow in rounded heads. Sun.

A. *alpestre*   2in. Close mat, L very small, grey. FL good yellow. May. Scree. C, D. Alps. (*A. serpyllifolium* is very similar; French Alps and Spain.)

A. *ovirense*   4in. Similar to *alpestre* but hoary L. *A. wulfenianum* even more so. Both SE Alps.

A. *saxatile*   12in. Shrubby. L rather coarse (to 6in). FL in golden masses, showy. Varies in compactness. Named forms include *citrinum* (lemon), *plenum* (double), and 'Dudley Neville' (ochre). May–June. C. C and SE Europe.

ANACYCLUS (*Compositae*)

A. *depressus*   Mat of feathery L and daisy-like FL, 1in, white, crimson-backed. May. Scree; needs protection in cold gardens, or AH. S, D. Morocco.

ANAGALLIS (*Primulaceae*) Pimpernel

A. *tenella*   Bog pimpernel. Creeping, stems rooting at nodes. L tiny, round, opposite. FL delicate pink, funnel-shaped, ½in, in pairs. Short-lived. June–July. Acid bog. D. W Europe including Britain. (Fig 24, see p 70.)

ANCHUSA (*Boraginaceae*)   Tufted perennials. L narrow, thick, wavy-edged, up to 3in. FL bright strong blue, ½in.

A. *angustissima*   12–18in. FL in branching sprays. April–June. S, C. Asia Minor.

A. *caespitosa*   Low mats 1–3in. FL nearly stemless, brilliant blue with white centre. May–June. Scree or AH. S, C. Crete.

ANDROMEDA (*Ericaceae*)

A. *polifolia*   Straggly shrub, 1ft. L small narrow whitish beneath. FL pink or white, ¼in long, urn-shaped. April–May. Rich lime-free soil. C, D. Temperate and Arctic zones of N hemisphere.

ANDROSACE (*Primulaceae*)   Beautiful dwarf plants in two main sections: (I) *Chamaejasme* L in small rosettes at ends of stolons. FL in umbels. Turf plants. Rich scree. S, ROSETTES. (II) *Aretia*. More or less tight cushions, L very small. FL single on very short stems. High alpines. Difficult; AH, moraine or scree, with protection from winter wet. C, S.

A. *alpina*. (Syn *glacialis*) (II) Dense cushions (in crevices) or diffuse (in wet scree). L tiny, hairy. FL ¼in, rose or white, almost stemless. April–July (in AH). Calcifuge, abundant moisture in growing season. High Alps.

A. *carnea*   (I) Densely tufted. FL ¼–⅓in, rose or white. April. Scree. Pyrenees, Auvergne, W Alps. (*brigantiaca, halleri, laggeri* are local forms differing slightly in foliage and size of FL.)

A. *chamaejasme*   (I) 4in. L ½in in small rosettes. FL ¼in, white; yellow or red eye. April. Alps.

A. *ciliata*   (II) Loose soft tufts. FL rose, ⅓in on 1in stems. March–June (in AH). Pyrenees.

A. *cylindrica*   (II) Dense tufts, old leaves not shed. FL ¼in, white stemless. April (in AH). Pyrenees. (Hybrids *cylindrica* × *hirtella* can be very good.)

A. *helvetica*   (II) Dense cushions. FL ¼in, stemless, white with yellow eye. Crevice-plant. Alps.

A. *hirtella*   (II) Dense hairy tufts. FL ⅓in, white. Crevice-plant. April (in AH) Pyrenees.

A. *lactea*   (I) Close tufts of smooth ¾in. L. FL white with yellow eye, ½in on 3in stems. March–May. Good and easy in scree. E Alps.

A. *lanuginosa*   (I) Loose mats of rosettes of silvery L on trailing stems. FL ⅓in pink with darker eye. June–Oct. Tolerates shade. Himalaya.

A. *primuloides*   (I) Mats of tight rosettes of silky hairy L. FL bright pink ⅓in in rounded heads on 4in stems. Excellent and easy. April–June. W Himalaya. (*chumbyi* is a good neat silky form.)

A. *pubescens*   (II) Similar to *helvetica*, but looser cushions of narrower L. Pyrenees, Alps.

A. *pyrenaica*   (II) Dense tufts of minute green narrow L. FL ¼in, white, yellow-eyed stemless. March–May. Less difficult in lime-free scree than most Aretians. Pyrenees.

A. *sarmentosa*   (I) Very similar to *primuloides*: both plants variable and *watkinsii* and *yunnanensis* are not very distinct forms.

A. *sempervivoides*   (I) Mats of neat green rosettes. FL pink ¼in in heads on 2in stems. April. Kashmir, Tibet.

A. *vandellii*. Syns *argentea*, *imbricata*   (II) Dense tufts of minute L, silvery with close hairs. FL ½in, white with yellow eye, stemless. April (in AH). Calcifuge. Pyrenees, Alps.

A. *villosa*   (I) Loose mats of small rosettes of silky ¼in L. FL ¼in, white with yellow or red eye in small heads on 2in stems. April–May. Turf or scree. Pyrenees to Himalaya. Variable: var *arachnoidea* is large-flowered and very silky; var *jacquemontii* (from Garhwal) very distinct with either purplish or rose FL.

A. *wulfeniana*   (II) Loose tufts of bright green smooth ¼in L. FL deep rose ½in on ½in stalks. May. Not too difficult in rich scree. Calcifuge. E Alps.

ANEMONE (*Ranunculaceae*)   Mainly spring-flowering, showy. Very variable in habit.

A. *apennina*   General habit of wood-anemone (*A. nemorosa*). Twig-like rhizomatous roots. Divided L. FL clear blue 1½in on 6–8in stems. Many narrow petals. March–April. Part-shade or woodland. D, S. S Europe. Variations in colour include white and rose; also doubles.

A. *baldensis*   6in. L deeply segmented. FL white, yellow boss. May. Stony turf, scree or moraine. Difficult. s. E Alps. (*A. pavoniana* from N Spain is very similar, taller, easier.)

A. blanda   Close to *apennina* but rounded tubers and L-segments more rounded. Feb–April. Sun or shade. D. SE Europe.

A. coronaria   Tubers. 6–12in. L finely cut incl the one on the FL-stem. FL solitary 2½in, petals about 6, broad, white, blue, purple or red, blue-black boss. Jan–May. Rich soil, sun. D, S. S Europe to C Asia.

A. hortensis. Syn *stellata*   Similar to *coronaria* but L less divided and those on FL-stem may be entire. FL more starry with narrower petals, pale purple. Rich loam, sun. D, S. Mediterranean.

A. narcissiflora   12in. Deeply cut L. Umbel of white, pink-flushed 1in FL with yellow boss. April–May. Rich well-drained loam. s. Pyrenees, Alps and into Asia.

A. nemorosa   Wood Anemone, Windflower. There are good soft-blue and lilac forms ('Allenii', 'Robinsoniana', etc), an exceptionally large white ('Wilkes' Giant') and dbl whites. Woodland. April–May.

A. obtusiloba patula   6in. L coarsely divided, hairy. FL ¾in on 6in stems, soft blue-violet with yellow boss. March–May. ?Calcifuge. Moist but well-drained position. s (sow fresh). Himalaya.

A. pavonina   Close to *hortensis* but fewer, broader petals in wide colour-range. s, D. Mediterranean. (*A. fulgens* is ?*hortensis* × *pavonina*—strong vermilion.)

A. ranunculoides   Similar to *nemorosa* but FL ¾in clear yellow. March. Woodland. D, S. Europe. (*A. seemannii*, soft sulphur-yellow, is *nemorosa* × *ranunculoides*. Good, and easier than *ranunculoides*.)

A. rivularis   15in. L coarsely cut. FL 1½in on thick branching stems, white with purplish reverse. May–June. Damp situation. s. India.

A. sylvestris   15in. Spreading rootstock. L coarsely toothed. FL 1½in white, yellow boss, drooping. May. Moist shade or sun. D, S. C, N and E Europe into Asia.

ANTENNARIA (*Compositae*)

A. dioica   Cat's-Ear. Close mat of small white woolly L. FL 'ever-lasting' greenish to deep rose in tight tufts on 4in stems. May–June. Dry soil; sun. D. Europe incl Britain, Asia, N America.

ANTHERICUM (*Liliaceae*)   Fleshy roots. L long narrow. FL white. Rich but well-drained soil; sun. S, D.

A. liliago   FL 1¼in in 15in spikes. May–June. Alps.

A. ramosum   Similar but L narrower, FL ¾in, petals narrower, loose panicle. July. S Europe.

ANTHYLLIS (*Leguminosae*)   Loose mats of L divided into opposite pairs of leaflets. Small vetch-like FL in crowded heads. D, S.

A. montana   3in mats. Leaflets many, small, narrow, silvery. FL pink to deep rose on 4in stems. May. Sun. Pyrenees, Alps, Mediterranean.

ANTIRRHINUM (*Scrophulariaceae*) Variable habit. 'Snapdragon' FL. Good drainage or crevice. C, S.

A. sempervirens   6in. Shrubby evergreen. L ¾in narrow-oval. FL ¾in creamy-white with lilac tache. May–Sept. Sun. Pyrenees.

APHYLLANTHES (*Liliaceae*)
A. monspeliensis   L rush-like. FL ¾in violet-blue on 6–9in stems. June. Sun. D. W Mediterranean.

AQUILEGIA (*Ranunculaceae*) Columbine. Fibrous or fleshy roots. Herbaceous. L divided into many stalked, lobed leaflets. FL large with 5 spurred petals. Rich but well-drained soil. S (may not come true), D.

A. alpina   18in. L finely divided. FL 2½in clear blue. May. Switzerland. (The true plant is rarely seen in gardens.)

A. bertolonii. Syn *reuteri*   6in. L small neat with rounded lobes. FL 1½in clear violet-blue. May–June. Scree. S. S France, Italy.

A. canadensis   12in. FL several to stem 1½in yellow, red-tinged; long-spurred. May–June. S. N America.

A. discolor   4in. L small neat glaucous. FL 1in blue and white. June. Scree. S. N Spain.

A. flabellata. Syn *akitensis*   12in. FL 1½in pale violet, white-centred, or white. April–May. S. Japan.

A. formosa   18in. FL several to stem 1½in scarlet, yellow-centred. May. S. Western USA.

A. pyrenaica   10in. L small neat. FL 2in soft clear blue. May. S. Pyrenees.

ARABIS (*Cruciferae*) Tufts or mats of rosettes of entire or toothed, usually hairy L.

A. blepharophylla   4in. FL ½in rose. March–April. Protected bed or AH. S, D, C. California.

A. caucasica. Syn *albida*   9in. Mats of rosettes of large soft L. FL white to rose, ½in in many-flowered trusses. Feb–May. C. S Europe. (Good double white form.)

A. × sturii   Loose tufted cushions 3in. L dark green glossy. FL in loose 6in trusses. D. Garden origin.

ARCTERICA (*Ericaceae*)
A. nana. Syn *Andromeda nana*   3in compact dwarf shrub. L small smooth elliptical dark green. FL white 'urns' with red calyces in small clusters on short

red stems, fragrant. Dec–April (in AH). Well-drained lime-free soil, peat-bed, or AH. c, s. NE Asia.

ARENARIA (*Caryophyllaceae*)   Tufts or mats. L small in pairs. FL solitary or in small, loose trusses. D, S.

A. *balearica*   Flat creeping mat of tiny rounded L on thread-like stems rooting at nodes. FL white ¼in on 1in stems. April–May. Shady wall or bank. Islands of W Mediterranean.

A. *montana*   8in. Loose mat, spreading by underground stems. L narrow 1in. FL white ¾in, several to a 4in stem. May–June. Sun or shade. SW Europe.

A. *purpurascens*   Mats of small pointed shiny L. FL ½in pale purple on 2½in stems. May–June. Sun or shade. Pyrenees.

ARMERIA (*Plumbaginaceae*)   Thrift. Close tufts of grass-like L. FL white to deep pink ¼in in tight rounded heads. C.

A. *caespitosa*   2in. Tight cushions. FL pink. March–May. Scree or AH. Spain.

A. *maritima*   Sea-pink. Close mats. FL-stems to 9in. Very variable in compactness and colour: '*corsica*' has brick-red FL. Sun. Europe incl Britain.

ARNEBIA (*Boraginaceae*)

A. *echioides*. Syn *Macrotomia echioides*   Prophet Flower. 12in herbaceous. L broadly lanceolate, to 5in, roughly hairy. FL ¾in bright yellow in loose heads on 10in stems with dark brown spots at base of each petal on opening, later disappearing. March–June. Sun. S, C. Armenia.

ASPERULA (*Rubiaceae*)   Mats of fine stems with small narrow L in whorls. FL small, cross-shaped, in tight clusters.

A. *hirta*   3in. Herbaceous. L narrow, hairy at margins, 6 in a whorl. FL white, pink-tinged. May–July. Sun. D, S. Pyrenees.

A. *lilaciflora*   2in. Mat of narrow L. FL pink in tufts on 2in stems. May–July. Sun. Scree. D, S. E Mediterranean.

A. *nitida*   2in cushions. L smooth narrow, 4 in a whorl. FL pink long-tubed in almost sessile clusters. June–July. Scree. C. Greece. (*gussonii*, Sicily, is similar.)

A. *suberosa*   Loose mats of soft hairy grey L. Stems fragile. FL pink long-tubed in 3in loose spikes. April–June. Scree or AH. Protect from winter wet. C. Greece. (*arcadiensis* is very similar.)

ASTER (*Compositae*)   Herbaceous. L oval to lanceolate, entire. FL daisy-like with yellow centres and blue to pink rays, heads solitary. D.

A. *alpinus*   9in. Spreading tufts. FL blue-purple to rose-purple, 1½in on 6in stems. May–June. Turf or scree. Protect from slugs. Alps, Pyrenees.

A. flaccidus. Syn *purdomii*   Similar to *alpinus* but rather coarser. L stalked 1½in hairy. FL 2½in on 8in stems. June. Himalaya, China, Siberia.

A. natalensis   9in. L neat in flat rosettes. FL 1½in clear light blue. May–June. Natal.

ASTILBE (*Saxifragaceae*)   Herbaceous. L divided. FL small in spikes or sprays. Rich moist soil. D, S, C.

A. chinensis pumila   12in. L coarsely toothed. FL pinkish-purple in branched dense spikes. July–Aug. Sun or shade. China.

A. glaberrima saxatilis   6in. L finely divided, reddish, glossy. FL pale pink in loose sprays. July–Aug. Japan.

AUBRIETA (*Cruciferae*)   Thick spreading mats of soft oval slightly toothed hairy L. FL blue-violet through purple to deep red, in short-stemmed sprays covering the mats. March–July. Best on lime in sun. D, C. Wide range of named garden hybrids of uncertain parentage but probably mainly the Greek *A. deltoidea*.

BERBERIS (*Berberidaceae*)   Spiny shrub with simple L.

B. × *stenophylla* 'corallina compacta'   10in. FL orange-yellow, cup-shaped, in short-stalked clusters along stems. May–June. C, LAYERS. Garden hybrid.

BORAGO (*Boraginaceae*)   Borage.

B. laxiflora   12in. Rosettes of rough oblong L. Spreading bristly stems with loose sprays of drooping pale blue FL with 'beak' of yellow anthers. Summer. Dry position. D, C, S. Corsica.

BOYKINIA (*Saxifragaceae*)

B. jamesii. Syn *Telesonix jamesii*   8in. L round blunt-toothed shiny. FL rose-purple, 1in, in short spikes. May. Moraine or AH; avoid winter wet. S, D. Colorado.

BRUCKENTHALIA (*Ericaceae*)

B. spiculifolia   6in. Needle-leaved spreading 'heather'. FL small pink bell-shaped in crowded tufts. June–July. Peaty lime-free soil. C, D, S. SE Europe, Asia Minor.

BULBINELLA (*Liliaceae*)   L long, narrow, glossy, hard. FL in close spikes.

B. hookeri   L to 12in. FL bright yellow ½in. June. Bog, but will tolerate drier conditions. D, S. New Zealand.

CALCEOLARIA (*Scrophulariaceae*)   Herbaceous. FL 2-lipped, the lower more or less inflated. Southern S America and Falkland Is.

C. biflora. Syn *plantaginea* 9in. L oval, strongly veined, toothed, glossy, in rosettes. FL yellow ¾in in pairs. May–June. Scree. s.

C. darwinii 6in. Tufts of glossy L to 3in long. FL 1½in long, grotesque; upper lip yellow, lower chestnut with white transverse band. May–June. Scree or AH. Difficult. s, c.

C. falklandica 5in. L rounded, shiny, in neat rosettes. FL yellow ¾in on 4in stems. May–June. Peat-bed. s.

C. polyrrhiza Spreading herbaceous mats. L lanceolate 2in in tufts at ends of underground runners. FL yellow ¾in one or few to a 6in stem. May–July. D, S.

C. tenella Close mat of tiny rounded L on slender stems, rooting at nodes. FL yellow, slightly spotted, ½in, several in loose cluster on 4in stem. May–August. Peat-bed. D, S.

CALLIANTHEMUM (*Ranunculaceae*) Dwarf high alpines with finely cut glaucous L and white FL with yellow boss.

C. coriandrifolium. Syns *C. rutifolium*, *Ranunculus rutifolius* FL to 1½in on spreading 6in stems. April. Lime-free scree or moraine. s. Pyrenees, Alps. (*C. anemonoides* and *C. kerneranum* are very similar: the latter grows on lime.)

CALLUNA (*Ericaceae*) Heather. Well-known dwarf shrub.

C. vulgaris Many garden forms, varying in height, habit, compactness, leaf-colour and flower-colour. 'H. E. Beale' is a good dbl pink. Aug–Oct. Sun. Sandy peat (calciphobe). c. Europe incl Britain.

CALTHA (*Ranunculaceae*) Kingcup.

C. palustris 12in. Herbaceous. L large, glossy, heart-shaped, bluntly toothed, on long stalks. FL to 2in deep bright yellow on branching stems. Showy dbl form. April–May. Water-side. D. Europe incl Britain. (*C. palustris alba*, white, is less robust.)

CAMPANULA (*Campanulaceae*) Usually herbaceous. FL nearly always some shade of blue, or white; and generally more or less bell-shaped. Stems and leaves with white 'milk'. Smaller species require special protection from slugs.

C. allionii. Syn *alpestris* 3in. Tufts of narrow 2in hairy L dispersed at ends of thin underground stolons. FL solitary, large, long (1½in) bells, grey-blue to rich violet. May–June. High scree-plant, calciphobe. Moraine or fast scree, or AH. Difficult. s. French Alps.

C. arvatica 3in. Thin underground stolons. Spreading tufts of small rounded toothed shiny L. FL flattish ¾in violet or white, 2 or 3 to a stem. July–Aug. Scree or AH. s, D. N Spain.

C. barbata   10in. Tap-rooted biennial. Rosette of long-oval hairy L. FL pendulous in long one-sided spike, clear light blue to white, bearded. May-Aug. s. Alps.

C. carpatica   12in. Clump of smooth rounded toothed L on long stalks. FL very open cups to 2in across, solitary. June–Sept. D, S. Carpathians. (Very variable; many named forms. Colour pale blue to deep violet, or white. *pelviformis* has very flat FL: *turbinata* is very compact.)

C. cenisia   2in. Sprawling, spreading by underground shoots. L small thick oval. FL solitary, starry, ¾in, slate-blue with red-violet stamens. June. High wet-scree plant, calciphobe. Moraine or AH. Difficult. D, C, S. Western Alps.

C. cochleariifolia. Syn *pusilla*   3in. Creeping and mat-forming. Rosettes of small, rounded, toothed, shiny, stalked L. FL ½in hanging in loose spikes on thin stems, bell-shaped, pale to deep blue or white. June onwards. D, S. Pyrenees, Alps. (Very variable; several named forms. 'Miranda' is silver-blue. 'Haylodgensis' and the similar 'Warleyensis' are doubles, ? hybrids with *carpatica*.)

C. garganica. Syn *istriaca*   4in. Dense tufts of rounded, blunt-toothed, stalked L. FL flattish, starry, violet with white centres, in dense clusters covering the mats. June–Aug. D, S. Adriatic coasts. (Variable.)

C. lasiocarpa   6in. Runs underground. Tufts of neat, narrow, toothed L. FL solitary, 1in, wide bell-shaped, China blue or white. June–Aug. Scree or AH. S. N America, Japan.

C. morettiana   3in. Small rounded toothed L in tufts on fine stems running in crevices. FL solitary, 1in, violet or white, bell-shaped. June–Sept. Dolomite crevice plant. Moraine, tufa or AH. Difficult in garden. S, C. Dolomites.

C. patula   12in. Biennial. Rosettes of soft narrow hairy L. FL 1in purple, open starry bells, in loose sprays on branching stems. June onwards. S (seeds itself). Europe incl Britain, Siberia.

C. pilosa   3in. Matted rosettes of neat, smooth L. FL 1in bell-shaped, China blue to deep purple, bearded. Variable. May–July. Scree. S, D. Japan to Alaska.

C. portenschlagiana. Syn *muralis*   4in. Wide spreading mounds of smooth rounded toothed L on long stems. FL strong purple, 1in, bell-shaped, in close clusters solidly covering the mats. Sun or shade: good on walls. D. S Europe.

C. poscharskyana   Included as a warning! Somewhat like *portenschlagiana* but coarser and looser in L and FL and latter of poorer colour. Indestructible and viciously invasive. Dalmatia.

C. pulla   3in. Habit of *cochleariifolia*, but FL solitary, 1in, deep rich purple. June–July. Scree. D, S, C. E Alps. (*pulloides* is a hybrid, *carpatica turbinata* × *pulla*, rather larger with lighter-coloured more rounded FL.)

C. raddeana   6in. Spreading mats of heart-shaped, coarsely toothed, dark, smooth long-stalked L. FL 1in, deep purple bells in loose spreading sprays. June–Aug. Sun or shade. D, S. Caucasus.

C. *raineri*   3in. L small hairy oval, slightly toothed, in tufts. FL solitary, large (1½in) light blue, upward-facing open bells. June–July. Rare crevice-plant. Moraine, scree, AH. D, S. Central Alps. (Garden plants are not always true.)

C. *sartori*   2in. L small, softly hairy, grey-green, rounded, in a central clump. FL ½in, numerous, pink, up-turned, funnel-shaped, on spreading leafy stems forming a mat. Annual or short-lived. June–July. Scree or wall. S (seeds itself). E Mediterranean.

C. *scheuchzeri*   8in. Loose tufts of narrow L from spreading underground stems. FL ¾in deep blue 'hairbells' in loose sprays on upright slender stems. June–Aug. D. European mtns. (C. *linifolia* is very similar, if not synonymous.)

C. *tommasiniana*   6in. L narrow, toothed, pointed, on stalks from a thick tap-root. FL pale blue narrow tubes with sharp-pointed petals, drooping, in close sprays on thin-branched stems. July–Aug. Scree. S, C. Italy.

C. *tridentata*   4in. Tap-root. Rosettes of stalked oval L, wider and slightly toothed at tip. FL 1in rounded, blue-violet bells with white base, solitary on spreading stems. April–June. Sun; scree. S. Caucasus. (C. *aucheri*, C. *bellidifolia* and C. *saxifraga* are very similar.)

C. *waldsteiniana*   Similar to *tommasiniana*, but L rounded and FL more open, erect. Scree. July–Aug. S, C. Dalmatia.

C. *zoysii*   3in. L small, narrow to oval or diamond-shaped, in small tufts on stems creeping through crevices. FL pale to deep blue ¾in long 'bells' closed at mouth with petal-tips puckered. July–Sept. Dolomite crevice plant. Scree, crevice, tufa or AH. Difficult: beware slugs! D, S. Italy, Austria. Yugoslavia.

CARDAMINE. Syn DENTARIA (*Cruciferae*)   Early flowering herbaceous plants for woodland or moist shade.

C. *kitaibelii*. Syn C. *polyphylla*   10in. L divided, toothed, 3in. FL cream, tubular in drooping clusters. March–April. Woodland. D. E Alps.

C. *pentaphyllos*. Syn *Dentaria digitata*   Similar in habit to the last. FL pinky-purple. April–May. Woodland. D. European mtns.

CASSIOPE (*Ericaceae*)   Low shrubs, with small close-packed overlapping L and white bell-shaped FL about ¼in. May–June. Calciphobe. Moist well-drained peat in half shade, or AH. Difficult in the open in dry districts. C, S, LAYERS. Some of the hybrids are better and easier than the species.

C. × 'Bearsden'   6in. Profuse clear white drooping bells on rounded hummocks.

C. × 'Edinburgh' (*fastigiata* × *saximontana*)   9in. Stems upright with FL in leafy spikes.

C. lycopodioides. Syn *Andromeda lycopodioides* Low mat of close wiry stems. FL small on red stems with red calyx. E Asia, NW America.

C. × 'Muirhead' (*wardii* × *lycopodioides*) 6in. Spreading with rooting branches. FL larger than *lycopodioides.*

C. saximontana 6in. Upright stems with dense-packed L and short-stemmed FL. Rocky Mtns. (Liable to be sold as *C. tetragona,* a difficult and inferior plant.)

C. wardii 9in. Underground runners. L hairy. FL large, open white bells. Offensive smell. Himalaya. (*wardii* × *fastigiata* is similar.)

CENTAUREA (*Compositae*) Knapweed.

C. simplicicaulis 12in. L 2in divided, silvery. FL 2in, lilac-pink, solitary on long bare stems. June–July. D. Armenia.

CENTAURIUM. Syn ERYTHRAEA (*Gentianaceae*)

C. portense. Syns *C. scilloides* var *portense, Erythraea diffusa* 3in. Neat tuft of small thick shiny L, narrow to rounded. FL clear pink, ½in in loose flattish heads. June onwards. Good drainage, sun. S. Europe incl Britain.

CHAENORHINUM. Syn LINARIA (*Scrophulariaceae*)

C. origanifolium 4in. L ½in oval, smooth, on brittle stems forming loose or dense tufts. FL ½in, purple with lilac throat, spurred, in loose sprays to solid mats. Variable. April onwards. S (seeds itself). Pyrenees, Spain.

CHAMAECYTISUS (*Leguminosae*)

C. pygmaeus Recently introduced under collectors' number, CMW 3818. 3in spreading shrublet. L small, smooth, narrow. FL ¾in yellow, Broom-like. May. Sun, scree. S, C. Yugoslavia to Turkey.

C. purpureus. Syn *Cytisus purpureus* 12in. L in three rounded leaflets on spread-ing branches. Spreads underground. FL 1in, pale or deep purplish-pink, or white, packed along the branches, facing up. April–June. Sun, D, C, S. S and E Alps.

CHAMAESPARTIUM (*Leguminosae*)

C. sagittale. Syn *Genista sagittalis* Spreading shrubby mat, herbaceous; winged green upright stems. L small narrow smooth. FL ½in pea-shaped yellow, in small dense heads. June. Sun. D, S. Central and S Europe. (Var *delphinense,* from the Pyrenees, has spreading stems in a flat mat.)

CHIASTOPHYLLUM (*Crassulaceae*)

C. oppositifolium. Syn *Cotyledon simplicifolia* 10in. L oval, bluntly-toothed, fleshy, in pairs on sprawling stems. FL small, golden-yellow, in branched hanging thin trusses. June–July. Wall or crevice. D. Caucasus.

CHIONODOXA (*Liliaceae*)   Bulbous. L narrow, few. FL tubular at base, blue, ¾in in loose sprays. Feb–April. OFFSETS, S.

C. *luciliae*   6in. FL blue, pale-centred, starry; also white and pink. Asia Minor, Crete.

C. *sardensis*   Similar without white centre. Asia Minor.

CISTUS (*Cistaceae*)   Shrubs with opposite entire L and large 5-petalled FL. Borderline hardy. C (easy), S. Mediterranean. Many good hybrids and cultivars.

C. *albidus*   2½ft. L 2in oval cottony. FL 2½in in few-flowered clusters, rosy-lilac. June–Aug. SW Europe.

C. *crispus*   2ft. L oval wavy-edged downy. FL 1½in rose-purple.

C. *laurifolius*   3ft (bigger in the wild). L oval pointed sticky. FL 2½in white, yellow-centred.

C. *monspeliensis*   3ft. L narrow, wrinkled. FL 1½in white in clusters.

C. × *purpureus* (*ladaniferus* × *villosus*)   2½ft or more. L to 3in, narrow. FL 3in deep rose with purple blotches.

C. *salvifolius*   2ft. L oval grey-green strongly veined. FL 1½in white, yellow-centred.

C. × 'Silver Pink'.   2ft. L narrow pointed. FL clear pink. (Garden origin; good.)

C. × 'Sunset' (? a form of *crispus*)   FL deep rose-purple.

CLEMATIS (*Ranunculaceae*)

C. *alpina*. Syn *Atragene alpina*   Climber and sprawler. L divided, coarsely toothed. FL solitary, nodding, violet (or white), bell-shaped with the 4 petals spreading at tips. April–May. Sun or shade but avoid drying at roots. S. European mtns, N Asia.

CODONOPSIS (*Campanulaceae*)   Herbaceous plants falling into two main groups. (I) Climbers with rounded tubers; very thin fragile stems, twining; heart-shaped, pointed, blunt-toothed, stalked L; and FL with spreading petals. (II) Sprawling clumps with large fleshy roots; thick upright or spreading stems crowded with nearly stemless oval L; bell-shaped nodding FL curiously marked within, stinking. The nomenclature of the latter group is confused, at least in gardens, where similar plants appear under several names.

C. *clematidea*   (II) 2ft. Smooth L. FL pale grey-blue patterned with orange and chocolate within. May–June. S, D. Asia.

C. *convolvulacea*   (I) FL 2in violet-blue, solitary at intervals on twining stems. Good but difficult; stems readily break away from tuber. S. Himalaya, W China.

C. *meleagris*   (II) 12in. L soft hairy. FL 1 or 2 to a stem. D, S. China.

C. ovata (II) *ovata* of gardens is similar to *meleagris*, but with many FL in a loose spike. The true plant is rare, smaller, daintier, with solitary, more funnel-shaped FL. D, S. Himalaya.

C. vinciflora (I) Similar to *convolvulacea* but FL smaller (1½in). July–Sept. Less difficult than *convolvulacea*; sun, good drainage, protection of fragile stems. S. Asia.

COLCHICUM (*Liliaceae*)   Corms. FL superficially crocus-like.

C. agrippinum 9in. L lanceolate 9in wavy, in spring. FL deep lilac with paler chequering, large (3in), somewhat starry, forming thick clumps. Aug–Sept. D. Uncertain origin (probably hybrid). (Fig 5, see p 33.)

C. autumnale 12in. The 'autumn crocus' of the Alps. L large (to 1ft) broadly lanceolate, in spring. FL 3in on long tubes, pale to deep rose-lilac, or white; many to a corm. Aug–Sept. Easy, but L too coarse for the small rock garden. Naturalises in grass if not mown while L are up. D, S. Europe incl Britain. (*byzantinum* and *speciosum*, and many cultivars and hybrids, are similarly large-leaved and larger flowered.)

CONVOLVULUS (*Convolvulaceae*)   Herbaceous. FL funnel-shaped.

C. cantabrica 12in. L 1½in lanceolate, along sprawling stems from a single root-stock. FL 1in, pale pink (resembling Lesser Bindweed) in loose sprays. June–Aug. C, S. S Europe.

C. elegantissimus. Syn *tenuissimus* Spreading underground, sprawling and climbing. L silvery, finely cut (lowest ones less so). FL 1½in clear pink. June onwards. Light soil in warm spot; slightly tender. C, D. Mediterranean. (*Althaeoides* is similar, with lower L less cut and FL purplish.)

C. mauritanicus 9in. Habit of *cantabrica*. L 1in oval. FL clear soft violet. June–Sept. Tender. Protected bed or AH. C (protect cuttings in winter). N Africa. Italy. (Plate p 35.)

CORTUSA (*Primulaceae*)

C. matthioli 8in. Herbaceous. L rounded, lobed, blunt-toothed, hairy, stalked. FL rose-purple or white ½in funnel-shaped with pointed petals, drooping, in bunched heads. May–Aug. Moist shade, woodland. S, D. Europe, Asia. (*pekinensis* and *pubens* are scarcely distinct forms.)

CORYDALIS (*Papaveraceae*)   Rhizome or tuber. Herbaceous. L much divided, usually glaucous. FL narrow tubular with blunt spur and two more or less distinct lips.

C. ambigua yedoensis 8in. FL 1in clear light turquoise-blue, white-centred, in solid close upright spikes. Jan–April. AH. D. Japan.

C. bulbosa. Syn *cava* 8in. Tuber becoming hollow; breaks into curved plates.

K

L ferny. FL 1in rose-purple through pale mauve to white, in dense upright or spreading spikes. Feb–April. Shade, woodland. D (pieces of tuber-plate). Europe. (*C. solida*, syn *densiflora*, with solid tuber, is very similar: both plants are variable.)

C. cashmiriana   4in. FL ¾in intense turquoise to Prussian blue in short spikes. April–May: L die down after flowering and reappear in Sept with a few dull slaty-blue FL! Temperamental in open garden, probably needing good drainage, humus, light shade; avoid drying out. AH. D (separate tubers in Sept). Himalaya.

C. lutea   10in. L ferny. FL ¾in yellow, gold-tipped, in tufts. April onwards. Sun, easy, suitable on walls. S (seeds itself), D. C and E Alps (and widely natural-ised incl Britain).

CRASSULA (*Crassulaceae*)   Semi-succulent, somewhat sedum-like.

C. milfordiae   2½in. Close mat. FL ⅛in, clear white, in tight heads on upright stems. July–Aug. Scree, AH. D. Basutoland. (Distributed as 'Crassula sp (Basutoland)'—not always true *milfordiae*.)

CREPIS (*Compositae*)   Hawksbeard.

C. incana   12in. L to 5in, lanceolate, toothed and cut, in basal tufts. FL 1in, shaped like small dandelions, pink, in loose branched sprays. July–Sept. Sun. D, S. SE Europe.

CROCUS (*Iridaceae*)   Corms. Long, very narrow, pointed L with white centre vein. FL 2in to 6in in height and 1in to 3in across, appearing (according to species) before, with or after the leaves, and from Sept to April. Some 50 wild species, and many garden forms. Most need light rich well-drained soil, and are better for summer baking. The late autumn and winter flowering species are best seen in the AH. D, S (slow). Some will naturalise in grass if not close-mown while leaves are up. The following are good and fairly easy: in addition to the petal colours given, many have showy red, orange or yellow stamens or pistils.

C. angustifolius. Syn *susianus*   Deep yellow, feathered brown. Feb. Caucasus.

C. biflorus   White, feathered purple. Feb. Italy to Persia.

C. chrysanthus   Wide range of colours—white, yellow, blue, multi-coloured; many named forms. Usually black barbs to anthers. Jan–March. E Medi-terranean.

C. corsicus   Clear rose-purple, externally buff-tinged and feathered dark purple. Jan–March. Corsica.

C. dalmaticus   Lilac, marked deeper purple. Feb–March. Dalmatia.

C. flavus. Syns *aureus*, *luteus*   Yellow to orange, large. Jan–March. E Europe.

C. imperati   Lilac, buff exterior with purple feathering. Large. Jan–Feb. Italy.

C. kotschyanus. Syn *zonatus*   Pale to deep lilac, with deeper veining; conspicuous yellow, orange-edged, central zone. Sept–Oct. Turkey, Lebanon.

C. laevigatus   White to lilac, generally feathered purple. Nov–March. Variable, with wide season. (Var *fontenayi* Nov–Jan has violet feathering on both sides of outer segments.) Greece.

C. medius   Rich violet, scarlet stigma. Oct–Nov. Riviera.

C. nudiflorus   Purple, long-tubed. Stoloniferous. Sept–Oct. L in spring. SW Europe (naturalised in N England).

C. purpureus. Syns *albiflorus, vernus*   White to purple. Feb–April. European mtns.

C. sieberi   White to purple, yellow throat, variable purple on exterior. Several named forms. Jan–Feb. Greece, Crete.

C. speciosus   Lilac, blue, or white, delicately veined; orange stigmas. Sept–Nov. W Asia. (Fig 6, see p 34.)

C. tommasinianus   Pale to deep purple. Jan–March. Spreads very freely. Dalmatia.

C. versicolor   Silver-white to purple with or without deep purple streaking. Feb–March. Maritime Alps.

CYANANTHUS (*Campanulaceae*)   Low, spreading, herbaceous. L small. FL solitary; calyx swollen, darkly hairy; spreading petals on narrow tube. S, C.

C. lobatus   6in mat. L oval, coarsely toothed. FL 1in blue-purple or white; petals rounded, bearded. June–Sept. Moist well-drained sandy peat. Himalaya.

C. microphyllus. Syn *integer* (of gardens)   3in. Flat mats. L tiny narrow entire. FL blue, starry. July–Sept. N India.

CYCLAMEN (*Primulaceae*)   Rounded tubers. Herbaceous. L all from base, more or less heart-shaped, leathery, smooth, dark green, usually patterned with light green or silvery-white above and dark red below. FL solitary, with strongly reflexed petals, usually twisted; FL-stalk usually contracts to a tight spiral when seed-pod is formed. Rich, well-drained soil, sun. S (sow fresh).

C. coum   4in. L 1in almost round, entire, deep green unpatterned. FL very squat, ¾in wide, ¾in long, white to deep rose-magenta with crimson or purple blotches at mouth. Jan–Feb. (Buds form before Christmas.) Fully hardy. E Mediterranean into Asia. (This is one of a confused group: the name *coum* is usually reserved for plants with unmarked L: other names in the group are *alpinum, atkinsii, hyemale, ibericum, orbiculatum, parviflorum, vernum.*)

C. cyprium   3in. L 1½in heart-shaped, coarsely-toothed, sage-green with lighter blotched pattern. FL narrow, ½–¾in, white with dark reddish-purple blotches between white auricles at mouth. Sl scented. Aug–Dec. Protected bed or AH. Cyprus.

C. europaeum. Syn *purpurascens*   5in. L 2in rounded slightly toothed, deep green with lighter markings round veins, almost evergreen. FL strong carmine, ¾in, very fragrant. June–Sept. Light shade. Hardy. Alps.

C. neapolitanum. Syn *hederifolium*   6in. L heart-shaped, pointed, very variable in size, shape and markings. FL 1in, pink to rose or white, streaked with deep carmine at mouth between prominent auricles. Aug–Nov. Hardy. Sun or shade. S Europe. (The easiest and best; will naturalise.)

C. repandum   9in. L 2½in, pointed, widely heart-shaped, very coarsely toothed, variably marked. FL long (to 1¼in), narrow, pale rose to deep carmine, sometimes deeper at mouth and tips of petals, style projecting; sl fragrant. March–May. Light shade or woodland. Borderline hardy. S France to Greece and Crete. (Fig 30, see p 94.)

CYPRIPEDIUM (*Orchidaceae*)   Rhizomatous, herbaceous. FL showy, with inflated pouch (lip). D in early spring.

C. calceolus   10in. L 6in, broadly lanceolate, strongly ribbed. FL usually solitary on leafy stem, 1½in; four long narrow, pointed red-brown sepals, large yellow pouch. May. Lime-rubble and leafmould. Light shade. Europe (incl Britain), N Asia. (Fig 12, see p 44.)

C. pubescens. Syn *flavescens*   18in. Similar to *calceolus*, but more FL (3 or 4) to stem, slightly smaller, sepals twisted, pouch marked reddish-brown at mouth. May. N America.

CYTISUS (*Leguminosae*)   Broom. Deciduous shrubs. L small, narrow, single or in three leaflets. FL pea-shaped C, S.

C. ardoinii   8in, spreading. FL ½in, yellow, in small clusters along stems. April–May. Sun. Maritime Alps.

C. × *beanii*   12in, spreading. FL deep yellow along leafy stems. Sun. Garden origin.

C. × *kewensis* (*multiflorus* × *ardoinii*)   18in, spreading. FL creamy-white, abundant. April–May. Sun. Garden origin. (Larger and more upright plants are sold under this name.)

DABOECIA (*Ericaceae*)   Low-growing evergreen calciphobe shrubs. L small, dark green, pointed. FL down-turned oval globes, ½in long, in loose spikes. Lime-free soil with sand and peat. D, C, S.

D. cantabrica. Syn *D. polifolia*   12–18in. L bristly. FL rose-purple or white. June–Sept. Sun or half-shade. SW Europe, Ireland. (Several named colour-forms, and also hybrids with the half-hardy *azorica*.)

DAPHNE (*Thymelaceae*)   Shrubs. FL tubular, usually fragrant.

D. *arbuscula*   10in. L ¾in narrow, thick, rolled edges, at ends of branches. Young shoots red. FL ½in pink, fragrant, in small clusters. June. Light limy soil. C. Czechoslovakia.

D. *blagayana*   12in, straggly. L 2in oval, in tufts at ends of branches. FL ¾in creamy-white, in close heads, fragrant. March–April. Shade, woodland. C. SE Europe.

D. *cneorum*   Prostrate to 10in. L ¾in narrow, crowded along stems. FL ½in, rose-pink, fragrant, abundant in dense tufts. April–May. Sun. Well-drained soil with grit, peat and lime. C. S and C Europe. (Very variable in height: *pygmaea* is prostrate; *eximia* upright; white-flowered *alba* is less vigorous. The best Daphne.) (*D. striata* is similar but more difficult.)

D. *mezereum*   To 2½ft or more. Deciduous. Open, upright. L 2in long-oval thin in tufts along stems. FL ½in, pink or white, often before L, fragrant, in tufts along stems forming spikes. Bright red berries. Feb–March. Sun or shade. S, C. Europe and into Asia.

D. *petraea*. Syn *rupestris*   4in compact mass of twisted branching stems. L ½in narrow. FL clear rose, ¼–⅓in, large for plant (especially in var *grandiflora*) in tight clusters, scented. May–June. Lime. AH. Difficult. C (usually grafted). N Italy.

D. *sericea*. Syn *collina*   2ft, rounded, leafy. L 1½in long-oval sl hairy. FL ½in, purplish-pink in round clusters, fragrant. April–May and at odd times. Rich, well-drained soil in sun; fully hardy. C. E Mediterranean.

DELPHINIUM (*Ranunculaceae*)

D. *tatsienense*   12in. Herbaceous. L deeply cut with narrow pointed segments. FL characteristic 'larkspur' shape, 1in, in few-flowered loose spikes, Prussian blue. June–Aug. Easy but short-lived. S. China.

DIANTHUS (*Caryophyllaceae*)   Pinks. Usually mats or cushions of narrow smooth opposite L, sheathing stems; and rounded flattened pink FL above narrow tubular calyx. Sun. C, S (may not come true in gardens.) Many hybrids and cultivars. Most have white forms.

D. *alpinus*   2½in cushion of shining ¾in L. FL 1¼in, petals full, toothed, cerise with central zone of white spots surrounded by darker band, bearded. May–June. Scree. E Alps. (Colour variants include *albus*; and also 'Boydii' —paler with more pronounced zoning.)

D. *arenarius*   10in. Close tuft of narrow L. FL ½in white with green spot, bearded, deeply fringed. June–Aug. E Europe.

D. *callizonus*   4in. Loose mat. L 1½in. FL single, 1in, pink with darker white-spotted centre-zone, petals toothed, June–Aug. Limy scree or turf. Carpathians.

D. carthusianorum 10in. L in grassy tuft. FL ¾in cherry red, toothed, bearded, among dark purple pointed bracts in dense heads at ends of long stems. June–Aug. European mtns. (Variable; good dwarfer forms.)

D. deltoides Maiden Pink, 7in. Loose hummocks of blunt 1in L. FL ¾in deep rose with white spots and dark centre-zone, toothed, bearded, several to a stem. Variable. April onwards. Europe incl Britain.

D. erinaceus 4in. Dense cushion of small prickly L. FL ½in bearded, toothed. June–July. Sharp scree or AH. Asia Minor.

D. glacialis 3in. Dense tuft of very narrow dark green 2in L. FL ¾in, single on short stems, chalky pink, unmarked, greenish on back, slightly toothed. May–July. Calcifuge. Scree or AH. E Alps. (*freynii* and *microlepis* are very similar, tending to smaller, better-coloured FL on longer stems.)

D. gratianopolitanus. Syn *caesius* Cheddar Pink, 10in. Loose mats of glaucous blunt-ended 2in L. FL 1in, single, pink, toothed, bearded, fragrant. May onwards. Europe incl Britain.

D. haematocalyx. Syn *pindicola* 5in. Tight tufts. L glaucous or not. FL 1in, deep pink, buff-backed, toothed, bearded. June–July. Scree. Albania, Yugoslavia, Greece. (Variable.)

D. monspessulanus. Syn *sternbergii* 10in. Loose mats. L narrow, pointed, curved, dark green. FL several to a head, 1¼in, pink, indistinctly zoned greenish or purple, deeply fringed, fragrant. June–July. European mtns.

D. myrtinervius 3in. Low loose mat of soft close-packed ¼in narrow L. FL ½in pink, bearded. May–July. Macedonia.

D. pavonius. Syn *neglectus* 3in. L narrow in grass-like tufts. FL 1in, rose-pink, buff-backed, toothed, bearded. May–June. Calciphobe. Lime-free scree. French Alps, Tyrol.

D. subacaulis 5in. Dense tuft of small narrow L. FL ½in pale pink. April–June. SW Europe. (Subsp *brachyanthus* is specially neat.)

D. superbus 12in. Like *monspessulanus*, but taller, looser, FL bigger and more deeply dissected. June onwards. Mountains of S and W Europe.

D. sylvestris. Syn *odoratus* 10in. Dense tufts of narrow dark green L. FL single on long or short stems, 1in, bright pink. May–July. Scree. European mtns. (Variable: forms from E Alps are brilliant in colour, and subsp *tergestinus* from Yugoslavia is very neat and dwarf.)

D. 'Whitehills' 2in. A mass of clear pink ¾in FL with deep red central zone on tight small-leaved tufts. May. Scree. (An exceptionally neat and beautiful cultivar for the rock garden. 'La Bourbrille' and 'Crossways' are also good.)

DIASCIA (*Scrophulariaceae*)

D. cordata 8in. Loose spreading clump of toothed heart-shaped ½–1in L. FL in loose heads, ¾in, rose-purple, lipped, 2-spurred. June onwards. Easy but ? tender. C, S. Natal.

DICENTRA (*Papaveraceae*) Herbaceous. L much-cut, ferny. FL in loose spikes; inner petals somewhat tubular, outer pair spreading and pouched at base. Rich light soil, sun or shade. D.

D. *eximia* 12in. FL purple or white, drooping. April onward. USA.

D. *formosa* 12in. Similar to *eximia* but outer petals rose, inner paler. (Subsp *oregana* has cream FL.) April onwards. W North America.

DIONYSIA (*Primulaceae*) Cushion-plants between *Primula* and *Androsace*. FL like small long-tubed primulas. Several recently introduced species, more or less difficult. AH. S, C. Iran to Pakistan.

D. *aretioides* 2½in. Soft mound of narrow greyish woolly slightly toothed L. FL ½in clear yellow, massed over the mound; petals notched. March–April. The least difficult. Iran.

DODECATHEON (*Primulaceae*) Shooting Stars. Herbaceous. FL with narrow pointed reflexed petals and a 'beak' formed by the pistil and stamens. Rich well-drained soil. S. N America. (Nomenclature confused, and plants from seed not always true.)

D. *meadia* 15in. L to 6in, lanceolate, smooth, in basal rosettes. FL ¾in rose to purplish, anthers yellow, in a loose umbel pendent on arching stems on a foot-high stalk. April–June.

D. *pauciflorum* 10in. Similar in habit to *meadia*, but smaller, anthers and throat purple (*macrocarpum* is similar). (Fig 27, see p 81.)

D. *tetrandrum* 15in. Rosettes to 1ft across. FL large, reddish-purple, marked yellow at mouth (*jeffreyi* is similar).

DORONICUM (*Compositae*) Leopard's Bane. Aster-shaped FL.

D. *cordatum* 8in. Leafy clumps. L heart-shaped. FL 2in, solitary. March onwards. D. SE Europe into Asia.

DOUGLASIA (*Primulaceae*)

D. *laevigata* 2in. Mat of small shining narrow L. FL ½in deep rose, in few-flowered heads on short stems. March–April. Rich scree. D, C, S. N America (Cascades).

DRABA (*Cruciferae*) Neat tufts or cushions. FL cross-shaped. S, C.

D. *aizoides* 2½in. Tufts of narrow pointed ½in bristly L. FL ½in, yellow, in loose heads. Jan–May. Scree. European mtns incl Britain. (Variable; and the following are very similar—*aspera, athoa, erioscapa, hispanica, longirostra*.)

D. *bryoides* 3in. Very dense cushions of minute hard L. FL ¼in, yellow, few to a loose head on slender stem. Var *imbricata* is even more compact. March–April. Scree, AH. Caucasus.

D. *dedeana* 2in. Very dense cushions of tiny narrow rigid hairy L. FL ½in, white in dense tufts. Feb–April. Scree or AH. Spain.

D. *mollissima* 2in. Close soft cushion. L tiny, greenish-white, velvety. FL ½in yellow, in loose heads on fine 1½in stems. March–April. Scree (protect from winter wet) or AH. Caucasus.

D. *rigida* 2½in. Close tufts of narrow bristly L. FL ½in golden-yellow in heads on slender stems. March–April. Scree or AH. Armenia.

DRACOCEPHALUM (*Labiatae*) Herbaceous. FL Dead-nettle-shaped. D, S.

D. *grandiflorum* 9in. L crowded, 3in, heart-shaped, blunt-toothed, stalked. FL 1in, blue with red calyces, in dense short spikes. June–Sept. Siberia.

DRYAS (*Rosaceae*)

D. *octopetala* 8in. Spreading prostrate shrub. Mats of oval round-toothed L, ½–1¼in, white beneath. FL solitary, 1½in, white with a boss of yellow stamens, like small dog-roses. April–June. Lime, sun. D, C, S. N Europe incl Britain; N America. (Var *minor* is especially small-leaved.)

EDRAIANTHUS (*Campanulaceae*) FL bell-shaped. S, C, D.

E. *caudatus*. Syn *dalmaticus* 5in. Rosette of hairy lanceolate L. FL-stems leafy. FL ¾in violet-blue, or white, in tight heads. June. Dalmatia.

E. *graminifolius* Similar to *caudatus*, but L very narrow and grass-like. Dalmatia. (Variable.)

E. *pumilio*. Syn *Wahlenbergia pumilio* 2in. Close cushion of ½in very narrow grey-green L. FL solitary, stemless, ¾in, violet, covering cushion. May–June. Scree. Dalmatia.

E. *serpyllifolius*. Syn *Wahlenbergia serpyllifolia* 3in. Low mat of 1in narrow dark green shining L. FL 1in (in form 'major' usually grown), rich purple, solitary on leafy stems. May–June. Scree. Albania, Yugoslavia. (Fig 20, see p 66.)

EPILOBIUM (*Onagraceae*) Two main groups, the European plants with FL like Rosebay Willow-herb, and the New Zealand plants with cross-shaped FL with notched petals. Nomenclature of latter is confused: pink-flowered plants are usually sold as '*kaikoense*' and white as *glabellum*.

E. *chloraefolium kaikourense* 3in. L ¾in oval, red-tinged, wavy-edged, on spreading stems. FL ½in, clear rose. May–July. S, D. New Zealand.

E. *fleischeri*. Syn *Chamaenerion rosmarinifolium* 8in. Spreading by underground runners. Herbaceous. Clumps of spreading stems with narrow pointed 1½in smooth L. FL in loose leafy spikes, 1in, 4 pale pink petals, purple sepals and stamens; narrow pods of fluffy seeds. River beds and glacier moraines. Moraine, wet scree. D, S. Alps. (*dodonaei* is very similar.) (Fig 22, see p 67.)

E. glabellum   9in. L 1in, oval, blunt-toothed. FL ¾in, creamy-white or pink. June–July. S, D. New Zealand.

EPIMEDIUM (*Berberidaceae*)   Creeping rhizomes forming clumps. Herbaceous, but dead or dying L retained till spring. Leaflets heart-shaped, pointed, more or less toothed, stalked, in 3's. FL in loose sprays, usually overtopping new but not old L. Sepals 8, inner 4 petal-like. Shade, woodland: cut off old L to display FL, but these are then at frost risk. D.

E. grandiflorum. Syn *macranthum*   15in. FL 1¼in, pendent; outer sepals rose-purple, inner pink; petals with long curved spreading white spurs. April–May. Japan, Manchuria. (Variable in colour: several named forms.)

E. × *rubrum* (? *alpinum* × *grandiflorum*)   10in. FL ½in, sepals red, petals cream or pink. April–May. Probably garden origin.

E. × *warleyense*   (? *alpinum* × *pinnatum colchicum*) 15in. FL ¾in, sepals copper, petals yellow. March–May. Garden origin.

E. × *youngianum* (*diphyllum* × *grandiflorum*)   10in. FL white (var *niveum*) or pinkish-purple (var *lilacinum, roseum* or *violaceum*). April–May. Garden origin.

ERANTHIS (*Ranunculaceae*)

E. hyemalis   Aconite. 6in. Small tubers. Herbaceous. L rounded, shiny, deeply dissected, forming a 'ruff' below the FL. FL solitary, 6-petalled, yellow, buttercup-like. Woodland. D, S. S Europe (naturalised in W Europe incl Britain). (*cilicicus* (Greece to Syria) and the hybrid × *tubergenii* are similar to *hyemalis* but a little larger.)

ERICA (*Ericaceae*)   Heath, heather. Low shrubs with short narrow pointed dark green L. FL more or less bunched in heads or spikes. FL urn- to bell-shaped, with protruding stamens. C, LAYERS.

E. carnea   Winter Heath. 3in mats to 12in rounded hummocks. FL all shades from dark red through rose to white: spikes often one-sided. Nov–April. Mountain plant, often in open woodland. Lime-tolerant; sun or half-shade. Alps. (Much variation in colour and flowering season—many named forms.)

E. vagans   Cornish Heath. 10in rounded shrub. FL pink to white, with dark purple projecting stamens, in close rounded spikes. July–Sept. Acid heaths. Calciphobe. Sandy peaty soil in dry position; sun. SW Europe, Cornwall.

ERIGERON (*Compositae*)   FL aster-like.

E. glaucus   9in. L 3in oval glaucous. FL 1½in solitary, purple, yellow-centred. June–Sept. D, S. N America.

E. karwinskyanus. Syn *mucronatus*   10in, sprawling. L 1in, narrow, soft, toothed.

FL in loose branching sprays. FL ½in, buds and young FL deep rose-purple, developing to white. May–Nov. Hardy. Sun, eg wall. D, s (seeds itself). Mexico; naturalised in SW Europe.

ERINACEA (*Leguminosae*)
E. *anthyllis*. Syn E. *pungens*   9in. Rounded spiny shrub. L tiny on branching green stems. FL ¾in soft violet, pea-shaped with swollen silky calyx, stemless. May–June. Scree in sun. s, c. Pyrenees to Tunisia.

ERINUS (*Scrophulariaceae*)
E. *alpinus*   3in. Rosette of 1in narrow blunt-toothed L. FL ¼in in open spikes on small-leaved stems, purplish to carmine, or white; almost regular, with 5 notched petals. May–June. Dry sunny position, walls. s (seeds itself). Mountains of W Europe. (Several named colour-forms.)

ERITRICHIUM (*Boraginaceae*)   Forget-me-not-like FL.
E. *nanum*. Syn E. *terglovense*   1in. Tight tuffet to loose mat of tiny oval pointed silky hairy leaves. FL ¼in intense blue with white or yellow raised inner ring and yellow stamens, buds purple; at first almost stemless on cushions, later lengthening and trailing. April–June: spring-germinated plants may FL in autumn. High alpine in rich screes, gritty turf or humuswads in crevices, on acid rocks or dolomite. Very difficult in open garden; vulnerable to winter wet; calciphobe. AH. s, c (difficult). European Alps; closely similar species or forms in high mountains elsewhere in northern hemisphere, and down to Arctic coast. (The doyen of European high alpines.)
E. *rupestre pectinatum*. Syns *strictum*, *wallichianum*, *Cynoglossum wallichianum* 9in. Herbaceous. Rosette of narrow somewhat silky 2in L. FL ¼in light blue in loose spikes on leafy stems. May onwards. Well-drained gritty soil. s. Asia.

ERODIUM (*Geraniaceae*)   Stork's-bill. L narrow, more or less finely cut. FL usually in loose few-flowered sprays, nearly regular but upper two petals often marked and lower three plain. Seeds with a long spiked 'beak', coiling when ripe. Some species are dioecious (ie male and female flowers on separate plants). Sun, good drainage.
E. *chrysanthum*   9in. Densely leafy mound. L finely cut, silky. FL ¾in sulphur, dioecious. May–Aug. Often shy-flowering. D. Greece.
E. *petraeum glandulosum*. Syn *macradenum*   9in. L slightly hairy, deeply cut. FL ¾in rose-pink, upper two petals blotched dark purple. May onward. s, c. Pyrenees. (Plants distributed as '*macranthum*' have unblotched FL.)
E. *reichardii*. Syn *chamaedrioides*   2½in. Close mats of oval blunt-toothed L. FL

½in pale to strong rose-purple, solitary. April onward. Slightly tender. Protected scree or AH. D. Balearics. There is a double form. (*E. corsicum* is very similar, with more elongated stems with two or three FL.)

ERYSIMUM (*Cruciferae*)   Short-lived perennials with wallflower-like FL. S, C.
E. helveticum. Syn *pumilum*   2½in. Close tuft of narrow 2in L. FL ½in bright clear yellow in close flat heads. May. Scree. European mtns.
E. linifolium   12in. Small tufts to large clumps of 3in narrow, slightly toothed, greyish L. FL ½in soft purple, in dense tufts among L, later extending into leafy spikes. April onwards. Spain, Portugal.

ERYTHRONIUM (*Liliaceae*)   Tuberous. L oval to lanceolate, usually mottled. FL 1½–2in, one or several, pendulous, on leafless stem; petals usually curled back, pistil and stamens projecting. Spring flowering. Part shade, light rich peaty soil. S, D. All but *dens-canis* are N American. There are several good named hybrids.
E. californicum   10in. L dark green with lighter mottling. FL cream with orange centre and yellow anthers, several to stem. April. California. (Plate, see p 107.)
E. dens-canis   Dogstooth Violet. 5in. L oval, pointed, variably blotched maroon on light green. FL rose-purple, solitary. Feb–April. Low woodland to high turf, blooming as snow recedes. Lime-tolerant. Sun or shade. Mountains of S Europe and Asia.
E. hendersonii   8in. L maroon netted with light green. FL lilac with blue-purple centre and anthers, several to a stem. April. Oregon.
E. oregonum   9in. L mottled light and dark green. FL several, white with orange centre and anthers, large, petals spreading. April. NW America.
E. revolutum. Syns *johnsonii*, *smithii*   Trout Lily. 10in. L veined and netted lighter green. FL several, white to rose, large. April–May. W America. (Plate, see p 107.)
E. tuolumnense   10in. L light green, unmottled. FL green-backed, bright yellow with yellow anthers, several to stem. California.

EUNOMIA (*Cruciferae*)
E. oppositifolia. Syn *Aethionema oppositifolia*   2½in. Mat of small oval opposite glaucous L. FL ½in pale pink, in close heads. April–May. Tender; buds frequently frost-damaged. Scree with protection, AH. D, C, S. Lebanon.

EURYOPS (*Compositae*)
E. acraeus. Syn *evansii*   12in rounded shrub; occasional underground runners. L 1½in, silvery blue-grey, narrow, ribbed, toothed at tip. FL solitary, golden-yellow 'daisies' on 3in stems. May–June. Sun, good drainage. C. Basutoland.

FRITILLARIA (*Liliaceae*)   Bulbous. Spring-flowering. L narrowly lanceolate. FL solitary or few on leafy stem, bell-shaped to tubular, pendulous. D, S. Light rich soil; sun or half-shade.

F. gracilis   10in. FL narrowly bell-shaped, maroon, blotched and tipped yellow. April–May. Dalmatia.

F. meleagris   Snakeshead. 10in. FL one or two, widely bell-shaped, 1½in long and wide, purple chequered green and white; or white. April–May. Damp meadows in the wild: tolerant of drier conditions. Europe incl Britain. (*F. tubiformis*, syn *delphinensis*, is very similar.)

F. pyrenaica   10in. FL solitary, long bell-shaped, chequered pattern of yellow-green and chocolate-purple in varying proportions; rarely yellow. April–May. Pyrenees and N Spain. (*hispanica* and *lusitanica*, rather dwarfer and wider-flowered, are generally similar.)

GALANTHUS (*Amaryllidaceae*)   Snowdrop. Bulbous. L basal, lanceolate to strap-shaped. Many species and vars with FL generally similar to common snowdrop but varying in size and in amount and distribution of green markings: variation also in L and flowering time. D (OFFSETS).

G. elwesii   8in. L 5in, broad glaucous. FL 1½in with green at both base and tip of inner petals. Jan–March. Sun. Asia Minor.

G. nivalis   Common snowdrop. 6in. L narrow strap-shaped, 4in at flowering time. FL 1in, green markings at tip only of inner petals. Jan–March. Half-shade, open woodland; will naturalise in grass. Europe, Asia Minor. Among many fairly distinct forms are:
  some doubles
  lutescens   yellow replaces green on stem and FL. Not robust.
  reginae-olgae. Syn *rachelae*   FL in Oct before L. Sun or shade. Greece.
  viridapicis   green tips to outer petals.

GAULTHERIA (*Ericaceae*)
G. cuneata   4in. Low, spreading, rooting shrub. L ¾in narrow-oval, blunt-toothed, netted, shiny. FL ¼in white globular, in small crowded bunches. Berries conspicuous, white, pink-tinged. June–July: berries on into winter. Calciphobe. Acid soil or peat-bed. D. China.

GENISTA (*Leguminosae*)   Broom. Low-growing shrubs with green stems and often small deciduous L. FL yellow, pea-shaped. Sun. S, C.

G. lydia. Syns *rhodopea*, *rumelica*   18in, spreading. L ¾in narrow, shining. FL ½in, profuse, along the branches. May–June. Balkans.

G. sylvestris. Syn *dalmatica*   6in, compact, spiny. FL abundant, bright yellow, in dense heads. June–July. Italy, Albania, Yugoslavia.

GENTIANA (*Gentianaceae*)   Many fine rock garden plants: considerable variation, falling into four main groups:

(I) evergreen, spring-flowering, usually blue; Europe

(II) herbaceous, summer-flowering, blue; Europe, Asia, N America

(III) herbaceous, autumn-flowering, blue; Asia

(IV) evergreen, FL cup-shaped, white; New Zealand

G. 'acaulis' Bell-Gentian. (I) 4in. Close mat of oval shining 1½in L. FL solitary
on short stalks, 2in tubes with spreading lobes, deep blue, throat streaked
and spotted green and indigo. April–May, and odd FL throughout year.
Rich, gritty, limy soil; sun. D, s. This most popular rock garden plant is a
mystery, (a) as to its precise identity—it corresponds closely but not totally
with some of the wild bell-gentians, (b) in its flowering, which is profuse
in some gardens but in others the buds are 'blind' with no blue corolla.

G. *alpina* (I) Like *acaulis* but L dull green, FL smaller, greenish-blue. Calciphobe,
shy-flowering. Lime-free well-drained turf, or sandy peat, in sun. D. W
Alps, Pyrenees.

G. *angustifolia* (I) Like *acaulis* but L narrow, almost strap-shaped. FL funnel-
shaped, wide-mouthed, deep blue with prominent green on throat.
March–July. Well-drained limy turf or scree. D, s. W Alps. (G. *clusii*, E
Alps, is very similar.)

G. *asclepiadea* Willow Gentian. (II) 2ft. L rounded at base, clasping stem,
tapering to point, ribbed. FL in sprays along leafy stems; 1½in tubular with
spreading pointed petals, purplish to greenish-blue, or white. July–Sept.
Streamsides and light woodland. Rich damp soil in sun or half-shade.
D, s Alps and into Asia.

G. *bellidifolia* (IV) 4in. Tuft of thick smooth spoon-shaped 1½in L. FL ¾in
white, cup-shaped. June–Aug. Calciphobe. Lime-free scree. Short-lived.
s. New Zealand.

G. × *carolii* (? *farreri* × *laurencei*) (III) 4in. Tuft of small narrow pointed dark
green L. FL solitary on spreading 6in leafy stems, 1¼in with narrow tube
striped dark and light green, and spreading petals clear coerulean blue,
white-centred. July–Sept. Calciphobe. Peat-bed; sun but avoid draught.
c (young shoots in early summer), D.

G. *cruciata* (II) 12in. Basal L lanceolate, 5in. FL grouped at tips and in leaf-axils
of leafy ascending stems; purplish 1in tube and 4 small blue petals. July–
Aug. s. Mtns of Europe and Asia.

G. *farreri* (III) 2½in. Central tuft of 1½ in very narrow curved L. FL solitary,
upturned at ends of 6in prostrate leafy stems; tube 2in, pale green, striped
indigo; petals Cambridge blue, white throat. Aug–Sept. Rich moist scree.
(Said to be lime-tolerant—doubtful.) Sun. D, c (young shoots), s. China,
Tibet.

G. *kochiana*. Syns *excisa*, *latifolia* (I) 4in. Like *acaulis*, but L widely oval, blunt, flaccid. FL at best very deep blue, green-spotted; can be purplish. D, S. Alps. Pyrenees.

G. *pneumonanthe* (II) 8in. L 1½in, narrow, pointed, dark green, shining. FL several in loose leafy spikes, tubular, 1½in long, dark blue, throat green with dark stripes. July–Sept. Acid bogs and heaths. Calciphobe. Bog or moist place, sun. D, S, C. N hemisphere incl Britain. (Fig 10, see p 42.)

G. *pyrenaica* (I) 3in. Close mat of narrow, pointed, ½in, shining L. FL solitary on short leafy stems, funnel-shaped, 1in, violet to purple with yellow stamens; large lobes between petals giving effect of 10 petals. April onwards. High turf on acid soil, tending to moist positions. Calciphobe. Acid scree or turf, avoid drying-out. Difficult. S, D. Pyrenees, E Europe, Asia.

G. *saxosa* (IV) Similar to *bellidifolia*, but slightly larger, with longer narrower petals. New Zealand.

G. *septemfida* (II) 10in. L 1in, long-oval, close-packed along stems ascending from a central tuft. FL in small groups at ends of stems, tubular, wide-mouthed, 1in, fringed between petals, rich blue. July–Aug. Sun, rich well-drained soil, lime-tolerant, easy. C (young shoots), S. Asia Minor to Persia. (Somewhat variable in cultivation: *lagodechiana*, with solitary FL, and × *hascombensis* (*lagodechiana* × *septemfida*) are very similar.)

G. *sino-ornata* (III) 4in. Central tuft of narrow pointed deep green 1in L. Mass of trailing stems with longer L, tending to root at nodes, forming wide loose mat. FL solitary, terminal, funnel-shaped, 2in long, wide-mouthed, Prussian blue, tube striped greenish-yellow and deep blue. Aug–Oct. Calciphobe, peat-bed, best in sun but avoid drying-out. D (separate thongs or rooted pieces in March), S. W China. (The best autumn species: many named vars incl *praecox* (earlier FL) and whites.)

G. *verna* Spring Gentian. (I) 4in. Rosettes of small smooth L forming loose tufts. FL solitary on upright stems, with narrow, more or less winged, calyx tubes and flat 1in deep royal-blue FL, often with white scales at throat. Variable in compactness, size and form of L, and FL-colour (many shades of blue, mauve, rich purple, white). April–May. Low alpine meadows to high turf. Rich well-drained soil. Short-lived. S. Europe incl Britain, Asia. (The best alpine! Many forms and related sp. *angulosa* is more robust, with broader shining L and very marked calyx-wings. *brachyphylla* is smaller, more compact; higher altitude, calciphobe, scree. *bavarica* has small more rounded L and var *subacaulis* is very compact; high altitude.) (Fig 1, see p 14.)

GERANIUM (*Geraniaceae*) Cranesbill. Herbaceous with thick rootstocks and dissected L. FL regular, 5-petalled, one to several in loose heads. Fruit in a 'beak'. Light soil, sun. D, S.

G. *argenteum*   6in. L round, deeply dissected, silvery. FL 1in, rose-pink with darker veins (deeper rose-purple in 'Lissadel's Var'). May–Sept. Italy, France, Yugoslavia.

G. *cinereum*   Similar but with greyish rather than silvery L.

G. *cinereum* subsp *subcaulescens*. Syn G. *subcaulescens*   6in. L clear green. FL brilliant magenta, black-centred. May–July. Italy, Greece, Yugoslavia. (G. × 'Ballerina' = *subcaulescens* × *cinereum*, an excellent plant with dark-centred FL pink with rose-magenta veining.)

G. *dalmaticum*   4in. L round, dissected, shiny. FL 1in, rose-pink; tuft of purplish stamens curved down. June–July. Yugoslavia, Albania.

G. *napuligerum*. Syn *farreri*   6in. L 1in, rounded, coarsely cut and toothed, in close tuft. FL 1¼in, pale clear lilac-pink, anthers black. May–June. Scree. SW China.

G. *sanguineum*   9in. Mounds of round deeply-cut L. FL usually solitary, 1¼in, strong purple-red. May onwards. Europe incl Britain, W Asia. (Var *lancastriense* forms closer mats and has pale pink darker-veined FL.)

GEUM (*Rosaceae*)   Creeping rhizomes. Clumps of divided L. FL regular with 5 petals, bunch of yellow stamens. Heads of feathery seeds.

G. *montanum*. Syn *Sieversia montana*   6in. L long, narrow, cut into rounded, toothed lobes, in pairs, with large lobe at end. FL yellow, 1–1½in, usually single on an upright stem. April–May. S, D. European mtns.

G. *reptans*. Syn *Sieversia reptans*   4in. Long leafy runners. L more finely and sharply cut than *montanum*. FL 2in, clear yellow, solitary on short stems. June–July. A high alpine of acid shales and screes. Calciphobe. Moraine or scree—avoid drying-out. Difficult. S, D. European mtns.

GLAUCIDIUM (*Podophyllaceae*)

G. *palmatum*   12in. Herbaceous. Tuberous rhizome. L two, 6in, rounded in outline, cut into pointed, toothed lobes, wrinkled. FL solitary 2½in; 4 pale violet petals and boss of yellow stamens. April–May. Half-shade, woodland. S. Japan.

GLOBULARIA (*Globulariaceae*)   Mats of small shining undivided L. FL in round tight heads. Sun. D, S.

G. *aphyllanthes*. Syns *vulgaris, willkommii*   9in. Basal L stalked, 1½in, oval. FL-heads ½in, blue, on stems with a few narrow L. May–June. Light soil. Sun. Alps. (*nudicaulis* is similar, slightly larger throughout.)

G. *cordifolia*   3in. Creeping mats of narrow 1in L notched at tips. FL-heads ¾in grey-blue, lilac or clear blue, on leafless stems. May–June. Light soil in sun. D, S. European mtns. (Subsp *bellidifolia* has unnotched L.)

G. *cordifolia* subsp *nana*. Syn G. *nana* ½–1in. Flat mat of narrow ½in L. FL lilac-blue in ½in heads. Hot sunny crevices. Spain, Pyrenees.

GYPSOPHILA (*Caryophyllaceae*)   Mat-forming. FL regular, 5-petalled. D, S, C.

G. *cerastioides*   L stalked, ¾in, soft oval light green. FL ½in, full-petalled, slightly notched, white, veined. April–June. Scree in sun. Himalayas.

G. *repens*. Syn *prostrata* 2in. Dense mat of trailing stems massed with small narrow, fleshy glaucous L. FL ¼in pink (deeper in vars *fratensis* and *rosea*) in loose flattish heads. Petals notched. June–July. Sun. Light soil or wall. Mtns of Europe.

HABERLEA (*Gesneriaceae*)   Packed rosettes of 3in, oval, bluntly toothed, wavy, hairy L. FL in heads, tubular, slightly irregular. Half-shade or north crevice in good soil. D, S.

H. *rhodopensis* FL pale lilac, 1in, April–June. Thrace. (Var *virginalis* is a good white; and *ferdinandi-coburgii* and *austinii*, slightly larger and with yellow markings on throat, are closely similar if not synonymous.)

HACQUETIA (*Umbelliferae*)

H. *epipactis* 8in. Herbaceous. L stalked, rounded, cut into coarsely toothed segments. FL bunched into small yellow heads, with a wide collar of leaf-like bracts: the effect is of a large green FL with yellow stamens. Feb–April. Half-shade or woodland. D. Eastern Alps.

HALIMIOCISTUS (*Cistaceae*)   Bigeneric hybrids between *Halimium* and *Cistus*.

H. *sahucii* (*Cistus salvifolius* × *Halimium umbellatum*) 18in. Shrub with 1in narrow L and heads of 1¼in white 'rockrose' FL, petals shallowly notched, yellow centres. May–Aug. Light soil in sun. Borderline hardy. C. ? Garden origin.

HALIMIUM (*Cistaceae*)   Evergreen shrubs near to *Helianthemum* (Rockrose).

H. *ocymoides*. Syns *Cistus algarvensis, Helianthemum algarvense* 15in L 1in, narrow, grey-green when young. FL 1in in small clusters at ends of spreading leafy stems; yellow, with or without chocolate centre ring. May–Aug. Good drainage, sun. Borderline hardy. C, S. Spain, Portugal.

HEBE (*Scrophulariaceae*)   Close to *Veronica*: the shrubby New Zealand 'Veronicas' are now usually called *Hebe*.

H. *bidwillii* 6in. Dense mat of slender rooting stems, thick-set with minute circular L. FL in loose heads on slender upright dark stems, ¼in, white, veined pink. June–Aug. Good and easy. D, S.

H. *catarractae* 15in. Rounded leafy bush. L 1in lanceolate coarsely toothed.

FL in elongated heads, ¼in white with or without rose-purple veining. D, C, S.

H. macrantha   18in. L 1in oval toothed shining. FL in clusters at ends of branches, 1in, clear white. May–July. ? Calciphobe: ? slightly tender. Rich soil or peat-bed. C, S.

H. pageana   9in. Loosely spreading shrub. L ¾in oval glaucous. FL ¼in clear white in dense terminal tufts. April–June. C, S.

HELIANTHEMUM (*Cistaceae*) Rock-rose. More or less shrubby, evergreen. Masses of regular 5-petalled FL. Sun, good drainage, lime. C (easy), S (may not come true).

H. apenninum. Syn *polifolium*   10in. Spreading. L 1in narrow grey, whitish below, downy. FL ¾in white or pink, yellow centred. April–Aug. Europe incl Britain, Asia Minor.

H. lunulatum   8in. Compact dwarf shrub. L ½in, narrow pointed green. FL ½in yellow with crescentic orange spot at bases of petals. May–Sept. Maritime Alps.

H. nummularium. Syn *vulgare*   Common rock-rose. Flat spreading mat to 15in dome. L oval to lanceolate, ½–1½in, usually smooth green above, greyish below. FL ¾in, wide range of colours but not blue or purple. April onwards. Europe incl Britain. (Very variable, even in the wild; several named subspecies and many cultivars: subsp *grandiflorum* with 1in golden FL is good distinct and permanent.)

H. oelandicum subsp *alpestre*, var *serpyllifolium*. Syn *H. serpyllifolium*   4in. Close mat of ½in elliptical green L. FL ½in yellow abundant. May–June. Mtns of S and C Europe.

HELICHRYSUM (*Compositae*) L whitish woolly. FL 'everlasting' because of persistent dry hard bracts.

H. bellidioides   4in. Herbaceous. Dense mat of fine woody stems, rooting down. L ¼in oval with a narrow point, green above, whitish below. FL ¾in solitary, white. April–June. Sun, good drainage. Hardy. D. New Zealand.

H. milfordiae. Syn *marginatum*   2in. Dense white woolly mat of broadly oval ½in L in rosettes. FL solitary on short leafy stems, 1¼in, shining white with yellow centre; outsides of bracts, hence buds and closed FL, crimson. June–July. Scree or AH. C, D. Basutoland.

HELLEBORUS (*Ranunculaceae*) Winter or early spring flowering woodland plants with large deeply divided L and more or less cup-shaped 5-petalled FL. S, D (they don't like it).

H. 'atrorubens'   12in. L divided into about 8 narrow, pointed, toothed, 7in leaflets, stalked but tending to lie low on ground. FL 2½in rose-purple,

L

pendent, 1 or 2 to a head. Feb–March. (Outstanding among the many hybrids and cultivars of *Helleborus*: uncertain origin, possibly deriving from *dumetorum* or *purpurascens*.)

H. *niger* Christmas Rose. 9in. L divided into about 8 thick, dark green, narrow, pointed, toothed 6in leaflets. FL 2½in white to rose with yellow boss of stamens, 2 to 3 in a cluster on a short stem. Dec–March. Rich soil in woodland. E Alps, W Asia.

H. *orientalis* 15in. L long-stalked, 5 slightly toothed 6in leaflets. FL 2in white or greenish yellow, with or without purple speckling inside (var *guttatus*) 2 or 3 to a leafy head. Feb–March. E Europe, Turkey, Russia. (Variable; several named subspecies and cultivars.)

HEPATICA (*Ranunculaceae*) Early spring flowering 'anemones'. Woodland or light shade. D, S.

H. *nobilis*. Syns *H. triloba*, *Anemone hepatica* 4in. L 2in with 3 angular lobes, sometimes variegated lighter or darker, or purplish beneath. FL solitary, ¾in, purple, blue, white or rose. Dec–April. Europe, Asia. *H. acutiloba* of N America is very similar. (Several named colour-forms and also doubles.)

H. *transsilvanica*. Syn *angulosa* 6in. Mat-forming. L 3in rounded, blunt-toothed. FL usually clear blue, 1½in. Rumania.

HORMINUM (*Labiatae*)

H. *pyrenaicum* 10in. Rosettes of 3in oval wrinkled toothed L. FL in close spikes, ½in, tubular, lipped, violet. May–July. Half-shade or sun. Pyrenees, E Alps.

HOUSTONIA (*Rubiaceae*)

H. *coerulea* 2½in. Mat of tiny narrow-oval L. FL ¼in, 4-petalled, light blue, yellow-centred, solitary. March–April. Short-lived and doubtfully hardy. Half-shade, light leafy moist soil. ? Calciphobe. D, S. Virginia.

HUTCHINSIA (*Cruciferae*)

H. *alpina* 3in. Mats of deep green shiny L cut into segments. FL ¼in 4-petalled, clear white, in rounded heads. March–May. Sun or half-shade, gritty soil. D, S. European mtns.

HYACINTHUS (*Liliaceae*) Bulbous plants with narrow L and spikes of tubular open-mouthed regular FL. D (OFFSETS), S.

H. *amethystinus* 9in. A small delicate pale blue version of the English bluebell. May–June. Good drainage, sun. Pyrenees.

H. *azureus*. Syn *Muscari azureum* 6in. L 3in. FL-spike *muscari*-like. FL clear Cambridge blue, or white. Feb–April. Asia Minor.

HYPERICUM (*Guttiferae*)   St John's Wort. Yellow 5-petalled FL with truss of stamens. C, S.

H. *coris*   8in. L ½in, thick, very narrow, furrowed, curved, crowded along stems. FL ¾ in starry pale clear yellow, sometimes streaked red, in mainly terminal clusters. June–Aug. Light soil; sun. Borderline hardy. SW Europe.

H. *olympicum*   12in. Rounded shrub. L crowded, 1in, narrow pointed glaucous. FL 1¼in golden or lemon (var *citrinum*); petals slightly oblique giving catherine-wheel appearance. June–Aug. SE Europe, Asia Minor.

IBERIS (*Cruciferae*)   Candytuft. FL in flat heads; 4 petals, the two outer larger.

I. *pruitii*. Syns *attica, carnosa, jucunda, tenoreana*   8in, dome-shaped. L 1in elliptical blunt-toothed near tip, glossy, fleshy. FL ¼in in 2in heads, white to deep lilac. May–July. Good drainage. S (sows itself), C. S Europe. (Variable; usually short-lived.)

I. *saxatilis*   4in. Prostrate shrub. L ¾in narrow. FL white in 1¼in heads. March–June. Sun. C, S. S Europe.

I. *sempervirens*   8in. Similar to *saxatilis* but less prostrate and slightly larger throughout. Mediterranean.

IPHEION (*Amaryllidaceae*)

I. *uniflorum*. Syns *Brodiaea uniflora, Triteleia uniflora*   Bulbous. Onion-smell. L 6in very narrow, flat, prostrate, appearing in late autumn. FL 1¼in star-shaped, white, pale blue or lilac, yellow-centred, solitary on 6in stems. Feb–May. Sun. D (OFFSETS). S America.

IRIS (*Iridaceae*)   Bulbous (I) or rhizomatous (II). L grass-like to sword-like. FL with outer petals with long 'haft' and usually down-turned 'fall', 3 more or less upright inner petals ('standards'), and 3 petal-like stigmas lying along the hafts. D, S.

I. *chrysographes* 'rubella'   (II) 10in. L narrow (½in). FL 2½in, standards spreading; maroon with very dark falls. June. Moist rich soil. China.

I. *cretensis*   (II) 6–12in. L very narrow (⅛–¼in) in dense clumps. FL 2½–3in; falls spreading, heart-shaped, rich purple, golden-yellow at base; standards upright, purple. Dec–March. Good drainage, hot position. Greece, Crete. (Possibly a small form of *unguicularis*: Cretan form has short grass-like L, Greek rather bigger.)

I. *danfordiae*   (I) 12in. L very narrow, grooved, with claw-point. FL 2in, clear yellow, with broad upright falls and standards, on 4in stems while L are still very small. Jan–Feb. Good drainage, sun. Bulb breaks into many minute bulblets after flowering: needs rich feeding. Turkey.

I. *gracilipes*   (II) 9in. L narrowly sword-shaped. FL 2in on slender stems, lilac (or white), falls with orange crest, standards spreading. May–June. Calciphobe. Rich acid soil or peat-bed; not too dry. Japan.

I. graminea (II) 10in. L narrowly sword-shaped. FL low down among L, 2½in; falls spreading, deep purple with yellow central band and very dark purple white-centred blades; standards small, purple; stigmas large, rose-purple. Scent of greengages. May–June. Sun. S Europe.

I. histrioides major (I) 6in. Light blue, fully hardy, and rapidly forms clumps of flowering sized bulbs. Feb–March. Sun. Asia Minor.

I. innominata (II) 8in. L grass-like. FL variable in colour; orange, buff or gold with darker brown markings, or various shades of violet with white markings on falls. May–June. Best in acid moist soil in sun or half-shade. Oregon. (Hybridises in cultivation with other American species, possibly accounting for some of the colour-variation.)

I. lacustris. Syn *cristata lacustris* (II) 4in. L sword-shaped, light green, in loose spreading mats. FL 2in; falls lilac with yellow and white crested ridge surrounded by darker purple zone; standards spreading, lilac. April onwards. Tolerates wide range of conditions but flowers best in sun. Eastern USA. (Plate, see p 108.)

I. laevigata (II) 2ft. L sword-like. FL 2½in, clear blue (also white and shades of pink and lilac). June–July. Moist places, water-side, sun. Japan.

I. pumila (II) 6in. Short sword-shaped L. FL 2½in; falls bearded, curled downwards; standards broad, upright; usually self-coloured, white, cream, yellow, blue or purple. April–May. Good drainage, sun. Mediterranean. (*chamaeiris* from France and Italy is very similar.)

I. reticulata (I) 9in. L as *danfordiae*. FL 3in. Falls deep blackish purple with white-edged orange blotch; standards upright purple. Feb–March. Good drainage, sun. Caucasus. Many named colour variants, eg 'Cantab' (light blue), '*J.S. Dijt*' (maroon), '*Royal Blue*' (dark blue), '*Springtime*' (violet-blue). Also several good robust hybrids with *histrioides* ('Joyce', 'Harmony') and *bakeriana* ('*Clairette*').

I. unguicularis. Syn *stylosa* (II) 12in. L long, narrow (½in). FL 3in, light violet. Falls spreading, rounded, white-blotched; standards also spreading and rounded. Very long flower-tube, replacing stalk. Scented. Dec–March. Arid spot in sun. N Africa, E Mediterranean. (Some colour-variation.)

I. xiphioides. Syn *anglica* (I) 12in. L very narrow, deeply grooved. FL 2 or 3 to stem, 3in, clear violet with white blotch on large down-turned falls; standards upright; stem sheathed with short broader leaves. July. Pyrenees.

Isopyrum (*Ranunculaceae*). Like small wood anemone.

I. thalictroides 4in. Herbaceous. Thin spreading rhizomes. L smooth, glaucous, divided into three 3-lobed ¾in leaflets on fine stems. FL ¾in, white, delicate, 2 or 3 in a loose spray. March–April. Dies down after flowering. Half-shade or sun. Europe. (There is a double form.) (*I. biternatum* from N America is very similar.)

JASIONE (*Campanulaceae*) Sheepsbit Scabious.
J. jankae 10in. Loose mat of strap-shaped 1¼in slightly toothed L. FL clear blue, tiny in dense flat 1in heads. June–Aug. S, D. Hungary.

JEFFERSONIA (*Berberidaceae*)
J. dubia 8in. Herbaceous. L 2in, round, heart-shaped at base, indented at tip, long-stalked. FL solitary, 1in, regular, pale mauvish blue. March–April. Half-shade or woodland. S, D. Manchuria.

JOVIBARBA (*Crassulaceae*) Like Sempervivum (Houseleek) but FL 6-petalled, bell-shaped.
J. heuffelii. Syn *Sempervivum heuffelii* 6in. 2½in rosettes of oval pointed thick L, glaucous. FL pale yellow in tight heads. May–July. Dry sunny position, eg crevice. D (the rosettes split and multiply themselves—no stolons).

KALMIOPSIS (*Ericaceae*)
K. leachiana 12in rounded shrub. L ¾in elliptical thick smooth. FL in loose trusses, rose-lilac, saucer-shaped, petals full, crinkled. Dec–April. Calciphobe, best in AH. C. Oregon.

LAPEIROUSIA (*Iridaceae*)
Lapeirousia laxa. Syn *Anomatheca cruenta* 8in. Bulbous. L narrow pointed ½in wide. FL in loose spikes ¾in on long tube, carmine, 3 lower petals blotched deep red. July–Sept. Doubtfully hardy. S. S Africa.

LATHYRUS (*Leguminosae*) Pea.
L. vernus. Syn *Orobus vernus* 15in. Herbaceous. L with three pairs of oval pointed 2½in leaflets. FL ½in pea-shaped, several in a loose head, rose, purple, white or blue. March–May. Light shade or woodland. D, S. Europe.

LEIOPHYLLUM (*Ericaceae*)
L. buxifolium 9in evergreen shrub. L ¼in oval glossy. FL ¼in in flat heads, white, pink-tinged. May–June. Calciphobe. Acid soil or peat-bed. C, S. N America.

LEONTOPODIUM (*Compositae*) Herbaceous. L felted, woolly. 'Everlasting flowers'. S, D.
L. alpinum Edelweiss. 6in. L 1in narrow, grey-green. FL heads 1½in, formed of

spreading white woolly bracts and central clustered heads of yellowish, scaly tiny FL. May–July. Good drainage. European mtns. (*nivale* is a high alpine form, dwarfer, with whiter L.)

LEUCOJUM (*Amaryllidaceae*)   Bulbous. S, D.

L. aestivum   Summer Snowflake. 18in. L long narrow. FL ¾in, bell-shaped, pendent in loose heads on tall stems, white, green-tipped. Feb–April. Rich moist soil or water-side; sun or half-shade. D, S. Europe incl Britain.

L. nicaeënse. Syn *niemale*   5in. L narrow grass-like. FL 1in, pendent, 1 to 2 on a stem, open, clear white with yellow anthers. May. Light soil, warm position or AH. S. Maritime Alps.

L. vernum   Spring Snowflake. 8in. L strap-shaped. FL ¾in, round bell-shaped, white with pointed green tips (yellow in var *carpathicum*), pendent, single (2-flowered in var *vagneri*). Feb–March. Rich soil, easy. D, S. Europe incl Britain.

LEWISIA (*Portulaceae*)   L fleshy mostly in basal rosette. FL regular with up to 16 narrow, usually notched petals. Probably calciphobe. Rich soil but perfect drainage. S, C. Western N America. Many hybrids and cultivars.

L. columbiana   8in. L 2in, narrow strap-shaped, numerous. FL ¾in bright or pale pink (rose-carmine in *L. c. rosea*—possibly a hybrid) in loose sprays. May–Aug. Tolerant of sun.

L. cotyledon   10in. L 3in, narrowly to broadly oval, edges sometimes wavy, crinkled or toothed. FL 1in, pale to strong rose or yellow, striped, in flattish heads. May–July. Part-shade, eg north-facing crevice or steep slope. (Very variable: many named varieties and cultivars, much colour and foliage variation. Named forms include *finchii, heckneri, howellii, purdyi*.)

L. pygmaea   2in. Thick tuberous root. L 2in narrow strap-shaped, dying down after flowering. FL 1 to 3 on 2in stems, ¾in, white or pink. May–July. High-level snow-watered plant. Best in AH.

L. 'Pinkie' (? *pygmaea* × *cotyledon*)   4in. L 2in, narrow. FL 1in in tight sprays, clear pink. May–July. Cultivation as for *cotyledon*. Good.

L. rediviva   2in. Root tuberous. L 1½in, narrow, disappearing at flowering-time. FL solitary on short stems, 2in, rose or white. June–July (earlier in AH). Sun; intolerant of wet while at rest; best in AH.

L. tweedyi   8in. L 4in, oval, blunt. FL 1 to 3 on a stem, 1½in, white, yellowish-pink, yellow or (*L. t. rosea*) rose-pink, yellow-centred. April–July. Perfect drainage.

LILIUM (*Liliaceae*)   Scaly bulbs. L pointed, crowded or in whorls up tall stems. FL large. Rich soil; sun or light shade. Buds subject to frost damage. SCALES, S.

L. bulbiferum 2ft. L 3in shiny, crowded, with bulbils in axils. FL in massive crowded spikes, 4in, open funnel shaped, broad petalled, vermilion with golden central area. June. BULBILS. Pyrenees, Maritimes, N Italy. (Var *croceum* lacks bulbils.)

L. martagon 2ft. L long-oval in whorls. FL in long loose spike, 2in, pendent, pale to deep maroon, or white. Petals strongly reflexed; protruding orange stamens. June–July. European mtns.

L. pomponium 18in. L 2½in, very narrow, densely crowded. FL on long stalks in open spray, pendent, 1½in, glossy vermilion, petals strongly reflexed, hanging orange stamens. June–July. Sun. Provence to Liguria.

L. pyrenaicum 2½ft. L 4in, narrow, densely crowded. FL pendent on long stems in loose open spike, 2½in, yellow, petals strongly reflexed, hanging scarlet stamens. Foetid. June. Pyrenees.

LINARIA (*Scrophulariaceae*) Toadflax. FL spurred 'snapdragons'.

L. aequitriloba 1in. Close spreading mat of ¼in kidney-shaped scalloped L on thin rooting stems. FL ¼in, purple, yellow at throat. April onwards. Creeper for crevices, rock-faces; sun or shade. D, S. Sardinia.

L. alpina 3in. Sprawling stems from central tuft. L ½in narrow fleshy glaucous, close-packed along stems. FL in terminal heads, ¾in, violet with bright orange throat (var *concolor* has lilac throat) or white or flesh-pink. April onwards. Scree or moraine; sun but not too dry; short-lived but seeds freely. S. European mtns.

L. supina Very similar to *alpina* but FL yellow with darker lip. Pyrenees, Spain.

L. triornithophora 10in. Spreads by underground thread-like roots. L pointed oval in whorls of 3 on upright stems. FL large (1¼in) in few-flowered heads, rose-purple with yellow throat. June–Sept. Sun or half-shade. S, D. Spain.

LINNAEA (*Caprifoliaceae*)

L. borealis 4in. Mat of ½in oval L in pairs along trailing stems. FL ½in, narrow funnel-shaped in pairs, pendent on upright slender stems, pale pink, veined deeper. June–Sept. Mossy banks in pinewoods. Calciphobe. Part-shade in acid soil or peat-bed. D, LAYERS, C. N Europe incl Britain, N America. (Var *americana*, syn *canadensis* is more robust.)

LINUM (*Linaceae*) Flax. Regular 5-petalled FL.

L. 'Gemmel's Hybrid' (?*flavum* × *arboreum*) 9in. Stems woody at base. L 1½in, pointed oval, glaucous. FL 1in in loose flattish heads, golden-yellow. April–June. Sun, good drainage. C. Garden origin. (The best and least tender yellow flax.)

L. narbonense 18in. L 1½in, narrow, pointed. FL 1in, bright deep blue in flattish sprays. May onward. Good and easy. D. S Europe.

L. *suffruticosum* subsp *salsoloides*   2½in. Mats of hard gnarled stems thickset with ½in narrow pointed hard L. FL 1in, very pale pink. May–June. Sun, scree. S, C. S Europe. (The species includes upright plants up to 18in.)

LITHOSPERMUM (*Boraginaceae*)   Gromwell. Regular 5-petalled blue FL.

L. *diffusum*. Syn *prostratum*   9in. Loose spreading mat. L 1in, narrow, bristly hairy. FL ¾in, clear blue, covering the mat. April–June. Calciphobe. Sun in acid soil. C. Spain, France, Portugal. (Variable in the wild. 'Heavenly Blue' and 'Grace Ward' are good garden forms.)

L. *oleifolium*   6in. Underground stolons. Loose mat of ½in oval shining L, silky-white beneath. FL tubular, ½in, China blue, in few-flowered clusters. April–June. Light soil in sun or half-shade. D, C. Pyrenees.

L. *purpureocoeruleum*   12in. L 1½in narrow pointed bristly. Non-flowering stems trail or arch and root at tips. FL tubular, ½in, dark blue, buds purple, in tight clusters. April–May. Sun or half-shade or woodland. D, ROOTING TIPS. Europe incl Britain. (Plate, see p 125.)

LOBELIA (*Lobeliaceae*)

L. *linnaeoides*. Syn *Pratia linnaeoides*   3in. Close mat of tiny round toothed dark purplish-green L on stems which root at nodes. FL ½in solitary on slender stems, 2 small upper petals and 3 larger lower, delicate pale pink, calyces and buds deep red. June onwards. Shade, peat-bed. Doubtfully hardy. D, S. New Zealand.

LOISELEURIA (*Ericaceae*)

L. *procumbens*. Syn *Azalea procumbens*   2in. Close mat of smooth thick narrow-oval ¼in L on woody stems. FL on short stalks, ¼in regular, pink with darker centres and calyces. May–July. Flat peaty areas on acid rocks. Calciphobe. Peat-bed or acid soil in sun, not too dry. Shy-flowering. D, C. Arctic-alpine, incl Britain.

LYCHNIS (*Caryophyllaceae*)

L. *flos-jovis*   12in. Basal rosette of 2in oval L, white-woolly. FL in flattish heads on leafy stems, 1in, dianthus-like, petals notched, clear rose. May–July. Light soil. Sun. D, S. S Alps.

MAZUS (*Scrophulariaceae*)   Close mats of creeping rooting stems. FL tubular with 2 smaller upper petals and 3 larger ones forming lip. D, S.

M. *radicans*. Syn *Mimulus radicans*   1in. L ½in oval shining olive-bronze, speckled. FL ¾in, upper petals violet, lip white. May–June. Sun or half-shade in moist peaty soil, or AH. New Zealand.

M. *reptans*   1in. L ¾in narrow oval, toothed. FL ¾in long, strong lilac, white bosses at throat flecked golden-brown. April onwards. Moist position in sun. Himalaya.

MECONOPSIS (*Papaveraceae*) Himalayan Poppies. Most of the fine 'blue poppies' are large.

M. *quintuplinervia* 12in. L narrow oval, 9in, bristly, in basal rosette. FL usually single, 1½in, wide bell-shaped, pendent, soft lavender. April onwards. Calciphobe. Half-shade or peat-bed. D, s. W China.

MERENDERA (*Liliaceae*)

M. *montana*. Syn *bulbocodium* 3in. Bulbous. L 3in narrow shining, appearing just after FL. FL up to 3in high and across, petals narrowly oval, pointed, rose-purple, yellowish at base. July–Sept. Good drainage, sun. s, D (OFF-SETS). Pyrenees, Spain, Portugal.

MERTENSIA (*Boraginaceae*)

M. *virginica* 18in. Basal L 6in oval blunt downy. FL pendent in large loose sprays on leafy stems, ½in wide on 1in tube, light blue. April–May. Rich soil in half-shade or woodland. s, D. Virginia.

MIMULUS (*Scrophulariaceae*) Herbaceous. FL tubular with 5 spreading petals, upper 2 turned back and lower 3 projecting forward as a lip. D, s.

M. *cupreus* 9in. Stems and L as *luteus* but smaller. FL 1in coppery-yellow to vermilion (many named colour forms). Waterside, wet soil. Annual or short-lived. s (seeds itself). Chile.

M. *luteus* Monkey Musk. 15in. Mats of fleshy stolons. L 1½in oval pointed toothed shiny. FL in loose heads on leafy succulent stems, 1½in, yellow with variable dark red markings (heavily spotted in var *guttatus*). May onwards. Waterside in wet soil. D, s. N America (naturalised in Europe incl Britain).

M. *primuloides* 4in. Rosettes of ½–1in narrow-oval L. FL solitary on thin stems, ⅓in, yellow. May–June. Peaty soil, well-drained but not too dry. D, s. Western USA.

MOLTKIA (*Boraginaceae*)

M. × *intermedia* (*petraea* × *suffruticosa*) 12in. Rounded dense shrub. L 1in narrow velvety. FL ¼in in short loose heads, strong clear blue. June–July. Light soil in sun. c.

MUSCARI (*Liliaceae*) Grape hyacinth. Bulbous. L generally very narrow. FL in spikes, globular, constricted at mouth. Light well-drained soil in sun. D (OFFSETS), s.

M. botryoides 6in. L thin, 4in. FL in dense conical spikes, violet-blue or white. March–April. S Europe.

M. tubergenianum (a garden form of *M. aucheri*) 8in. L 6in, ½in broad. FL deep blue in close spike, but sterile florets at tip pale blue. Feb–April. (An improvement on the common *M. atlanticum*, syn *racemosum*, which is too invasive for the rock garden.)

MYOSOTIS (*Boraginaceae*) Forget-me-not. Low-growing plants with narrow-oval softly hairy L and ¼in FL.

M. alpestris var *rupicola* 1in. Tight cushions. L ½in. FL almost stemless, brilliant blue with white or yellow scales in throat. April–May. Scree or AH. s. European mtns. (A high-altitude form of *M. alpestris*, which is taller and looser.)

M. australis var *conspicuus* 5in. L 1½in. FL in tight sprays, bright yellow, or white. May–June. Short-lived. Scree. s. New Zealand.

M. explanata 1in. L ¾in, silky in rosettes on creeping rooting stems. FL stemless, clear white with yellow throat. April–June. Scree. D, s. New Zealand.

NARCISSUS (*Amaryllidaceae*) Bulbous. L long narrow. FL 6-petalled with central corona. D (OFFSETS), s.

N. asturiensis 5in. L strap-shaped. FL 1¼in, yellow, corona long-conical (a tiny daffodil). Feb–April. Rich scree or AH. N Spain. (Variable: the garden form *minimus* is better and easier than the wild type.)

N. bulbocodium Hoop-petticoat daffodil. 8in. L very thin, cylindrical. FL 1in, petals thin and inconspicuous; corona large, funnel to bell-shaped, strong yellow (pale yellow in var *citrinus*). March–May. Rich moist position in sun. S France to N Africa. (Several named hybrids and vars; some, eg *romieuxii* and *mesatlanticus*, very early-flowering and better in AH.)

N. cantabricus Similar to *bulbocodium* but FL clear white and corona widely open and more or less pleated. Oct–Feb. AH. Summer baking. N Africa. (Var *petunioides* has corona almost flat, 2in across, with prominent stamens.)

N. cyclamineus 6in. L very narrow but flat. FL narrowly tubular, with 1in corona and 1in petals laid back in a tube, clear yellow. Jan–April. Moist position. Spain, Portugal.

N. juncifolius 6in. L narrow, rush-like. FL one or several, ¾in, with long thin tube, spreading oval petals and small cup-shaped corona, clear yellow. April–May Rich scree or AH. Pyrenees to Portugal.

N. rupicola 10in. Similar to *juncifolius* but larger with narrow flat L and 1in FL, usually solitary. Spain, Portugal.

N. triandrus Angel's Tears. 9in. L narrow, shining, grooved. FL 1½in long, 1 to 3, pendent, white (var *albus*) through cream to yellow (var *concolor*), petals reflexed but not so strongly as in *cyclamineus*, corona bell-shaped, slightly pleated. March–April. Rich scree. Spain, Portugal.

NOMOCHARIS (*Liliaceae*)   Scaly bulbs. Large open FL, one or few to a leafy stem. Half-shade; peat, sand and lime-free leafmould. S, SCALES. W China.

N. aperta   12in. L 3in, lily-like, pointed, shiny, not whorled. FL 2½in, soft rose-pink with a few dark spots near centre, boss of yellow stamens. May–June.

N. mairei   L narrower and sharper, whorled. FL white to pale pinkish purple, spotted deep purple, inner petals broader, fringed. June.

OENOTHERA (*Onagraceae*)   Herbaceous or nearly so. Plants very variable in appearance and habit. FL 4-petalled. Some confusion over nomenclature, the genus having been split up by some botanists in America, whence the species come.

Oe. caespitosa   3in. Almost stemless overground, but underground stolons. L in rosettes, narrowly lance-shaped, sinuous to toothed, softly hairy. FL 3in, opening white in evening, pink on second day. May onwards. Well-drained soil, sun. Protect from winter wet and cold. S, D. Western N America.

Oe. mexicana rosea   3in. Biennial or short-lived perennial. L 1in, narrow-oval, shining, slightly toothed. FL ½in, clear rose, in axils at ends of leafy stems. Light soil, sun. S (Resembles an *Epilobium*, and a plant distributed as *E. niveum* appears to be identical).

Oe. ovata   3in. L in crowded rosettes, 5in, narrow, sinuous to slightly toothed, prominent central white vein. FL 1–2in, clear yellow with rounded ribbed petals, opening in evening. May onward. Dry poor soil (flourishes in gravel drives). S. California.

Oe. taraxacifolia. Syn *acaulis*   6in. L deeply and irregularly toothed (dandelion-like) in rosettes. FL on sprawling stems which gradually lengthen throughout summer, 3in, like *caespitosa*. June onwards. Dry poor soil. S. Chile.

Oe. tetragona. Syn *Kneiffia tetragona*   Loose trailing mat. L 2½in, narrow, pointed, entire, turning red. FL in loose terminal trusses on trailing leafy stems, yellow, 1¼in, petals notched. June–Aug. Light soil, sun; bank or rock face. D, C. N America.

OMPHALODES (*Boraginaceae*)

O. cappadocica   6in. Herbaceous. Creeping rhizome. Tufts of 3in stalked L, oval to narrow heart-shaped, pointed, strongly veined. FL ½in Forget-me-not-like, blue, white-centred, in loose sprays. March–May. Light shade or sun. D. Cappadocia.

O. luciliae   4in. L 1¼in, oval smooth glaucous, in basal tuft. FL in short trailing leafy sprays, ½in, pale clear china blue, petals dimpled, cream-centred. April onwards. Scree or AH; guard against slugs. S, C. Greece, Asia Minor.

O. verna   Blue-eyed Mary. Very similar to *cappadocica*, increasing by runners and forming mats. Feb–April. There is a white form. Half-shade. D. S Europe.

ONONIS (*Leguminosae*)
O. fruticosa   2ft. Leaf-losing woody shrub. L with 3 1in dark green toothed leaflets, crowded towards ends of stems. FL pea-shaped, 1in, clear rose, in small tight bunches. June–July. Light soil in sun. S. Maritime Alps, Spain.

ONOSMA (*Boraginaceae*)   Bristly hairy, FL tubular, pendent. Sun, good drainage. S, C.
O. albo-roseum. Syn *cinerara*   12in. L 1½in narrow, hoary-grey. FL 1in long, opening white, turning rose. April–June. Well-drained bank or rock face. Asia Minor. (Plate, see p 126.)
O. tauricum   Golden Drop. 12in. L 2in, narrow, grey-green. FL 1¼in golden-yellow. Bank or rock face. SE Europe.

OURISIA (*Scrophulariaceae*)
O. caespitosa gracilis   2in. Close mats of tiny rounded shining L on creeping rooting stems. FL ½in, white with yellow centre, lower 3 petals projecting forward as a lip. Half-shade in acid soil or peat-bed, or AH. D. New Zealand.

OXALIS (*Oxalidaceae*)   Herbaceous. Rhizomes fleshy or corm-like. L rounded, ½–1in, divided into lobes or segments. FL wide funnel-shaped. Gritty or sandy soil, usually in sun. D, S.
O. adenophylla   3in. Rhizome corm-like. L grey-green, divided into many segments, each deeply notched and folded. FL 1in, rose, centre paler. April–June. Chile.
O. enneaphylla   3in. Rhizome horizontal; otherwise very similar to *adeno-phylla*. FL white or rose. April–June. Half-shade. Falkland Is, Patagonia.
O. inops   3in. Root a small corm. L in 3 rounded overlapping leaflets. FL 1in rose, petals folded back. Appears late, flowers June–Aug. Multiplies abundantly by offsets. S Africa.
O. laciniata   2½in. L silver-grey, segments narrow and wrinkled. FL 1¼in, white, purple or blue-violet, darker in centre, veined. May–June. Scree or AH. Patagonia.
O. lobata   3in. Round corm. L ¾in, glaucous, 3 rounded notched lobes. FL golden-yellow with broad reflexed petals. Sept–Oct. Underground most of the year, so mark the spot! S America.

PAPAVER (*Papaveraceae*)   Poppy. Short-lived perennials. Scree or moraine. S.
P. myabeanum   8in. L coarsely cut, bristly. FL 1½in, lemon-yellow with green boss; buds pendent, brown-furred. June onwards. Japan.

P. sendtneri. Syn *alpinum*   10in. L glaucous, finely divided, in basal tufts. FL solitary 1½in, pendent in bud, white, pink or yellow with yellow boss. Alps. (*P. rhaeticum* from Pyrenees and E Alps is generally similar with yellow FL and long tap-root; more difficult.)

PARADISEA (*Liliaceae*)
P. liliastrum   St Bruno's Lily. 12in. Rhizome. L long narrow, grooved. FL narrow funnel-shaped, 1½in long, white with prominent stamens, in short one-sided spike. May–June. Rich soil in sun. D, S. European mtns.

PENSTEMON (*Scrophulariaceae*)   FL tubular, lower 3 petals turned down to form lip. Light well-drained soil in sun. Tend to be short-lived. C, S. N America.
P. albertinus   9in. L oval, pointed, smooth, long-stalked in basal tuft. FL ¾in long, ½in across, in close spike; lilac-blue with purple tube and throat. June–July.
P. heterophyllus   12in. L 2in very narrow, pointed. FL 1in long, blue with lilac tube and throat, in close leafy spike. June–July. Short-lived or frost-tender; best treated as annual. California.
P. menziesii   4in. Woody, prostrate. L small thick oval, toothed. FL 1½in, reddish-purple, profuse. June.
P. newberryi ('*roezlii*' of gardens)   6in. Shrubby, spreading. L small leathery oval, toothed, tinged red. FL 1in carmine, buds coral. May–June. (There are also taller forms of *newberryi*: true *roezlii* is blue and quite different.)
P. pinifolius   8in. Spreading rooting loose mat. L 1in, very narrow, pointed. FL ¾in, thin-tubed, coral, in few-flowered spikes. June–July. Scree. D, C.
P. scouleri   12in. Shrubby. L 1½in narrow-oval. FL large, lavender. May–Sept.

PETROCALLIS (*Cruciferae*)
P. pyrenaica. Syn *Draba pyrenaica*   1in. Flat neat mats. L ¼in deeply toothed in tight rosettes. FL ¼in 4-petalled, pink, scented. March–May. Scree or crevice. D. European mtns.

PETROCOPTIS (*Caryophyllaceae*)   Perennials with smooth L in basal tufts. FL ½in in loose sprays. S. N Spain, Pyrenees.
P. glaucifolia. Syns *P. lagascae*, *Lychnis lagascae*   6in. L 1in, oval, glaucous. FL rose-purple. May–June. Crevice or scree.
P. pyrenaica   3in. L ½in narrow-oval, pointed. FL white or pale pink. May–June. Crevice or scree.

PETROPHYTUM. Syn SPIRAEA (*Rosaceae*)   Close shrubby mats of L with sparse silky hairs. FL creamy-white with prominent stamens, in tight bottle-brush tufts. C, D, S. Western N America.

P. caespitosum   Similar to *hendersonii* but smaller in all its parts. AH.

P. hendersonii   3in. L 1in, oval in rosettes, pink-edged. FL-spikes 2in long. May–June. Scree.

PHLOX (*Polemoniaceae*)   FL with narrow tube and 5 flat open petals. D, C. N America.

P. adsurgens   8in. Loose straggling mats of 1in oval pointed shining L. FL ¾in, salmon-pink with darker striping. May–June. Calciphobe. Half-shade in acid soil or peat-bed.

P. bifida   6in. Lax mats of narrow pointed rough-edged 1½in L. FL 1in clear white or violet-tinged; petals deeply divided, Y-shaped. April–May. Sandy soil or scree. Sun.

P. divaricata. Syn *canadensis*   9in. L 1½in oblong in pairs on ascending stems. FL 1in, pale violet, petals notched, in loose heads on erect stems. April–May. Sun or half-shade.

P. douglasii   6in. Dense mats. L ½in narrowly triangular, pointed, rough-edged. FL nearly stemless covering the mats, ½in, white through lilac to violet. April–July. Light soil; sun. (Many named colour-forms, eg 'Snow Queen', 'Rose Queen', 'Violet Queen'.)

P. stolonifera   9in. Overground stolons. L 1½in, oval. FL 1in, lavender, in flattish heads on upright leafy stems. April–May. Half-shade.

P. subulata   8in. Large mats. L ¾in narrow pointed, crowded on stems. FL ¾in, wide colour-range, darker in centre, petals notched; solidly covering the mats. April–June. Light soil, sun. The best and easiest. Many named colour forms, eg 'Betty' (rose-pink), 'Four Winds' (salmon-pink), 'G. F. Wilson' (blue), 'Temiscaming' (magenta) and 'alba'.

PHUOPSIS (*Rubiaceae*)

P. stylosa. Syn *Crucianella stylosa*   9in. Long stems spreading from central tuft to form loose mat. L 1in narrow, pointed, hispid, in whorls. FL small 4-petalled pink in dense 1in heads. Attractive but smelly. May–June. Light soil in sun. D, S. Caucasus.

PHYLLODOCE (*Ericaceae*)   Small heath-like calciphobe shrubs for peat-bed. C, S.

P. coerulea. Syn *Menziesia coerulea*   8in. L ⅛in narrow thick blunt, in tufts at ends of stems. FL ⅓in, egg-shaped, pink to purple, pendent on separate stems in loose few-flowered terminal clusters. March–May. Alpine-Arctic, incl Scotland.

P. nipponica   5in. Similar to *coerulea* but FL bell-shaped, white or pale pink. Japan.

× PHYLLOTHAMNUS (*Ericaceae*)

× *P. erectus* (*Phyllodoce empetriformis* × *Rhodothamnus chamaecistus*)   8in. L ⅓in narrow, pointed, crowded. FL ½in cup-shaped, rose, erect on separate stems in clusters. April–May. Peat-bed. Garden origin. Better garden plant than either parent.

PHYTEUMA (*Campanulaceae*) Herbaceous. FL in tight heads, narrow tubular, often curved, petals joined at tips, separated at base; stigmas protruding: effect is of spiky heads.

P. comosum 6in. L 1¼in narrow-oval, pointed, toothed. FL-heads globular, 2in; FL lilac at expanded base, the joined petals forming a purple-black curved beak. June–July. Limestone crevice, scree or AH: protect from slugs. S. E and SE Alps on dolomite. (Fig 3, see p 21.)

P. scheuchzeri 12in. Fleshy roots. Basal L in rosettes, stalked, long heart-shaped, pointed, toothed; stem-L narrow, pointed. FL in dense spherical 1in heads, deep blue. May–July. Light soil; easy. Alps.

POLYGALA (*Polygalaceae*)

P. chamaebuxus 3in. Loose spreading shrubby, with underground stolons. L 1¼in narrow-oval, blunt, smooth. FL in loose clusters; petals in a narrow tube, clear yellow ageing to reddish-brown; sepals upright prominent, either creamy-white or rose-purple. Feb–May, and sometimes in autumn. Light shade or woodland; ? best in acid soil. C. European mtns. (Fig 13, see p 45.)

POLYGONATUM (*Liliaceae*)

P. hookeri 2in at flowering to 4in later. White fleshy roots. L 1½in narrow-oval, pointed, in rosettes forming close mats. FL ½in lilac, flat on short stems. May. Easy with good drainage. Appears late, dies down early. D. W China.

POLYGONUM (*Polygonaceae*)

P. affine 8in. L 3in narrow-oval, pointed, on spreading red stems. FL rose-pink, buds deeper, in dense 2½in spikes. May–July. Calciphobe. Acid soil or peat-bed. Forms dense mats when happy. D. Nepal. (Variable: 'Donald Lowndes' is a compact deep-coloured form.)

POTENTILLA (*Rosaceae*) Symmetrical 5-petalled flat to cup-shaped FL with central boss of stamens.

P. alba 3in. L in 5 spreading long-oval leaflets, toothed at tip, silvery below. FL ¾in white in loose sprays. March–May. S, D. E Europe.

P. eriocarpa 2in. Low tufts of glaucous L in 3 oval ¾in leaflets notched at tip. FL ¾in, light yellow, solitary on 2in stems. May–Sept. Good drainage; sun. D, S. Himalayas.

P. fruticosa Almost prostrate to erect (4ft) leaf-losing shrub. L divided into about 5 1in narrow blunt hairy leaflets. FL ½–1½in, yellow, abundant. April–Oct. C. N hemisphere incl Britain. Very variable; many named forms include:

> *arbuscula* Low, spreading. FL 1in, clear pale yellow.
>
> *beesiana* 12in. L silvery. FL ½in, mid-yellow.
>
> *farreri* 3ft upright. L small, dark green. FL ½in strong yellow, profuse.
>
> 'Tangerine' FL variably tinged orange.

P. glabrata 'Veitchii'. Syn *P. fruticosa* 'Veitchii' Very similar to *fruticosa* but FL white. China.

P. megalantha 8in. Herbaceous. L 2in in 3 broad overlapping ribbed coarsely toothed silky leaflets. FL 1¼in clear creamy-yellow in few-flowered leafy heads. April–June. Good drainage. D, S. Japan. (Plants sold as *fragiformis* and *villosa* appear to be very similar.)

P. nitida 2½in. Herbaceous. Flat dense mats of silvery L divided into three ¾in leaflets, notched at tips. FL 1 or 2 to a stem, rose-pink, darker centred, petals notched, ¾in. May–Sept. Scree. D, S. S Europe, usually on dolomite.

P. × tonguei 3in. Mats of green L with 3 to 5 toothed 1in leaflets. FL on short trailing branches, ¾in orange-yellow, red-centred; petals notched. June–Aug. Good drainage. D. Garden origin.

PRATIA (*Lobeliaceae*)

P. angulata. Syn *treadwellii* 2½in. Herbaceous. Mat of creeping rooting succulent stems. L thick oval coarsely toothed, ½in. FL ½in white starry; 5 petals, the two upper widely separated. Purple berries. May–Aug. Moist half-shady position in peaty soil. Slightly tender. D, S. New Zealand.

PRIMULA (*Primulaceae*) Mostly more or less herbaceous, dying down to resting bud. L all basal, generally in rosettes. FL regular 5-petalled, with narrow tube: shape as given under the species refers to the corolla beyond the tube, flat or nearly so unless otherwise stated. Many are covered with farina (white, sometimes yellow, fine powder) on flower stems and calyces as well as leaves.

P. auricula 4in. Rosette of oval to diamond-shaped blunt L, 1½–3in; with or without coarse teeth, white margin and farina. FL in one-sided umbel, ½–¾in, yellow, with spreading notched petals; fragrant. March–April. Crevice or scree. D, S. European mtns.

P. capitata 8in. Rosette of narrow-oval wrinkled coarsely toothed farinose 2½in L. FL in round heads, ¼–½in, flattish to cup-shaped, petals notched, deep purple with yellow central ring. May–July. Sandy peaty moist soil in sun or half-shade. Short-lived. S. SW China.

P. chionantha 10in. L upright in rosettes, 8in, narrow, farinose beneath, edges wavy and curling under. FL on short stalks in round head, ¾in, white, fragrant. April–June. Rich moist well-drained soil. s. Yunnan. (Lilac to purple forms may arise from seed—? hybrids with the closely related but more difficult species *melanops, sino-plantaginea, sino-purpurea*.)

P. *cockburniana*   10in. L 6in oval, wrinkled. FL short stemmed in loose whorls on long stalk, ½in, bright orange, petals notched. May–June. Rich moist soil; sun or half-shade. Short-lived. s. W China.

P. *denticulata*   10in. L up to 6in at flowering time, much bigger later, oval, wrinkled, slightly toothed. FL in tight round heads, ½in, lilac to purple, white, rose or deep red, yellow eye, petals notched. Feb–April. Rich soil; sun or half-shade; easy. s, D. Himalaya.

P. *farinosa*   Bird's-eye primrose. 8in. L in rosettes, 2½in, narrow-oval, bluntly toothed, white farinose. FL in round heads, ½in, pale to deep rose or white, yellow eye, petals notched. April–June. Wet scree, turf or bog. Short-lived. s. Europe incl Britain, Asia.

P. *frondosa*   6in. L 3in, oval, wrinkled, toothed, farinose. FL in loose heads, ½in, chalky pink with yellow eye and dark rose ring round it. Feb–April. Easy with good drainage; sun or half-shade. s, D. Balkans.

P. *glaucescens*   6in. L 2½in, narrow-oval, pointed, deep green, smooth, shining. FL 1in, primrose-like, pale to deep rose-purple with cream eye, in loose few-flowered heads. April–May. Rich well-drained soil. D, s. N Italy. (P. *spectabilis* is closely similar.)

P. *hirsuta*. Syn *rubra*   4in. L in rosette, 2in, broadly oval, coarsely toothed in upper half, narrowing with smooth edges to stalk. FL ¾in, primrose-like, pale pink to deep rose, white-centred, in loose umbel. March–April. Calciphobe. Lime-free scree or crevice. D, s. European mtns.

P. *ioessa*   9in. L in rosette, 3in, narrow-oval, wrinkled and toothed. FL pendent in close few-flowered head, bell-shaped, ¾in long, lilac or white. April–May. Rich soil in half-shade. Short-lived. s. Tibet.

P. *japonica*   18in. L in rosette, up to 12in, narrow-oblong, coarsely wrinkled and toothed. FL ¾in in whorls (tiers) on stout stems, primrose-shaped, white through rose to purple. April–June. Moist rich soil; sun or half-shade; ? calciphobe. s. Japan.

P. *marginata*   4in. L in rosettes, 3in, narrowly to broadly oval, coarsely toothed with white or yellow margin and farina. FL ½–¾in, flat to funnel-shaped, in loose heads, pale to deep blue-lilac with white or yellow eye, petals notched: variable. March–April. Scree or crevice. D, s. W Alps.

P. *nutans*   10in. L 5in narrow-oval, softly hairy. FL in very tight short heads, bell-shaped, ½in, soft violet-blue, scented. May–June. Monocarpic. Moist rich soil; sun or half-shade. s. China.

P. *polyneura*. Syns *lichiangensis, veitchii*   9in. L 3in, stalked, heart-shaped with large rounded teeth, downy. FL in loose rounded heads, 1in, primrose-

M

shaped, pale to deep rose-carmine with yellow eye. May–June. Rich moist soil; sun or half-shade. s, D. China.

P. pulverulenta 20in. L 8in long-oval, tapering to long stalk, wrinkled. FL in whorled tiers, ¾in, varying shades from purplish to brick red, pink or white. May–June. Moist rich soil, half-shade. s. China.

P. rosea 6in. L 3in at flowering time, narrow-oval, pointed, reddish with wide white centre vein, smooth. FL in loose head, 1in, primrose-shaped, glowing rose-carmine with yellow eye. March–April. Shallow water or bog. s, D. Himalaya.

P. secundiflora 18in. L 6in, upright, narrow, pointed. FL pendent in bunch on long stem, ¾in, bell-shaped, wine-red. May–June. Moist position, waterside. s, D. China.

P. sieboldii 10in. Spreading clump. L 6in, triangular with coarse round teeth, wrinkled, downy. FL in loose heads, 1in, primrose-shaped, pale to deep rose, purple or white, with white eye. April–May. Moist peaty soil. D, s. Japan.

P. sikkimensis 2ft. L to 12in, elliptic, coarsely toothed. FL pendent in loose tuft on tall stem, 1in, sulphur-yellow, bell-shaped. June. Rich soil, waterside. s, D. Himalaya, S China. (*P. s. pudibunda* is an alpine form, 1ft.)

P. vialii. Syn *littoniana* 12in. L upright, 8in, narrow, pointed, wrinkled, with rolled margins, downy. FL in tight spike, ¼in, bell-shaped, lilac; sepals and buds, and hence upper part of spike, rich crimson. May–July. Rich moist well-drained soil. s. S China.

P. viscosa 6in. L 3in oval, slightly sticky glandular, leathery, coarsely toothed, smelly. FL in round bunched head, 1in, wide funnel shaped, soft violet, fragrant, petals notched. April–May. Crevice or scree. ? Calciphobe. s. Pyrenees, W Alps.

PTEROCEPHALUS (*Dipsaceae*)

P. parnassi 2½in. Mat of 1in oval toothed L. FL-heads like scabious, 1¼in across, lavender-pink. July–Sept. Scree, crevice or wall; sun. D, s. Greece.

PTILOTRICHUM (*Cruciferae*)

P. spinosum. Syn *Alyssum spinosum* 9in. Rounded shrub, tips of old wood spiny. L 1in narrow, pointed, silvery. FL ¼in, 4-petalled, white or purplish-pink, in tight rounded 1in heads. May–July. Sun. c, s. Spain, S France.

PULMONARIA (*Boraginaceae*)

P. angustifolia 9in. L 7in, narrowly elliptic, pointed, soft, bristly. FL tubular opening to ½in at mouth, brilliant blue, rose-purple in bud, in one-sided heads. March–April. Half-shade. D. C Europe.

PULSATILLA (*Ranunculaceae*) 'Anemones' with stout root-bundles and close tufts of hairy dissected L. FL 5 or more petals with boss of stamens, showy. Ring of dissected L forming 'ruff' below FL. Seeds with long plumes. More or less herbaceous, old L mostly dying in autumn. S (sow fresh), D (in early spring: they resent disturbance).

P. *alpina*. Syn *Anemone alpina* 18in. L 12in ferny. FL solitary, to 2½in, white, backed grey, blue, green or purple. May. Deep rich limy soil. European mtns. (Ssp *apiifolia*, syn *sulphurea* is very similar, with sulphur-yellow FL: calciphobe. Both plants very variable in size and height.)

P. *vernalis* 6in (more in fruit). L 2½in, stalked, cut into blunt toothed segments , usually persisting in winter. FL 2in, globular, white inside, externally green, blue, pink or purple with sheen of golden hairs. 'Ruff' densely covered externally with golden-brown silky hairs. April. Rich scree or AH; shy-flowering in open. European mtns.

P. *vulgaris*. Syn *Anemone pulsatilla* 10in. L 6in, more or less finely dissected. FL 2in, pale to rich purple, stamens golden. March–May. Rich limy soil in sun. Europe incl Britain. (Variable in size and colour: there are white and wine-red forms.)

PUSCHKINIA (*Liliaceae*)

P. *scilloides*. Syn *libanotica* 4in. Bulbous. L few, 4in, ¾in broad, shining, blunt. FL ¾in, pale bluish-white with blue central line down each petal; column of white stamens; loose short spikes: scilla-like. Feb–April. D, S. Asia.

RAMONDA (*Gesneriaceae*)

R. *myconi*. Syn *pyrenaica* 6in. L 3in in rosette, broadly oval, coarsely toothed, wrinkled, softly hairy. FL 2 or 3 to a stem, 1in, 5-petalled, regular, bluish to reddish-violet, pink, or white, with yellow 'beak' of stamens. May–June. Humus-containing north-facing crevice: avoid drought. S, LEAF-CUTTINGS. Pyrenees. (*nathaliae* from Macedonia and Bulgaria, and *serbica* from Macedonia are very similar.) (Fig 4, see p 24.)

RANUNCULUS (*Ranunculaceae*) L mostly at base. FL regular, buttercup-shaped: the white-flowered species often produce small or defective petals.

R. × *ahrendsii* (*amplexicaulis* × *gramineus*) 9in. Herbaceous. L 6in, up to ½in wide, grass-like or broader. FL 1in, several to stem, cream with orange stamens. Somewhat variable. March–May. D. Garden origin.

R. *alpestris* 3in. Herbaceous. L ¾in, rounded in outline, deeply dissected but segments overlapping. FL ¾in, white. April–June. Scree, moraine or turf; avoid drought. European Alps. Generally similar are *traunfellneri* (L deeply cut, segments thinner), *crenatus* (L toothed rather than cut) and *bilobus* (L lobed)—all from E Alps.

R. *amplexicaulis* 9–18in. L to 6in, narrow-oval, sometimes heart-shaped at base, tending to sheathe stem. FL to 1½in, white, solitary or several on a branching leafy stem. Variable. April–May. Turf; avoid drought. S. Pyrenees, N Spain.

R. *asiaticus* 9–15in. Herbaceous. Basal L uncut or few segments, stem L finely divided. FL ¾–2in, white, pink, rose, scarlet, cream or yellow, with black central boss. Jan (in AH)–May. Tender: protected bed or AH. Summer 'baking'. S, D. E Mediterranean.

R. *gramineus* 10in. L 9in, grass-like. FL 1in clear yellow buttercups. April–May. Easy. S, D. SW Europe.

R. *parnassifolius* 3in. L ¾in, round heart-shaped, ribbed, silky. FL several to a stem, ¾in, cup-shaped, white with pink veining. April–May. High screes. Moraine or AH. S, D. European mtns. (Fig 2, see p 20.)

R. *pyrenaeus* 4in. L 3in, narrow, more or less grass-like. FL like *alpestris*. March–May. Flowers at edge of snow. Scree, damp turf or moraine. S. European mtns.

R. *seguieri* 4in. L 1½in, rounded in outline, deeply and finely cut. FL 1in, clear white with golden boss. April–May. Limestone moraine. S. High altitudes in European mtns.

RHODODENDRON (*Ericaceae*) Evergreen shrubs with more or less bell-or funnel-shaped FL in clusters. Generally calciphobe, requiring acid soil or peat-bed. A large genus with many species and hybrids suitable for a large rock garden on lime-free soil. D, C. The following are selected as especially dwarf and suitable for a small rock garden or peat-bed.

R. *ferrugineum* 'Alpenrose'. To 3ft but usually much smaller. L 1¼in, narrow-oval, dark green and shiny above, rusty brown below. FL 6 to 12, ¾in, pale to deep rose-scarlet. June. Sun; good drainage. Alps.

R. *hanceanum nanum* 12in. L 1½in oval. FL 1in yellow. March–April. Buds subject to frost damage. China.

R. *hirsutum* 'Alpenrose.' Like *ferrugineum*, but L 1in, pointed oval, bright green, long hairs on margins. June. Turf or scree in sun; *not* calciphobe. Alps.

R. *impeditum* 12in, compact, rounded. L ½in, oval, grey-green. FL 1 or 2, in mauve. May. China.

R. *keleticum* To 12in. L ¾in, pointed oval, shining. FL 1 or 2, ¾in, reddish-purple. May–June. Tibet.

R. *leucaspis* 18in, open spreading. L 1¼in, round-oval soft hairy. FL 2in, white with dark brown anthers, opening almost flat: distinct. March in AH. Borderline hardy: protected bed or AH. Tibet.

R. *pemakoense* 10in, spreading and rooting. L ¾in, oval. FL 1 or 2, 1¼in, funnel-shaped, pinkish-purple. March–April. Buds liable to frost damage. Tibet.

R. *radicans* 4in, prostrate. L ⅓in, narrow oval, slightly hairy. FL solitary, 1in, purple, opening nearly flat. May–June. Tibet.

R. *scintillans* 2ft, erect. L narrow-oval, pointed, ¾in, shiny, grey beneath. FL in clusters, ¼in, pale to deep blue-purple. April. China.

RHODOHYPOXIS (*Hypoxidaceae*)

R. *baurii* 4in. Small round tuber. L grass-like, softly hairy. FL solitary, ¾in on 4in stems, 6-petalled, the inner 3 narrower, opening flat from a short tube, pale to deep rose. April–June. ? Calciphobe: sun or half-shade in peaty soil, moist in summer. Hardy but vulnerable to winter wet. S, D. S Africa. (Var *platypetala* is white.)

RHODOTHAMNUS (*Ericaceae*) Near to *Rhododendron*.

R. *chamaecistus* 8in, straggly shrub. L ½in, narrow-oval, hairy-edged. FL 2 to 4 in a loose cluster, ¾in, flat with projecting stamens, pink to rose-purple. April–May. Buds frost-tender. On dolomitic limestone in the wild, but best treated as calciphobe in well-drained peaty soil in half-shade. S, C, LAYERS. E Alps, Siberia.

ROMULEA (*Iridaceae*) Corms. Crocus-like, but L do not have central white vein and flowers have short stalks. S, D.

R. *bulbocodium* 3in. FL 2in, violet with yellow centre, inner 3 petals smaller than outer. March–May. Rich well-drained soil. Fully hardy. Mediterranean.

R. *clusiana* 4in. FL larger and more yellow. May. Doubtfully hardy. Protected bed or AH. Spain.

R. *longituba alticola*. Syn '*Syringodea sp*' 2in, but L to 9in, spreading. FL 2in, clear yellow, darker centred. Sept–Oct. Hardy. Sun; good drainage. Basutoland.

ROSA (*Rosaceae*)

R. *pendulina pyrenaica*. Syn *R. alpina pyrenaica* 10in. A low-growing spreading form of the almost thornless alpine rose. FL like dog-roses, 2in, deep rose. Hips narrowly flask-shaped, coral. Easy with good drainage. C, S. Pyrenees.

ROSCOEA (*Zingiberaceae*) Fleshy roots. L lance-shaped clasping stem. FL few in leafy spike, more or less crowded; 'orchid-like' with long tube, erect upper petal, 2 lateral petals and broad lip. Rich moist soil in part-shade; plant deeply. D, S. China.

R. *cautleoides* 15in. L narrow (½in). Buds and calyces red, FL 2½in long, sulphur-yellow. May–July.

R. *humeana* 9in. L broader (1in). FL 2in long, pale to deep purple. July–Sept.

SANGUINARIA (*Papaveraceae*)
S. canadensis   8in. Thick rhizome with red sap. L to 4in, I per flower, heart-shaped, blue-grey, scalloped, sheathing stem. FL 1½in, white; petals narrow, about 10; central boss of stamens. (*S. c. plena* has rounded tufts of many petals.) May (FL are very transient). Rich soil, half-shade or woodland. S, D. Eastern N America.

SAPONARIA (*Caryophyllaceae*)   Mats or cushions. FL 5-petalled, regular, flat on tubular calyx.
S. caespitosa   3in. L 1in, narrow, pointed, in tufts. FL ½in, pink, with purple hairy calyx, in small heads, trailing. June–July. Scree. S, C. Pyrenees.
S. ocymoides 'ruba compacta'   3in loose mat. L ¾in, oval hairy. FL ½in, crimson, in flat heads covering mat. May–June. Sun; scree or rock face. C. European mtns. (The type plant is very variable, often looser, larger, paler-flowered.)
S. × *olivana* (*pumilio* × *caespitosa*)   2in. Close firm cushion. L 1in, narrow, pointed, shiny. FL 1in, chalky pink, with baggy calyx, on short few-flowered stems trailing round edge of cushion. May–June. Scree. C (Occasionally sets a few seed, which produce interesting hybrids.) Garden origin. (Better and easier than either parent.)

SATUREJA (*Labiatae*)
S. subspicata   9in. Aromatic herb, shrubby at base. L 1in, narrow, pointed. FL rose-purple in best forms, tubular with hood and 3-lobed lip, ¼in across, in short close spikes. Aug–Sept. Sun. C, S. Balkans.

SAXIFRAGA (*Saxifragaceae*)   A large genus of plants many of which are suitable for the rock garden. FL 5-petalled, usually regular and flat to saucer-shaped. The genus is divided into 15 sections: most of the species, hybrids and varieties here described fall into three of these sections, viz Kabschia, Encrusted and Mossy. The Kabschias are conveniently subdivided into the true Kabschias and the Englerias, though the two hybridise.
   (I)   Kabschias. Compact, often hard, mats or cushions of tiny rosettes of hard, often lime-encrusted L. One to several large FL on short stems. Jan–March. Better with lime except *lilacina*; sharp scree in sun or light shade (avoid scorching); or AH in view of early flowering. A few good species and a vast range of hybrids of which a small selection are here included.
   (II)   Englerias. Tight or loose mats of small-leaved rosettes. FL-spikes curled over in bud. FL small, petals inconspicuous, but stems and swollen calyces deep red. March–April. Scree, crevice or AH.
   (III)   Encrusted (Silver) saxifrages. Small to large rosettes. L silvery with lime-incrustations, usually more or less strap-shaped. FL in long arching sprays. May–June. Mostly better on lime; sparse soil or crevice; sun.

(IV) Mossy saxifrages. L cut into segments. Large loose spreading mats. FL in flattish sprays, solidly covering the mats. April–May. Good soil in light shade; avoid scorching. Most of the Mossies grown are hybrids of mixed parentage and garden origin: there are a great many and only a few examples are named here. The species are rarer, more difficult and generally less showy.

The unnumbered species fall into other sections. Except where stated, all saxifrages are hardy, and can be propagated by cuttings (usually isolated rosettes) or division, and the species by seed.

S. *aizoides* 4in. Loose mats of narrow blunt thick shiny ¾in L. FL ½in, narrow-petalled with prominent ovary, yellow, often with red spots, or orange or blood-red. April–June. Gritty soil, damp; N-facing or by waterside. N hemisphere, incl Britain, arctic to alpine.

S. × *apiculata*. (I) (*S. marginata rocheliana* × *sancta*) 5in. Firm mats. L ½in, green, smooth, blunt, slightly encrusted. FL ½in, clear pale yellow (white in var *alba*) in rather tight heads on leafy stems. Good, easy. ? Garden origin.

S. 'Bridget'. (I × II) (*marginata* × *stribrnyi*) 6in. Small hummocks of tiny hard rosettes of glaucous blunt ¾in L. FL several on red hairy leafy upright stems, ½in, pale pink, cup-shaped, calyces red.

S. *burserana* (= *burseriana*) (I) 2in. Neat mats. L ¼in, narrow, pointed, glaucous, inwardly curved in tight small rosettes. FL ½in, white (sulphur yellow in *S. b. sulphurea*, probably a hybrid) in few-flowered sprays on red stems. Variable in size. E Alps, usually on dolomite.

S. *callosa*. Syn *lingulata* (III) 12in. Hard mats of 2in rosettes. L narrow, broadening towards tip. FL ½in, white, sometimes red-spotted, on graceful loose red-stemmed sprays. W Mediterranean.

S. *cebennensis* (IV) 3in. L ½in with three blunt teeth, light green, glandular hairy. FL ¾in, clear white, full-petalled, 2 to 3 on a stem. Cevennes.

S. *cochlearis* (III) 6in. Tight hard mats. L ¼–½in, narrow, blunt, silver glaucous. FL white, rather narrow-petalled, funnel-shaped, in loose sprays on red stems. (Variable. *S. c. minor* is very small and compact.) Maritime Alps.

S. *cotyledon* (III) 18in. L 2in strap-shaped, round-tipped. FL ½in, variously marked or spotted with red, along the length of large pyramidal arched and branching sprays. Variable. N hemisphere, arctic and alpine.

S. 'Cranbourne' (I) 1in. Close hummocky mats of ⅛in glaucous lime-encrusted down-turned L. FL ½in rose-pink, stemless. Garden origin.

S. *exarata* (IV) 2½in. Close soft mat. L ¼in wedge-shaped, 3-lobed, in congested rosettes. FL ¼in, creamy white, several to a stem. Not easy. Scree or AH. European mtns.

S. *ferdinandi-coburgii* (I) 2in. Hard compact cushions, L ¼in glaucous, narrow, pointed, curved inward. FL golden-yellow, ½in, several to a reddish stem. Balkans.

S. 'Flowers of Sulphur'   (IV) 4in. Pale yellow-flowered mossy hybrid.

S. fortunei   12in. L 2½in, round, blunt-toothed, glossy, leathery, long-stalked, green becoming red, under-sides red. FL ½in white, the lower petals longer and toothed; in loose many-flowered sprays. Oct. Liable to frost damage. Rich moist soil in half-shade; calciphobe. China, Japan.

S. grisebachii   (II) 6in. L heavily silvered, especially at edges, neatly arranged in many-tiered pyramidal rosettes, lowest L larger (1¼in). FL-stems leafy, hooked at tip; stems, bases of L and buds and calyces deep crimson with velvety hairs. ('Wisley form' is usually grown—rosettes larger and fewer, stem-leaves totally red.) Balkans.

S. 'Iris Pritchard'   (I) 2½in. Generally like *burserana* but FL an unusual apricot colour.

S. 'Jenkinsae'. (I) (*burserana* × *lilacina*)   1½in. Wide, close hummocky mats. L tiny, pointed, silvery glaucous. FL ½in, solitary, rose-pink, darker centred. Very early; weather-resistant. Excellent.

S. juniperifolia sancta   (I) 2½in. Thick mat of rosettes of narrow pointed ½in emerald L. FL ¼in, strong yellow in bunched heads. Robust: starve for free flowering. Greece, Asia Minor.

S. 'Kathleen Pinsent'   (III) A *callosa* hybrid. FL rose-pink in loose sprays. Good but not robust.

S. lilacina   (I) 1½in. Spreading hummocky mat of minute rosettes of ⅛in down-turned silver glaucous L. FL ½in, solitary, lilac-pink, darker centred, almost stemless. Calciphobe. Not easy. Scree in half-shade (avoid drought), moraine, or AH. Himalaya.

S. longifolia   (III) 2ft. L very long, narrow, strap-shaped, blunt, glaucous, lime-edged, in beautiful tight flat spiral rosette up to 1ft across. FL ½in, white sometimes spotted red, in huge pyramidal branching spray. Flowers after 5–7 years, then dies. Crevice or wall. Pyrenees, E Spain.

S. marginata   (I) 6in. Tight rosettes of ¼in oval blunt glaucous pitted L (larger in var *rocheliana*). FL ¾in, white, funnel-shaped, several to a flattish spray. Apennines to Carpathians.

S. 'Maria Luisa'   (I) 2in. Clumps of ½in rosettes of small spiky glaucous en-crusted L. FL ¾in, white, flat, full-petalled, stems and buds reddish. Early.

S. media   (II) 4in. Similar to *grisebachii* but L pointed and FL-spikes shorter and less red. Pyrenees.

S. × *megasaeflora*   (I) 2½in. Foliage like *burserana*. FL 2 or 3 to a stem, ¾in, warm pink, darker centred, petals separated and clawed.

S. oppositifolia   Purple saxifrage. 1½in. Loose trailing mats. L tiny, oval, lime-encrusted, tightly packed in alternating pairs towards ends of stems. FL ¾in, full-petalled, cup-shaped, solitary on very short stems, pale clear pink to deep rose-purple, or white. Very variable in size, colour and compact-ness. March–April. Not always easy: probably clones vary; some at least are calciphobe. Scree or crevice facing N or W; avoid drought or scorching. N hemisphere, incl Britain; arctic to alpine.

S. paniculata. Syn *aizoon* (III) To 12in. Rosettes ½–2in. L oblong, wider and blunt at tip, encrusted round edges. FL usually creamy white (rose and pale yellow in forms 'rosea' and 'lutea'), ½in, in flattish sprays towards ends of more or less upright stems. Variable; many named forms. (*S. a. baldensis* from Monte Baldo is particularly compact.) Europe and N America; arctic to alpine.

S. pentadactylis (IV) 4in. Loose domes, small for a 'mossy'. L thin, hard, dark green, with stalk-like blade dividing into 3 to 5 long thin straight fingers. FL to ½in, white, several in a flattish head on red wiry stems. Variable. Calciphobe. Scree. Spain.

S. retusa 1in. Flat spreading mats of minute curved triangular dark green pitted L. FL ¼in, several on a flat 1in spray, clear rose-pink with darker centre and stamens, narrow petalled. March–April. Calciphobe. Very gritty soil. Best in AH. High altitudes in European mtns.

S. 'sanguinea superba' (IV) 9in. Hybrid mossy with large (⅜in) cup-shaped, deep crimson, non-fading FL.

S. scardica (I) 4in. Mats of rosettes of ¾in narrow, spiky, encrusted L. FL ½in, white or pinkish, several to a head; stems and calyces red. Avoid full sun. Macedonia.

S. sempervivum. Syn *porophylla thessalica* (II) 4in. Tufts of tight rosettes of hard pointed silvery ½in L. FL similar to *media*. Balkans.

S. 'Stormonth' (IV) 3in. Neat small-leaved compact hybrid mossy, with abundant small (¼in) FL, creamy-white or rose.

S. 'Tumbling Waters' (*longifolia* × *callosa*) (III) Similar to *longifolia* but FL-sprays are laxer and should be allowed to hang; and offsets are produced, allowing propagation. Slow-growing.

S. umbrosa 'primuloides' 10in. Mats of 2in rosettes of oval blunt-toothed glossy L. FL ½in, white with pink spots, in loose sprays on upright wiry red stems. A small 'London Pride'. May–June. Light soil in sun or half-shade. D, C. Pyrenees. ('Elliott's Variety', neater and with rose-pink crimson-centred FL, is better.)

S. 'Wallacei' (IV) Similar to 'sanguinea superba' but FL clear white

S. 'Winifred' (I) 2in. Like 'Cranbourne' but FL larger, fuller, good rose, deeper centred.

SCABIOSA (*Dipsaceae*)

S. graminifolia 12in. Loose tufts. L to 6in, narrow, pointed, silvery, grass-like. FL-heads typical scabious, 2in, lilac. June onwards. Light soil; sun. S. S Europe.

SCHIZOCODON (*Diapensiaceae*)

S. *soldanelloides* 3in. Mat of round or heart-shaped, glossy, red-tinged, bluntly toothed, 1in L, turning crimson in autumn. FL 1in, bell-shaped, fringed, pale pink, deeper centred, in few-flowered heads. March–April. Calciphobe. Rich moist, peaty soil, well-drained, in shade. S, D, C. Japan.

SCILLA (*Liliaceae*)   Bulbous. L long, narrow, glossy. FL flat to cup-shaped, petals separate to base. S, OFFSETS.

S. *autumnalis*   Autumn squill. 9in. L 6 × ⅛in, following FL. FL ¼in in tight spikes, lengthening as seed develops, reddish-lilac or white. July–Sept. Light soil. Europe incl Britain, N Africa.

S. *bifolia*   4in. L two, 4 × ½in, folded, hooded at tip. FL ½in, bright blue with blue stamens (or white or rose) in loose one-sided sprays. Feb–April. Easy in light soil; sun or shade; spreads abundantly. Jura to Mediterranean.

S. *italica*   9in. L bluebell-like. FL ¼in in dense 3in spikes, china blue. March–May. Light shade or woodland. S France, Italy.

S. *messeniaca*   Similar to the last, but spikes looser and fewer-flowered. Greece.

S. *pratensis*   9in. L 9in, narrow, grass-like. FL less than ¼in, lilac-blue, tubular at base, starry, in short close heads. May–June. Sun. Yugoslavia.

S. *siberica*   6in. L 4 × ½in, folded. FL ¾in, strong greenish-blue with darker centre stripe on petals, broad funnel-shaped, down-turned, few to a loose spike. Feb–April. Easy in good soil in sun. Siberia.

S. *tubergeniana*   Generally like *siberica* but L flatter and FL very pale blue with darker central stripe. (Superficially identical with *Puschkinia scilloides*.) Feb–March. Persia.

S. *verna*   Spring squill. 6in. L 9 × ⅛in, arching downwards. FL ½in, very pale china blue with dark blue stamens, starry cup-shaped, in flat heads just clear of L. May–June. ? Calciphobe. Sandy peaty soil; sun. Europe incl Britain.

SCORZONERA (*Compositae*)

S. *rosea*   9in. L 4in grass-like. FL-heads like a hawk-weed, 1in, pale to deep rose. June–July. Light soil in sun. D, S. SE Alps.

SCUTELLARIA (*Labiatae*)   Herbaceous. FL tubular with lip, upper petals joined to form a 'beak'. Light soil in sun. D, S.

S. *alpina*   6in. Loose mats of oval, toothed, wrinkled 1in L. FL 1in long in bunched heads, lip lilac, beak purple. May–Oct. European mtns, Asia.

S. *scordiifolia*   6in. Little white knobbly rhizomes. Loose mats. L narrow-oval, toothed, wrinkled, ¾in. FL ¾in, deep purple with white streaks on lip, in loose leafy spikes. June–Oct. N Asia.

SEDUM (*Crassulaceae*) L more or less fleshy. FL regular, usually 5-petalled, starry, in flattened heads. Dry light soil in sun. D, C, S. Nearly all kinds are more or less rampant.

S. *album*   White stonecrop. 6in. Loose mats. L to ½in, succulent, cylindrical, in crowded non-flowering spikes. FL white with red stamens, ½in in loose heads on upright pink stems. June–Aug. Europe incl Britain, W Asia, N Africa. (Var *murale* has brownish foliage.)

S. *cauticola*   4in. Loose hanging mat of round, slightly toothed 1½in L, glaucous, crimson-tinged. FL ½in, rose-purple, in flat trailing trusses. Aug–Oct. Wall or rock-face. Japan.

S. *ewersii*   6in. Mat of trailing stems with pairs of 1in glaucous, red-edged, rounded L. FL ⅓in, purplish-pink in flat sprays on upright crimson stems. July–Sept. Himalayas.

S. *kamtschaticum*   8in. Mound of more or less upright stems set with narrow, toothed, glossy 1½in L. FL ½in, golden-yellow 'fading' to reddish-brown. June–Aug. Kamchatka. (There is a variegated form, less robust.)

S. *middendorffianum*   6in. Like a smaller, neater, more compact *kamtschaticum*. NE Asia.

S. *oreganum*   6in. L ¾in, fat, spoon-shaped, shiny, red-tinged, in tight rosettes. FL ½in, golden-yellow, somewhat funnel-shaped, on red-brown stems. June–Aug. Western N America.

S. *populifolium*   To 1ft. Loosely spreading, twiggy at base. L diamond to heart-shaped, to 1½in, jagged toothed, stalked. FL ½in pale pink in dense flat heads on leafy stems. Aug. Siberia.

S. *reflexum*   9in. Mats of upright stems. L ¾in, cylindrical, pointed, dense on non-flowering stems. FL ½in, yellow, in flat sprays on red upright stems with down-turned L. June–Aug. Europe incl Britain.

S. *spathulifolium*   3in. Mats of rosettes of rounded, flat, thick, smooth, glaucous, white-bloomed L. FL ½in, yellow, in flat sprays, May–June. Western N America. (Var *purpureum* has purplish L, and 'Capablanca' is very neat with small densely white L.)

S. *spurium*   6in. Mats of bright green, glossy, 1in, close-packed, round, blunt-toothed L. FL ⅔in, rose-pink in flat heads. June–July. Caucasus.

SELLIERA (*Goodeniaceae*)

S. *radicans*   2in. Rooting mat of 1in narrow smooth L, broader towards tip. FL single, white, half-funnel-shaped with the 5 narrow petals pointing downwards. July. Moist peaty soil. Slightly tender. D. New Zealand, Australia, Chile. (Fig 26, see p 75.)

SEMIAQUILEGIA (*Ranunculaceae*)

S. *simulatrix*. Syns *Aquilegia ecalcarata*, *Semiaquilegia ecalcarata*   12in. Habit, and divided L, like a small columbine. FL in loose sprays, 1in, pendent, dark reddish-violet, like a columbine without spurs. May. Light soil in sun. S. China.

SEMPERVIVUM (*Crassulaceae*) Houseleek. L fleshy, in tight rosettes, spreading by stolons. FL regular with 6 to 20 petals, usually starry, in flat, sometimes branched, cluster on leafy stem. Sun; dry soil, rock or crevice. D.

S. *arachnoideum* 4in. Rosettes ¼–2in. L soft, green, oval, pointed, curled into rosette, the tips connected with cobweb-like hairs. FL ¾in, petals rose-pink with darker centre streak; yellow central boss. June–Aug. European mtns.

S. *ciliosum* 4in. Rosettes globular, 1½in. L many, narrow, pointed, incurved, red-tipped, fringed with white bristles. FL ¾in, lemon-yellow. Macedonia.

S. *montanum* 4in. Rosettes 1¼in, flattish. L often red-tipped, minutely downy. FL 1in, few to a head, wine-red. May–July. European mtns.

S. *tectorum* Common houseleek. 10in. Rosettes to 4in, flattish, of relatively few thick, flat, hard, oval, concave, pointed, glaucous, red-tipped, smooth L. FL 1in, dull purplish-red, numerous in flat branching sprays. June–July. European mtns incl Britain. (Variable, with many named varieties and cultivars.)

S. *wulfenii* 8in. Rosettes 2in. L like *tectorum* but paler bluish-green and hairy at edges. FL ¾in, yellow, purple-centred. July. ? Calciphobe. E Alps.

SHORTIA (*Diapensiaceae*)

S. *uniflora* 4in. Mat of oval, blunt-toothed, glossy, 1in L, bright green, red-tinged, red in autumn. FL 1½in, wide funnel-shaped, white or pale pink, petals irregularly toothed. March–May. Calciphobe. Sandy peaty soil, well-drained, in half-shade. D, C (resents disturbance). Carolina, Formosa, Japan.

SILENE (*Caryophyllaceae*) L opposite, entire. FL 5-petalled, regular, flat on tubular calyx.

S. *acaulis* Moss campion. 2in. Close mat of narrow glossy pointed ¼–½in. L. FL ¼–½in solitary, stemless in *S. a. exscapa* to 1in stems in *S. a. longiscapa*; pale to deep pink, or white, petals slightly notched. April–June. Scree or well-drained turf, AH. D, C, S. N hemisphere incl Britain; arctic to alpine.

S. *alpestris*. Syn *Heliosperma alpestre* 6in. Loose mats. L ¾in, narrow, pointed. FL in loose sprays, ½in, petals 4-toothed. May–June. Well-drained soil or scree in sun. D, S. E Alps.

S. *armeria* 9in. Annual. L 1½in, oval, smooth glaucous. FL ½in, brilliant cerise to magenta, in flat branching sprays. June onwards. Light soil; sun. Maintains itself by seeding. Europe. (*S. compacta* from W Asia is almost identical.)

S. hookeri Syn *Melandrium hookeri* 2½in. Herbaceous. L 2in, narrow-oval, slightly downy, on sprawling 4in stems. FL single, 1½in, salmon-pink with darker scales at throat, each petal cut into 2 main lobes and 2 short narrow side-lobes, giving a slashed appearance. May–July. Moraine or AH; protect from winter wet; not easy. S. California.

S. pusilla   4in. A smaller and neater version of *alpestris* from S and C Europe.

S. schafta   6in. Herbaceous. L 1in, narrow-oval, in soft loose mat. FL 1 or 2 to a stem, 1in, carmine, petals narrow at base and separated, notched. July–Sept. Light soil; sun. S, D. Caucasus.

SISYRINCHIUM (*Iridaceae*)   Thick fibrous roots. L folded, sheathing stem like *Iris*. FL regular 6-petalled. S, D.

S. angustifolium   Blue-eyed grass. 9in. L narrow, grass-like. FL ½in, flat, starry, pale to deep blue, or white, in small clusters at tip of stem, only one open at a time. May–June. Sun. N America, naturalised in Britain. (A sterile form of this or *bermudianum* is a better garden plant.)

S. bermudianum   10in. Similar to the last, but L a little broader and FL slightly fuller, violet. Bermuda.

S. brachypus   4in. L to ½in wide. FL clear yellow. June–July. SE USA.

S. douglasii. Syn *grandiflorum*   9in. L narrow, grass-like. FL narrow funnel-shaped, 1in long, rich satiny violet, or white. Feb–April. Well-drained peaty soil in half-shade. N America. (Fig 25, see p 73.)

S. filifolium   9in. L cylindrical, rush-like. FL ¾in, white, purple-veined, bell-shaped. May. Well-drained peaty soil. Falkland Is.

SOLDANELLA (*Primulaceae*)   Flat clumps of small, thick, flat, round, stalked L. FL pendent, tubular to funnel-shaped, fringed. Buds form in autumn and are frequently destroyed (? slugs) in winter. Wet turf, bog, moraine or AH; difficult to flower well. D, S.

S. alpina   3in. L to 1in, mostly smaller. FL 2 or 3 to a stem, ⅔in, funnel-shaped, fringed to half their length, violet. Feb–March. European mtns.

S. montana   6in. Similar but larger. L shallowly toothed. Petals more deeply fringed. Feb–March. European mtns. (Subsp *villosa*, Pyrenees, is more robust and easier.) (Fig 7, see p 37.)

SPIRAEA (*Rosaceae*)   Deciduous shrubs. FL ¼in, regular 5-petalled, in many-flowered flat clusters. Good soil in sun. D, S.

S. bullata   12in. L 1in, rounded, toothed. FL rose-pink. July–Aug. Japan.

S. japonica 'Bumalda'   12in. L 1½in, oval to heart-shaped, coarsely toothed. FL rose-pink. June–Aug. Japan.

STERNBERGIA (*Amaryllidaceae*)

S. lutea   6in. Bulbous. L 6in, narrow, strap-shaped. FL crocus-like but shortly stalked, clear yellow, 2½in. Sept–Nov. Sparse soil; sun. D (OFFSETS). C and S Europe.

SYRINGA (*Oleaceae*)

S. palibiniana   To 3ft. Like common lilac but smaller in all its parts. FL-trusses 3in, pale lilac, May–June. Light soil in sun: prune to required size. C. Korea.

TEUCRIUM (*Labiatae*)   FL. Upper lip usually very inconspicuous, lower long with 2 side-lobes. Light well-drained soil in sun. D, C, S.

T. ackermannii   8in. Herbaceous. Mat of 1½in narrow, silvery, blunt-toothed L. FL ½in, dark reddish-purple, in flattened many-flowered heads. June–Aug. Asia Minor.

T. chamaedrys   Wall germander. 10in. Herbaceous. L 1in oblong, blunt-toothed. FL in loose whorls on leafy stems, ½in, pale to deep purplish-pink. July–Sept. Dry places, walls; sun. Europe incl Britain.

T. marum   8in. Old branches spiky. L ¼in, narrow-oval, whitish beneath, with distinctive strong aromatic smell. FL ⅓in, rose-purple, in narrow spikes. July–Sept. Beloved of cats. W Mediterranean. (This or a closely allied species is frequently offered as '*Micromeria corsica*'.)

T. polium.   Syn *aureum*   6in dome of hoary-white ¾in oval, toothed L on woolly white stems. FL ⅓in, yellow, in flat 1in heads. July–Aug. W Asia.

T. pyrenaicum   4in. Herbaceous. Spreading rooting mat of ¾in rounded, blunt-toothed, wrinkled, glossy L. FL ½in, lip cream, upper petals purple, in flat 2in heads. June–July. Pyrenees, French Alps.

THALICTRUM (*Ranunculaceae*)

T. kiusianum   3in. Herbaceous. L divided into ⅓in, lobed, fine-stalked leaflets. FL ⅓in, pendulous, in few-flowered loose clusters; petals small, purple; stamens prominent, purple. May–July. Scree or AH. D. Japan. (*T. coreanum* is very similar.)

T. orientale   6in. Leaflets ½in, divided, lobed, glaucous. FL ¾in, deep lilac, 3 or 4 in a loose spray. April (in AH). Scree or AH. S. Greece, Asia Minor.

THLASPI (*Cruciferae*)

T. rotundifolium   2in. Roots fleshy. Small dense tufts of ¼in smooth, round, thick, stalked L. FL ¼in 4-petalled, pale to deep lilac, in tight flattish heads, scented. Feb–April. Moving screes at high altitudes. Scree (avoid drought), moraine or AH; difficult. S. European mtns.

THYMUS (*Labiatae*)   Thyme. More or less shrubby, usually aromatic. FL with small upper and larger 3-lobed lower lip. Light soil; sun. D.

T. caespititius. Syns *azoricus, micans*   2in. Dense hummocky mats of narrow ¼in L, hairy on edges. FL ⅓in, rose-lilac, in small heads flattened against the mat. May–Aug. Carpeter; paths, etc. SW Europe.

T. herba-barona   3in. Loose straggly mat. L ⅓in, oval, pointed, strongly scented of caraway when bruised. FL small, pink, in loose heads. May–July. Paths (grown for scent). Corsica, Sardinia.

T. integer   2½in. Spreading gnarled branches. L ¼in, pointed, thick-edged, with white woolly hairs. FL tubular, ½in long, clear pink, calyces brown-purple. Feb–May. Doubtfully hardy. Protected bed or AH. Cyprus.

T. serpyllum   1in. Dense flat spreading rooting mats. L ¼in, narrow-oval, smooth or hairs on edges. FL ⅓in in small tight heads. Pale rose to strong carmine, or white. May–July. Europe. (Variable, several named forms.)

TRIFOLIUM (*Leguminosae*)
T. alpinum   Alpine clover. 6in. Herbaceous. Mat of spreading leafy branches. L in 3   1in, narrow, pointed, folded leaflets. FL ¾in long, narrow, in loose few-flowered heads, rose or white; fruity fragrance. May–June. Well drained soil or scree; sun. S. European mtns.

TRILLIUM (*Liliaceae*)   L 3 in a whorl on upright stem. FL 3-petalled. Moist leafy or peaty soil in half-shade or woodland. S, D. Eastern N America.

T. erectum   9in. L 2½in, broadly diamond shaped, deep glossy green. FL solitary, close to the leaves, 2in, petals broadly oval, pointed, deep wine-red, stamens cream. April–May.

T. grandiflorum   12in. L 4in, broadly oval, pointed, ribbed, glossy. FL 2½in, petals broadly oval, white 'fading' to rose-pink. April–May.

T. undulatum   9in. L 2½in, oval, narrowly pointed, matt, red-tinged. FL 1½in, very pale pink with deep rose-purple ring at centre. May.

TRITELEIA (*Liliaceae*)   Corms. L all from base, to 1ft, very narrow, sprawling, sometimes dying before flowering. FL in open flat umbel on upright stem. Rich well-drained soil; sun or half-shade. D (OFFSETS), S. California.

T. lactea. Syns *Brodiaea lactea, Hesperochordon lacteum*   12in. FL ¾in, white, wide funnel-shaped. July–Aug. (*T. hyacinthina* is very similar or synonymous.)

T. laxa. Syn *Brodiaea laxa*   10in. FL narrow funnel-shaped, 1in long, pale to deep violet with darker central line on outside of each petal; many-flowered umbels. June–July. (Var *maxima* is much larger.)

TROLLIUS (*Ranunculaceae*)   Herbaceous. L rounded in outline, more or less deeply dissected. FL like large buttercups. Rich moist soil in sun. D, S.
T. acaulis   9in. L 2in, finely divided and toothed. FL 1½in, golden-yellow, flat. May–July. Himalaya.

T. europaeus Globe-flower. 18in. L 3in, divided to base in about 5 toothed segments. FL solitary on long stems, 1¼in, many-petalled, globular, creamy-yellow. April–July. Europe incl Britain.

T. yunnanensis. Syn T. *pumilus yunnanensis* 12in. L 2in in about 5 broad coarsely toothed lobes; a few stem-leaves. FL 2 to a stem, 2in, flat, golden-yellow. June–July. China.

TULIPA (*Liliaceae*) Bulbous. L more or less narrow, pointed, mostly from base. FL 6-petalled, starry when fully open. Rich well-drained soil in sun; species suitable for the rock garden are hardy but need a summer baking. D (OFFSETS), S (slow).

T. aucheriana 4in. L 6 × ½in, folded, prostrate. FL 1 to 3, 2½in, purplish-rose with yellow-brown centre and white middle zone; petals pointed, opening flat. April–May. Persia, Syria.

T. batalinii 9in. L 6 × ¾in, folded, slightly wavy. FL solitary, 2in, cup-shaped, creamy yellow. April–May. Bokhara.

T. clusiana Lady tulip. 10in. L 9 × ½in, glaucous, prostrate. FL solitary, starry when open but tending to remain half-closed, petals 1½in, narrow, pointed, curving out at tips, white, the 3 outer petals crimson on outer surface. April. Middle East. (Fig 28, see p 86.)

T. linifolia 6in. L 4 × ¼in. FL solitary, 2½in, opening flat, bright red with black-purple central blotch. May. Bokhara.

T. stellata chrysantha 9in. Rather like *clusiana* but FL clear yellow with outer 3 petals russet externally. April–May. Afghanistan, Kashmir.

T. sylvestris 15in. L 10 × 1in. FL usually solitary, 3in, long, narrow, clear yellow, red-tipped, russet or green externally, pendent in bud, scented. April–May. Europe incl Britain, and into Asia and N Africa. (*T. australis*, dwarfer and redder externally, may be thought of as a montane southern form of *sylvestris*.)

T. tarda. Syn *dasystemon* 4in. L 4 × 1in, glossy, down-curved. FL several to a bulb, 2in, white with rich yellow centre, reddish externally. March–April. Turkestan.

T. turkestanica 8in. L 6 × 1in, prostrate. FL several to a stem, 1¼in, white, yellow centred, opening flat. March–April. Turkestan.

T. urumiensis 6in. L 8 × ¾in, folded, prostrate, tending to curl. FL 2½in, star-shaped, clear yellow, outer petals red externally. April–May. Persia.

TUNICA (*Caryophyllaceae*)

T. saxifraga 8in. Central tuft of 1in very narrow L. Loose sprawling mat of fine-leaved flowering stems with many ¼in regular 5-petalled pink FL in loose sprays. May–Sept. Light soil in sun; rock face or wall. S, C. S Europe and W Asia. (*T. s.* 'Rosette' is a good double.)

UVULARIA (*Liliaceae*)
U. grandiflora   10in. Rhizomatous, herbaceous. L 3in, narrow-oval, pointed, the lower sheathing stem, the upper tending to clasp it. FL in a small hanging cluster, narrowly bell-shaped, 1in, yellow. May. Leafy soil; light shade or woodland. D, S. N America.

VERONICA (*Scrophulariaceae*)   FL usually 4-petalled, one slightly narrower. Light soil; sun. D. (See also Hebe.)
V. austriaca   10in. Herbaceous. Mat of dissected downy L. FL ⅓in in narrow branching spikes. June–July. SE Europe.
V. cinerea   8in. L 1in, narrow, pointed, silvery grey with short hairs. FL ¼in, china blue in loose trailing spikes. May–June. Asia Minor.
V. fruticans. Syn *saxatilis*   3in. Woody at base, stems flopping. L ⅓in, oval, glossy. FL 2 or 3 at tips of stems, ½in, brilliant blue, crimson central ring; evanescent. May. Scree. European mtns incl Scotland.
V. gentianoides   10in. Flat rosettes of 2in oval, glossy, slightly toothed L. FL in upright leafy dense spikes, ½in, clear china blue, evanescent. May. Caucasus. (There is a form with variegated L.)
V. incana   12in. Herbaceous. L 3in, narrow, pointed, blunt-toothed, grey with silver margins and mid-vein. FL in dense 6in spikes on upright leafy stems, ¼in, deep purple with prominent stamens. June–Sept. Russia.
V. kellereri   3in. Loose mats of prostrate stems, woody at base, crowded with ⅓in oval glossy L. FL ¼in, in dense short spikes, deep violet-blue with prominent stamens. April–May. Bulgaria.
V. nummularia   2in. Loose mat of short sprawling woody stems. L ¼in, round, glossy. FL ¼in in short tight heads, light clear blue. April–May. Scree. Pyrenees.
V. pectinata   3in. Soft spreading dense mat. L ½in, oval, toothed, hairy. FL deep blue, or pale rosy-lilac (var *rosea*), ⅓in, in loose sprays covering mat. April–May. Asia Minor.
V. prostrata. Syn *rupestris*   5in. Herbaceous. Dense spreading mat. L 1in, narrow-oval, toothed, FL ⅓in, brilliant blue, in 3in prostrate spikes. May–June. Europe, N Asia. (Also several named colour-forms, eg 'rosea', 'Silver Queen', 'Spode Blue'.)
V. telephiifolia   1in. Creeping loose mat of ¼in round-oval, thick, glaucous L. FL ¼in, mid-blue, in small groups in axils. April–Sept intermittently. Scree or AH; not easy. Armenia.

VIOLA (*Violaceae*)   Most fall into two main types—(I) 'violets' with side petals directed downwards, generally smaller-flowered; (II) 'pansies' with side petals directed upwards, larger. L usually with prominent stipules (leaf-like appendages at base of leaf-stalk) which may be as big as the L. FL spurred.

V. aetolica. Syn *saxatilis* (II) 3in. Close neat tufts of ¾in narrow-oval blunt-toothed L; stipules ½in, divided. FL ¾in, rounded, golden-yellow with short brown central streaks. April–May. Scree. Short-lived. s. Balkans.

V. biflora (I) 4in, herbaceous. L 1in, kidney-shaped, blunt-toothed, stalked. FL ½in, strong yellow, brown-veined; spur short. April–May. Crevice in half-shade. s. N hemisphere.

V. calcarata (II) 4in. Thin spreading rhizomes. L 1in, narrow, pointed, stalked, blunt-toothed; stipules long, narrow, toothed. FL 1½in, violet, blue, yellow, or white; spur thin, ½in. April–June. High alpine meadows. Rich scree or turf; not easy. s, D. Alps.

V. cazorlensis 4in. Herbaceous. Stems woody at base. L ½in, narrow, pointed, stalkless, crowded on upright stems. FL intense crimson-purple, ¾in, narrow-petalled; spur 1in, thin, curved. June–July (earlier in AH). Well-drained soil in protected bed or AH. Not easy. s, D, C. Spain (Sierra Cazorla). (*V. delphinantha*, Greece, is very similar.)

V. cornuta (II) 8in. Herbaceous. Thin rhizomes forming spreading loose mats. L 1in, narrow-oval, pointed, toothed; stipules ½in, divided. FL 1¼in, light purple, or white; spur ½in. Variable in colour and compactness. April onwards. Light soil; sun. D, s. Pyrenees.

V. gracilis (II) 6in. Loose mat. L 1 × ½in, blunt, smooth. FL 1¼in, clear violet with small yellow centre and a few dark central streaks. April–May. Scree. D, s. Macedonia, Bulgaria.

V. papilionacea (I) 4in. Herbaceous. Thick branching rhizome. L 3in (less at flowering time), round heart-shaped, shallow-toothed, glossy. FL 1in, full-petalled, clear white with dark central streaks, sometimes lined or speckled with violet, or violet throughout. April–June. Good soil in light shade or woodland. s (seeds around). Eastern N America. (*V. cucullata* and *V. septentrionalis* are very similar.) (Plate, see p 143.)

V. tricolor subsp *curtisii alba* (II) 3in. L ¾in, oval to heart-shaped, blunt toothed; upper narrower; stipules deeply divided. FL ¾in, creamy white with dark central streaks; upper petals sometimes purple. March onward. Light soil; sun. Short-lived but seeds abundantly and mainly comes true. s. W Europe incl Britain, Balkans. (Plate, see p 144.)

VITALIANA (*Primulaceae*)

V. primuliflora. Syn *Douglasia vitaliana* 1in. L ¼in, narrow grey, in tight rosettes forming spreading close mat. FL stemless in small groups, ¾in long, tubular calyx, petals ½in, yellow, not opening wide. April–May. Scree, AH; not always free-flowering. D. European mtns.

WAHLENBERGIA (*Campanulaceae*) Herbaceous. FL solitary, open bell-shaped. s, D.

W. albomarginata   3in. L ¾in, narrow, broader towards tip, glossy, wavy-edged, in rosettes. FL ¾in, pale clear blue, petals opening flat. June onwards. Peaty soil in half-shade. New Zealand.

WALDSTEINIA (*Rosaceae*)

W. ternata. Syn *trifoliata*   4in. Loose spreading mat with stolons. L on long stalks, divided into 3 1in, coarsely toothed, glossy leaflets. FL ¾in, yellow with boss of stamens, in few-flowered pendent sprays. April–May. Light soil; sun. D, S. Balkans to Japan.

WELDENIA (*Commelinaceae*)

W. candida   3in. Thick tuber, herbaceous. L in rosette, 5 × 1in, blunt, sinuous, glossy. FL 1½in, cup-shaped with 3 broad petals, white with yellow stamens, solitary, stemless but long-tubed, in cluster from centre of rosette. May–July. AH. ROOT CUTTINGS. Mexico.

ZAUSCHNERIA (*Onagraceae*)   Herbaceous. FL tubular, the 4 petals splayed at the mouth, notched. Light soil in sun in warm position; hardy but FL subject to damage by early frosts. D. NW America. The species and varieties are not clearly defined.

Z. californica   10in. Loose clump of flopping stems crowded with L 1in long, variable in width, more or less grey-hairy. FL 1in long in loose leafy spikes, scarlet to vermilion. Aug–Oct. (Var *angustifolia* has narrower, *latifolia* broader, and *cana* greyer L. A particularly good early and fine form is available as 'Dublin'.)

Nine
Lists of Plants for Special Positions

The following lists relate not only to the rock garden proper, but also to the woodland and water which so often, and so effectively, go with it. They include many of the plants described in the previous chapter, as well as a great many more not included there. The lists are not exhaustive—they number only some hundreds out of thousands of rock plants—nevertheless the rock garden which included them all would be by any standards a well stocked one.

Plants in the descriptive list which do not appear in any of the following lists require 'ordinary' rock garden conditions—that is to say they grow without difficulty in a well-drained soil and are not particularly fussy as to aspect.

There is a good deal of overlap between the lists: many rock plants fortunately are happy in a variety of environments. It should not be too readily assumed that a plant appearing in only one list is intolerant of any other conditions: if a plant does not grow well in one situation it is always worth trying it in another.

No separate list is given of plants suitable for troughs or sinks, since this must depend on the soils and situation provided: however, plants which are sufficiently small and compact to be suitable for culture in a small trough are marked with an asterisk.

WATERSIDE
Plants for wet soil at the water's edge.

Caltha palustris	C. palustris alba
C. palustris fl pl	Cardamine pratensis fl pl

Epipactis palustri
Fritillaria meleagris
Gentiana asclepiadea
Iris laevigata
Leucojum aestivum
Mazus reptans
Mimulus cardinalis
M. cupreus
M. luteus
Primula bulleyana
P. cockburniana
P. florindae
P. helodoxa

P. japonica
P. luteola
P. pudibunda
P. pulverulenta
P. rosea
P. secundiflora
P. sikkimensis
P. sinopurpurea
P. vialii
P. waltonii
Saxifraga aquatica
S. geranioides

WOODLAND

Plants suitable for, and in most cases naturally growing in, copses or the edges of woodlands.

Actaea spicata
Ajuga reptans atropurpurea
A. triquetrum
Allium ursinum
Anemone apennina
A. nemorosa
A. ranunculoides
A. seemannii
A. sylvestris
A. trifolia
Arisarum proboscideum
Aruncus sylvestris
Asarum caudatum
A. europaeum
Astrantia major
Cardamine bulbifera
C. kitaibelii
C. pentaphyllos
C. trifolia
Cyclamen repandum
Daphne blagayana
Eranthis spp
Gagea lutea
Gentiana asclepiadea

Glaucidium palmatum
Helleborus spp
Hepatica spp
Maianthemum bifolium
Melittis melissophyllum
Montia (Claytonia) siberica
Orchis maculata
O. mascula
Ornithogalum umbellatum
Podophyllum emodi
P. peltatum
Polygala chamaebuxus
Polygonatum spp
Pulmonaria angustifolia
P. officinalis
Pyrola spp
Ranunculus aconitifolius
R. ficaria cupreus
Scilla liliohyacinthus
Streptopus roseus
Stylophorum diphyllum
Symphytum grandiflorum
Tiarella cordifolia
T. wherryi

Trillium spp
Uvularia grandiflora
Vinca minor

Viola papilionacea
V. septentrionalis

LIGHT SHADE

Plants tolerant of, and in some cases preferring, a shady position. Grading into the 'Woodland' group. Some 'Waterside' plants, eg Primulas, are happy also in half-shade away from water.

*Androsace lanuginosa
Arenaria balearica
Cardamine pratensis* fl pl
*Clematis alpina
*Corydalis cashmiriana
Cyclamen europaeum
C. neapolitanum
Cypripedium calceolus
C. pubescens
Epimedium* spp
Erythronium spp
*Galanthus nivalis
Hypsela longiflora
Isopyrum thalictroides
Jeffersonia dubia
Leucojum aestivum
*Lewisia cotyledon
*L. pygmaea
Linnaea borealis
Mazus reptans
Mentha requienii
Mertensia virginica
Omphalodes cappadocica

O. verna
Phlox adsurgens
P. amoena
P. divaricata
P. stolonifera
Polygala chamaebuxus
Polygonatum hookeri
Sanguinaria canadensis
Saxifraga aizoides
S. fortunei
*S. oppositifolia
S. rotundifolia
S. umbrosa
Selliera radicans
Shortia uniflora
Synthyris reniformis
S. stellata
Thalictrum diffusiflorum
Vancouveria hexandra
*Viola biflora
V. papilionacea
V. septentrionalis*

BOG

Continuously wet, acid, peaty soil, rich in humus, poorly drained.

*Anagallis tenella
Bulbinella hookeri
*Gentiana pneumonanthe
*Parnassia palustris
Pinguicula spp
*Primula clarkei
P. farinosa

P. halleri (*longiflora*)
*P. rosea
*P. scotica
*P. warshenewskiana
*Ranunculus pyrenaeus
Wahlenbergia hederacea*

PEAT

Or acid peaty soil.

Andromeda polifolia
Arctostaphylos uva-ursi
Arthropodium candidum
Bruckenthalia spiculifolia
Calceolaria falklandica
*C. tenella
Calluna vulgaris
Cassiope spp
Clintonia borealis
Cyananthus spp
Cypripedium reginae
Daboecia cantabrica
Diplarrhena moraea
Erica vagans
Erythronium spp
Gaultheria cuneata
*Gentiana carolii
*G. farreri
*G. sino-ornata
Hebe macrantha
*Houstonia coerulea
Iris gracilipes
I. innominata
Jeffersonia dubia
Leiophyllum buxifolium
Leptospermum scoparium prostratum
*Lewisia columbiana
*L. cotyledon
*L. pygmaea
Lilium formosanum pricei
Linnaea borealis
Lithospermum diffusum
*Lobelia linnaeoides
*Loiseleuria procumbens
Mazus pumilio
M. radicans
Meconopsis spp
*Mertensia echioides

*Mimulus primuloides
Mitchella repens
Nomocharis spp
Ophiopogon planiscapus
*Ourisia caespitosa gracilis
O. coccinea
Perezia recurvata
Pernettya mucronata
P. tasmanica
Phlox adsurgens
Phyllodoce spp
Phyllothamnus erectus
Pimelea coarctata
Polygonum affine
P. vaccinifolium
Pratia angulata
Primula capitata
P. ioessa
P. muscarioides
P. nutans
Reineckia carnea
Rhododendron spp
*Rhodohypoxis baurii
Rhodothamnus chamaecistus
Schizocodon soldanelloides
Selliera radicans
Shortia uniflora
Sisyrinchium douglasii
S. filifolium
Symphyostemon biflorum
Thalictrum diffusiflorum
Trillium spp
Tropaeolum polyphyllum
Vaccinium vitis-idaea minus
Vancouveria hexandra
Viola eizanensis
*Wahlenbergia spp

TURF AND SCREE

There is a gradation (see Chapters One and Three) from relatively stoneless, humus-rich 'turf' through 'rich scree' and 'fast scree' to 'moraine'. For the purposes of these lists three grades are distinguished; but so much depends upon the nature of the soil, the climate, and the aspect that frequently only personal experiment will determine a plant's needs in a particular garden. Wherever possible the inclusion of a plant in one of these lists has been based upon its choice of habitat in the wild.

(i) 'TURF'

*Androsace carnea
*A. chamaejasme
*A. hedraeantha
*A. lactea
*A. primuloides
*P. villosa
*A. wulfeniana
Anemone baldensis
*A. obtusiloba patula
Aquilegia alpina
A. pyrenaica
*Aster alpinus
Bulbocodium vernum
Campanula alpina
C. barbata
C. betulifolia
C. pilosa
*Centaurium portense
Colchicum alpinum
Crocus purpureus
*Cyananthus integer
C. lobatus
Cytisus (Chamaecytisus) hirsutus
Daphne cneorum
*Dianthus alpinus
*D. glacialis
*D. neglectus (pavonius)
*D. 'Whitehills'
*Diascia cordata

*Dryas octopetala minor
Erythronium dens-canis
*Gentiana 'acaulis'
*G. alpina
*G. angustifolia
*G. bellidifolia
*G. clusii
*G. farreri
*G. froelichii
*G. pumila
*G. pyrenaica
*G. saxosa
*G. verna
Gymnadenia conopsea
*Iris lacustris
*Isopyrum thalictroides
*Leontopodium alpinum
Linum alpinum
*Loiseleuria procumbens
*Lychnis alpina
*Narcissus asturiensis
N. bulbocodium
*N. cyclamineus
Nierembergia hippomanica
N. rivularis
*Omphalodes luciliae
*Oxalis adenophylla
*O. enneaphylla
*Potentilla eriocarpa

*Primula clarkei
*P. farinosa
*P. frondosa
*P. glutinosa
*P. halleri (longiflora)
*P. hirsuta
*P. integrifolia
*P. minima
*P. pedemontana
*P. scotica
*P. viscosa
*P. warshenewskiana
*Pulsatilla vernalis
Ranunculus ahrendsii
*R. alpestris
R. amplexicaulis
*R. bilobus
*R. crenatus
R. montanus
*R. parnassifolius
*R. pyrenaeus
*R. traunfellneri
Rhododendron ferrugineum

R. hirsutum
*Romanzoffia sitchensis
*R. unalaschkensis
*Romulea bulbocodium
*R. clusiana
*R. longituba alticola
*R. zahnii
*Saponaria pumilio
Saxifraga aizoides
*S. cebennensis
*S. crustata (incrustata)
*S. oppositifolia
*S. retusa
*Soldanella spp
Synthyris reniformis
S. stellata
Trifolium alpinum
*Veronica aphylla
*Wahlenbergia albo-marginata
*W. matthewsii
*W. tasmanica
Wulfenia carinthiaca
W. orientalis

(ii) SCREE

Alyssum repens
*A. serpyllifolium
A. wulfenianum
*Anacyclus depressus
*Androsace hedraeantha
*A. lactea
*A. sempervivoides
*A. villosa
*Aquilegia bertolonii
*A. discolor
*Arabis androsacea
Arenaria aggregata
*A. tetraquetra
*Armeria caespitosa
Asperula lilaciflora caespitosa
A. nitida
*A. suberosa

Callianthemum rutifolium
*Campanula allionii
*C. arvatica
*C. caespitosa
*C. cenisia
C. excisa
*C. hercegovina nana
*C. morettiana
*C. piperi
C. pulla
C. pulloides
*C. raineri
*C. tommasiniana
C. tridentata (group)
C. waldsteiniana
*C. zoysii
Carduncellus rhaponticoides

Chamaecytisus pygmaeus
*Convolvulus nitidus
*Corydalis rutifolia
Crepis incana
*Dianthus alpinus
*D. callizonus
*D. erinaceus
*D. glacialis
*D. haematocalyx
*D. microlepis
*D. subacaulis
*D. 'Whitehills'
*Douglasia laevigata
*D. montana
*Draba aizoides
*D. bryoides imbricata
*D. dedeana
*Edraianthus pumilio
*E. serpyllifolius
*Erigeron aureus
Erinacea anthyllis
*Eritrichium nanum
Erysimum helveticum
E. linifolium
*Eunomia oppositifolia
*Gentiana froelichii
Geum montanum
Gypsophylla cerastioides
Hutchinsia alpina
Hypericum nummularium
*Linaria alpina
*L. supina
Linum suffruticosum salsaloides
Melandrium elisabethae
Minuartia laricifolia
M. verna
*Morisia monanthos (hypogea)
Myosotis alpestris
M. australis conspicuus
*M. explanata
*M. rupicola
*Narcissus juncifolius

N. rupicola
*N. scaberulus
N. triandrus
*N. watieri
Oenothera caespitosa
*Omphalodes luciliae
*Oxalis laciniata
Papaver sendtneri (alpinum)
P. myabeanum
P. rhaeticum
Penstemon pinifolius
*Petrocallis pyrenaica
Petrocoptis glaucifolia
*P. pyrenaica
*Petrophytum caespitosum
P. hendersonii
Phyteuma comosum
*P. pauciflorum
*P. sieberi
*Polygala calcarea
*P. vayredae
Potentilla alchemilloides
P. clusiana
P. nitida
Primula allionii
P. auricula
P. clusiana
P. glaucescens
*P. marginata
*P. pedemontana
P. spectabilis
*P. tyrolensis
*P. viscosa
P. wulfeniana
Pterocephalus parnassi
Ptilotrichum macrocarpum
Ranunculus ahrendsii
*R. alpestris
*R. bilobus
*R. crenatus
*R. parnassifolius
*R. pyrenaeus

R. seguieri
Salvia caespitosa
Saponaria caespitosa
*S. olivana
S. pulvinaris
*S. pumilio
*Saxifraga aspera bryoides
*S. caesia
*S. exarata
*S. (Englerias)
*S. (Kabschias)
S. 'Kathleen Pinsent'
S. pentadactylis
*S. 'Primulaize'
*S. retusa
*S. squarrosa
Senecio carniolicus
S. incanus
S. uniflorus
*Silene acaulis
S. hookeri

S. ingramii
Teucrium montanum
*Thalictrum kiusianum
T. coreanum
Thlaspi bulbosum
T. kurdicum
*T. rotundifolium
*Townsendia formosa
*Trifolium uniflorum
Veronica allionii
*V. aphylla
V. fruticans
*V. nummularia
*V. telephiifolia
*Viola aetolica
V. bubanii
V. calcarata
*V. cenisia
*V. dubyana
V. gracilis
*Vitaliana primuliflora

(iii) MORAINE

*Anchusa caespitosa
Boykinia jamesii
*Campanula cenisia
Epilobium fleischeri
Geum reptans
*Linaria alpina
Papaver sendtneri (alpinum)

P. rhaeticum
Ranunculus glacialis
*R. parnassifolius
*R. pyrenaeus
R. seguieri
Thlaspi rotundifolium

CREVICES

*Antirrhinum sempervirens
Campanula cochlearifolia
*C. morettiana
*C. zoysii
*Erinus alpinus
Haberlea spp
*Jovibarba heuffelii
*Lewisia columbiana
*L. cotyledon

*L. pygmaea
Narcissus canaliculatus
Paederota bonarota
*Petrocallis pyrenaica
Petrocoptis glaucifolia
*P. pyrenaica
Phyteuma comosum
Potentilla alba
P. caulescens

P. clusiana
P. nitida
Primula auricula
P. clusiana
P. glaucescens
*P. hirsuta
*P. marginata
P. spectabilis
*P. tyrolensis
*P. viscosa
P. wulfeniana

Putoria calabrica
*Ramonda spp
Rhodiola rosea
Saxifraga callosa
S. cochlearis
*S. crustata (incrustata)
S. longifolia
S. mutata
S. paniculata
*Sempervivum spp

TUFA

Most plants which are reasonably neat and compact, which naturally grow in screes or fissures, and which present difficulties in cultivation are worth trying in tufa.

*Androsace spp (Aretians)
*Arenaria tetraquetra
*Armeria caespitosa
*Asperula suberosa
Boykinia jamesii
*Campanula hercegovina nana
*C. morettiana
*C. piperi
*C. raineri
*C. zoysii
*Convolvulus nitidus
*Douglasia laevigata
*D. montana
*Draba aizoides
*D. bryoides imbricata
*D. dedeana
*D. mollissima
*D. polytricha
*D. rigida
*Edraianthus pumilio
*E. serpyllifolius
*Eritrichium nanum
*Lewisia brachycalyx
*L. columbiana

*L. cotyledon
*L. pygmaea
*L. rediviva
*L. tweedyi
*Myosotis rupicola
*Petrocallis pyrenaica
*Petrocoptis pyrenaica
*Petrophytum caespitosum
Phyteuma comosum
Potentilla clusiana
P. nitida
Primula auricula
P. clusiana
*P. marginata
*P. tyrolensis
P. wulfeniana
Saxifraga aretioides
*S. caesia
*S. cochlearis minor
*S. (Englerias)
*S. (Kabschias)
*S. squarrosa
*Silene acaulis

HOT DRY POSITIONS

Acantholimon spp
Alyssum saxatile
Antennaria dioica
Aphyllanthes monspeliensis
Arabis caucasica
Asarina procumbens
Carmichaelia enysii
Chamaespartium sagittale
Cistus spp
Convolvulus cantabrica
*Crassula milfordiae
Cytisus spp
Erinacea anthyllis
Genista spp
*Globularia spp
Halimiocistus sahucii
Halimium ocymoides
*Helichrysum milfordiae
Hypericum empetrifolium
H. coris
H. olympicum
Hyssopus officinalis
*Iris cretensis

I. pumila
I. unguicularis
Ononis fruticosa
Onosma cinerara (albo-roseum)
O. echioides
O. tauricum
Penstemon spp
Phlox bifida
P. douglasii
P. subulata
Phuopsis stylosa
Prunus prostrata
Ptilotrichum spp
Rhamnus pumila
Satureja subspicata
Saxifraga (Encrusted)
Scorzonera rosea
Sedum spp
*Sempervivum spp
Teucrium polium
Verbascum pestalozzae
V. spinosum
Zauschneria spp

PROTECTED BED

This refers to protection against winter cold (see Chapter Four). Many plants commonly grown in the alpine house are worth trying in a protected bed in the open: those here listed are in the main unsuitable, chiefly because of size, for the alpine house. It should not, of course, be supposed that the plants listed can all be grown in the *same* protected bed—they are diverse in their requirements as to soil, etc.

Allium subhirsutum
Alyssoides cretica
*Anacyclus depressus
Arabis blepharophylla
Asphodeline liburnica
Bletilla striata
Briza maxima
Campanula rupestris
Commelina coelestis

Convolvulus althaeoides
C. cneorum
C. elegantissimus
C. mauritanicus
Crassula sarcocaulis
Digitalis obscura
Gladiolus spp
Gynandriris sisyrinchium
Helichrysum virgineum

Hermodactylus tuberosus
Lapeirousia laxa
Lavandula stoechas
Leptospermum scoparium praestratum
Linum monogynum
L. viscosum
Lotus creticus
Mandragora officinarum
Ophrys spp

Parochetus communis
Scilla reverchonii
Serapias spp
*Stachys corsica
Tanacetum pallidum spathulifolium
Thalictrum tuberosum
Verbascum spinosum
Zephyranthes candida

ALPINE HOUSE

Almost any rock or alpine plant can be grown in an alpine house. The following list is restricted to plants which are best grown there for one or other of the reasons given on p 121.

*Allium callimischon
Alstroemeria hookeri
A. pygmaea
Anchusa caespitosa
*Androsace (Aretians)
*A. villosa
Arcterica nana
*Arenaria tetraquetra
Arthropodium candidum
*Asperula suberosa
Asphodelus acaulis
Boykinia jamesii
Calceolaria darwinii
*Campanula allionii
*C. arvatica
C. cashmiriana
*C. cenisia
C. excisa
C. fragilis
*C. morettiana
*C. piperi
*C. raineri
*C. zoysii
Cassiope spp
Conandron ramondioides
*Convolvulus nitidus
Corydalis ambigua yedoensis
Crocus banaticus (iridiflorus)

C. crewei
C. cyprius
C. niveus
*Cyclamen cilicium
*C. cyprium
C. graecum
C. libanoticum
C. persicum
C. pseudibericum
C. repandum
Daphne jasminea
*D. petraea
Dicentra peregrina pusilla
Dionysia spp
*Draba bryoides imbricata
*D. mollissima
*D. polytricha
*D. rigida
*Erigeron aureus
*Eritrichium nanum
*Erodium reichardii
Erysimum helveticum
*Eunomia oppositifolia
*Gentiana froelichii
*G. pyrenaica
*Gladiolus triphyllus
*Helichrysum frigidum
Helleborus lividus

Hypericum aegypticum
*Iris histrio aintabensis
Jankaea heldreichii
*Jasminum parkeri
Kalmiopsis leachiana
Leucogenes grandiceps
L. leontopodium
*Leucojum autumnale
*L. hyemale
*Lewisia brachycalyx
*L. rediviva
*L. tweedyi
Lithospermum rosmarinifolium
L. zahnii
*Lloydia graeca
*L. serotina
Mazus radicans
*Morisia monanthos (hypogaea)
Narcissus bulbocodium romieuxii
N. cantabricus
*N. scaberulus
*N. watieri
*Oxalis laciniata
*O. lobata
*Petrophytum caespitosum
Phlox nana ensifolia
*Polygala paucifolia
*P. vayredae
Primula allionii
P. edgeworthii
*P. glutinosa
*P. marginata
*P. minima
P. reidii
P. suffrutescens
*P. tyrolensis
*P. viscosa
*Pulsatilla vernalis
Putoria calabrica
Ranunculus asiaticus
R. calandrinioides
R. glacialis

*R. parnassifolius
R. seguieri
Rhododendron leucaspis
*Romulea clusiana
*R. zahnii
Saxifraga aretioides
S. brunoniana
*S. caesia
*S. (Englerias)
S. flagellaris
S. florulenta
*S. (Kabschias)
*S. oppositifolia
*S. retusa
*S. squarrosa
Scilla adlamii
Senecio leucophyllus
S. uniflorus
Silene hookeri
S. ingramii
Sisyrinchium depauperatum
*Soldanella spp
*Talinum okanoganense
Tecophilea cyanocrocus
T. violacea
Teucrium aroanium
*Thalictrum kiusianum
*T. coreanum
*T. orientale
*Thlaspi rotundifolium
*Thymus integer
Trachelium asperuloides
Tsusiophyllum tanakae
Verbascum dumulosum
Veronica bombycina
*Viola cazorlensis
*V. cenisia
*V. delphinantha
*V. dubyana
*Vitaliana primuliflora
*Weldenia candida

Bibliography

There is a considerable literature on alpine plants. The small selection which follows is mainly of books which I have found particularly valuable and interesting in constructing and maintaining my garden and getting to know my plants. A few of these books are out of print but are nevertheless included as they are well worth seeking out. In addition to the publications listed, there is a wealth of material of special interest to alpine and rock gardeners in the journals of the specialist alpine and rock garden societies. The Alpine Garden Society and the American Rock Garden Society each publish a quarterly *Bulletin*, and the Scottish Rock Garden Club a half-yearly *Journal*.

GENERAL

Clay, Sampson. *The Present-Day Rock Garden* (1954), supplement to 'Farrer'
Farrer, Reginald. *The English Rock Garden* 2 vols (1918)
Royal Horticultural Society. *Dictionary of Gardening*, 4 vols (1951; supplement 1969)

CULTIVATION

Elliott, J. G. *Bulbs Under Glass* (Alpine Garden Society, 1970)
Heath, Royton E. *Collectors' Alpines* (1964)
Hills, Lawrence D. *The Propagation of Alpines* (1950)
Hulme, J. K. *The Propagation of Alpine Plants* (Alpine Garden Society, 1970)
Jackson, Robert. *Gardening on Chalk and Lime Soil* (1940)
Symons-Jeune, B. H. B. *Natural Rock Gardening* (1932)

SPECIAL GROUPS OR GENERA

Anderson, E. B. *Dwarf Bulbs for the Rock Garden* (1959)
Bowles, E. A. *A Handbook of Crocus and Colchicum for Gardeners* (1924)

Crook, H. Clifford. *Campanulas* (1951)

Elliott, R. C. *The Genus Lewisia* (Alpine Garden Society, 1966)

Evans, R. L. *A Gardener's Guide to Sedums* (Alpine Garden Society, 1971)

Grey-Wilson, C. *Dionysias* (Alpine Garden Society, 1971)

Harding, Winton, *Saxifrages* (Alpine Garden Society, 1970)

Lilley, S. E. *Ericaceous and Peat Loving Plants* (Alpine Garden Society, 1969)

Synge, Patrick M. *Collins' Guide to Bulbs* (1961)

Wilkie, David. *Gentians* (1936)

MOUNTAIN FLORAS

Craighead, John J., Craighead, Frank C., and Davis, Ray J. *Field Guide to Rocky Mountain Wildflowers* (Cambridge, Mass, 1963)

Huxley, Anthony. *Mountain Flowers, Europe from the Pyrenees to the Julian Alps* (1967)

Philipson, W. R., and Hearn, D. *Rock Garden Plants of the Southern Alps* (Christchurch, NZ, 1962)

Some rock and alpine garden societies

British Columbia: The Alpine Club of British Columbia. Sec: Mrs O. W. Sherlock, 590 E Kings Road, North Vancouver, BC. Canada

England: The Alpine Garden Society. Sec: Mr E. M. Upward, Lye End Link, St John's, Woking, Surrey

France: Société des Amateurs de Jardins Alpins, 84 Rue de Grenelle, Paris VII

New Zealand: The Canterbury Alpine Garden Society, c/o Mrs B. Hannan, 157 Hackthorne Road, Christchurch 2

Scotland: The Scottish Rock Garden Club. Hon Sec: Mrs L. C. Boyd-Harvey, Boonslie, Dirleton, North Berwick, East Lothian

USA: The American Rock Garden Society, Sec: Richard W. Redfield, Box 26, Closter, NJ 07624

Vancouver: The Vancouver Island Rock and Alpine Garden Society, 5021 Prospect Lake Road, RR 1, Royal Oak PO, Sannion, BC, Canada

Index of Plant Names

(† indicates a recent name-change: see Addendum to this Index)

227

Addendum to the Plant Index

Since this book went to press the third volume of *Flora Europaea* has been published. The following changes in classification or nomenclature, which it has not been possible to correct in the text, have been made. **New correct names** are shown in bold type.

General Index